ROUTLEDGE LIBRARY EDITIONS:
ECONOMICS AND SOCIETY

Volume 11

THE ECONOMICS OF HUMAN HAPPINESS

THE ECONOMICS OF HUMAN HAPPINESS

COLLIN BROOKS

Routledge
Taylor & Francis Group
LONDON AND NEW YORK

First published in 1933 by George Routledge & Sons, Limited

This edition first published in 2026
by Routledge
4 Park Square, Milton Park, Abingdon, Oxon OX14 4RN

and by Routledge
605 Third Avenue, New York, NY 10158

Routledge is an imprint of the Taylor & Francis Group, an informa business

British Library Cataloguing in Publication Data
A catalogue record for this book is available from the British Library

ISBN: 978-1-032-97576-4 (Set)
ISBN: 978-1-041-14347-5 (Volume 11) (hbk)
ISBN: 978-1-041-14354-3 (Volume 11) (pbk)
ISBN: 978-1-003-67401-6 (Volume 11) (ebk)

DOI: 10.4324/9781003674016

Publisher's Note
The publisher has gone to great lengths to ensure the quality of this reprint but points out that some imperfections in the original copies may be apparent.

Disclaimer
The publisher has made every effort to trace copyright holders and would welcome correspondence from those they have been unable to trace.

THE ECONOMICS OF HUMAN HAPPINESS

BY

COLLIN BROOKS

AUTHOR OF "THE THEORY AND PRACTICE OF FINANCE," "HOW THE STOCK MARKET REALLY WORKS," "SOMETHING IN THE CITY," "THIS TARIFF QUESTION," "THE ROYAL MAIL CASE," ETC.

LONDON
GEORGE ROUTLEDGE & SONS, LIMITED
BROADWAY HOUSE: 68-74 CARTER LANE, E.C.
1933

Printed in Great Britain by
HEADLEY BROTHERS
109 Kingsway, London, W.C.2; and Ashford, Kent

TO
HILAIRE BELLOC

" Politics is the Science of Human Happiness "

Joseph Chamberlain, at Glasgow, in 1885

CONTENTS

FOREWORD

THERE is nothing original in this book. It is, in the best meaning of the term, a commonplace book. If it fails to say for half-a-guinea what a multitude of men are saying in pub and club, tavern and train, for nothing, it will be because I have an impediment in my speech arising from the need for controlling the epithets which they can use freely.

It is agreed on all hands that society is sick, perhaps sick unto death. As the visible representative of society the plain man, the average citizen, is the victim of a malaise which has drawn about him a horde of economic busybodies eager to explain the cause of the seizure and to suggest and administer remedies. This book suggests but one remedy, the age-old advice of the onlooker—" give him air ". Ignoring the Heath-Robinson-like contraptions of the currency cranks, this book advises the stricken wayfarer to take up his bed and walk. Deriding the nostrums of the rival schools of rejuvenators and the profferers of economic trusses and crutches, it suggests to that smitten traveller to " get up and work it off ". It is, however, something different from a course of economic Couéism. It preaches not a faith cure, but a lack-of-faith cure—a cure to be induced by a healthy scepticism about those who have hitherto been the witch doctors of the tribe.

When the British Broadcasting Corporation sent into the homes of its licence-holders a Grand Good-night on New Year's Eve, 1932, its spokesman, after dwelling upon the imminent disasters which menaced those homes from the economic maladministration of the world, concluded by insisting that the only cure for world depression was the Christian religion, a point of view which must have sounded odd to many citizens of a great Moslem Empire with its sprinkling of Jews, Buddhists, agnostics, atheists and indifferentists. The following morning *The Times* newspaper insisted that the only salvation lay in a theistic belief in a benign personal God. Mr. Ramsay MacDonald suggested that belief in the National Government was sufficient, while Sir Josiah Stamp and Mr. Keynes respectively advised a régimen of saving and spending, and Mr. John Strachey and Mr. Murry pinned their faith to an adoption of Communism, ignoring the New Year hopes of Sir Oswald Mosley for a Fascist State to end all ills. Lord Melchett and Sir Basil Blackett find a panacea in planned money. Mr. Chesterton and Mr. Belloc demand a return to Distributism—three acres and a cow for the new English peasant and, perchance, three parlours and a Morris-Cowley for the urbanite. Mr. Baldwin desires low tariffs as a means to no tariffs, and Colonel Amery wants high tariffs as a means to higher tariffs and a self-sufficient Empire which shall include self-sufficient components. Major Walter Elliot is for quotas, and Sir Walter Layton is for free imports. Mr. Montagu Norman hankers after the gold standard which Mr. Churchill found lying upon a stricken field in 1925 and raised again in the economic wilderness to which we were then so rapidly and joyously advancing. Sir Robert Horne, understandably in view of his business attachments, advocates bimetallism and Major Douglas, Mr. Taylor Peddie, and Mr. Kitson sweep both gold and silver into the contemptuous category of the base metals and suggest currency standards of their own, which would supplant the golden calf of our exodus from prosperity by the book of index numbers. The practical bankers speak with a divided voice, with that powerful overlord, Mr. McKenna, leading the revolt against the Norman conquest. The " productionists " want more looms per weaver and the ca' canny school wants more weavers per loom. Mr. Maxton wants monopoly under the title of Nationalization, and Sir Harry McGowan wants monopoly under the title of Rationalization.

The function of applied economics is to make contemporary wants coincident. No economist, as statesman, could possibly make all these wants coincident. There is no political eclecticism which could build a platform from the planks offered by so many different log-rollers. But there is one want that is universal. It is expressed at its broadest in the words of a popular song. Although we flatter ourselves that we are a politically minded race, the average citizen does not think politically. He does not say, " I want this fiscal system or that," or, " I want this mode of government or the other." He says, quite simply, " I want to be happy," and on the promise of what he conceives to be a wider or narrower chance of happiness he votes at the polls or in his union chapel or lodge.

This book, it may be said, is a loose treatise on how to be happy though civilized. It is an expansion of the thought that a " managing " Government is as great an affliction as a " managing " wife into the suspicion that a Planning Body is only a new-fangled name for an old-fangled affliction, a busybody. It is based on the conviction that what is really wanted is not better leadership, more scientific leadership, reformed leadership, dictatorial leadership, democratic leadership, or any other qualified leadership—but less leadership. It enunciates the doctrine that we are suffering not so much from faulty organization as from organization without any adjective whatsoever. It also suggests, with courtesy, as I hope, and in a Pickwickian sense, that in the thieves' kitchen of modern " leadership " too many crooks have spoilt our broth.

The book is no manifesto for perfect freedom. It does not clamour for a return to cut-throat competition. It is not a pleasing fable from the Blue Book of the Laissez-fairies. It is only an expression of Individualism inasmuch as it suggests mildly that the individual should be the starting-point of political thought, and not the trade union, or the joint stock company, or the Empire, or the whimsies of some dead dreamer. We live in the age of George V, not in that of Thomas More, or of Utopia, or even of Oliver Twist. This book derides the idea that we shall attain happiness by Marxing through Georgia or merely—as Mr. Chesterton might say[1] and advise—by asking for More.

Individualism is not enough. Socialism is too much. No " ism " is necessary. The individual cannot do everything alone ; he must indulge in communal co-operation for common purposes. But the individual does not need a Government Department or a Board of Governing Directors to spend his wages for him ; educate his children for him ; select and " vet " his mate for him before those children are begotten ; form his habits for him ; arrange his dietary for him ; construct his morals for him ; select and censor his amusements for him ; standardize the commodities of his daily life for him, and arrange his contribution to a burial club for him. He needs a Government which will govern, in the old sense of maintaining law and order and the enforcing of contracts, and which will stand in relation to his life as the policeman theoretically stands in relation to his home—ready at call, but unable to enter without an invitation.

The over-organized, beswaddled and dragooned citizen of to-day will not find it easy to attain to sufficient freedom in which to work out his own economic salvation. The dons of a man's alma mater will tell him that mother

[1] Or, indeed, may have said.

knows best, whether that alma mater be a university or a trade union. The common room and the board room will not lightly forgo their recent command of men's minds and actions. There is an old Lancashire proverb to the effect that " changes are likesome, and fools like 'em ", and it is not easy to persuade a voting citizen to apply to a proposed change Melbourne's test of " why not leave it alone ? " It is less easy to obtain the repeal of restrictive laws.

The State will give more readily than it will relinquish. The State gives the law, and does not like to have a gift ass looked in the mouth. As most truths have been enshrined in jests, it may be recalled that thirty years ago it was said of the Nihilists of Russia that they asked for nothing and got knout. The traders and workers of a modern industrial community who ask for nothing but the freedom to work their way out of a world slump, are much more likely to get licences than liberty.

None the less, the people of Britain having long ago learnt to put not their trust in princes, may come to learn to put not their trust in pedants and pedagogues. They may learn that you cannot have a prescribed régimen, without regimentation, and that the effects and reactions of regimentation are precisely those factors in recovery or retrogression which the prescriber cannot foresee. They may learn that in the application of an economic plan the psychological factor is an imponderable, and come again to trust their own native commonsense and mother wit in preference to placing a blind faith in the academic costiveness of professors or the inherent ineptitude of Parliamentarians whose political mechanism prohibits the timely application of a stimulant or repressant which, even if promptly applied, might have proved the wrong prescription.

C.B.

CHAPTER I

THE DECAY OF HAPPINESS

IN an age whose culture has substituted for that blessed word Mesopotamia the still more comforting word Relativity it is a little perturbing to find in circulation verbal tokens which are readily taken at face value though to the simplest test they show as spurious. Cataloguers of our present discontents are many and wide ranging. They include personalities as different as George Lansbury and John Maynard Keynes, Joseph McCabe and Commander Kenworthy, Sir Basil Blackett and Lord Melchett, the contributors to *Economica* and to the *Daily Mail*. Each has his diagnosis and his remedy. Only Mr. Montagu Norman, supported by the prestige of his great office as Governor of the Bank of England, confesses to a human inability to discern the vital causes and inevitable effects of the troublesome situation in which, at the beginning of the fourth decade of the twentieth century, mankind in general and the inhabitants of the British Isles in particular find themselves. But if the causes and cures of the prevailing world malaise are many, the descriptions of the disease are not varied. We are suffering, it would seem, from " want in the midst of plenty " or, alternatively, from " the chaos of capitalism ".

Either phrase runs from the tongue trippingly, but neither is more than a base verbal token having no genuine content of truth behind it. By any reasonable and traditional use of language we are not suffering from want, and, whatever capitalism is, it is not the father of chaos.

" Want " is a word that must always be relative to its context, but chaos is an absolute. As Morley said of the elephant we may not be able to define a chaos, but we know it when we see it. If any indefatigable Arthur Young of our own time reported upon a tour of Great Britain in the nineteen-thirties, confining himself exclusively to a description of what he saw and excluding rigorously any discussion of what he heard or felt, his testimony to the material state of Britain would show a land gratifyingly free from individual penury and collectively over-organized.

The signs of want were common enough at the opening of this century. Mendicants whose rags ill concealed their sores or their emaciated bodies, and dispossessed workers dying from under-nourishment ; sweated workers whose minds were closed to any contact with life but that of the more brutal satisfactions ; children born of untended mothers and bred without care to a shiftless or debased adolescence ; men and women homeless and dependent upon the vagaries of private charity for a continuance of existence—these portents were commonplaces of social life within living memory. Our own time knows them not as our fathers knew them.

In our day the touring enquirer would look vainly for the " Poor Joe " of Dickens. He would find newspaper vendors well clad in somebody's " fifty-shilling " suiting and flower girls brave in rayon stockings and artificial fur coats. He would find some millions of persons wholly relieved from the grinding toil of manual labour by modern machinery to enjoy the plentiful amenities of modern communal life—the parks, the art galleries, the libraries, the dog-racing tracks, the cinematograph theatres, and the broadcast—and in receipt of a weekly income some 25 per cent higher than an agricultural labourer's wage in 1911. We would find that even those toilers not so relieved from all work were employed for an average eight hours a day only and were in enjoyment of amenities of housing and eating more varied and rich than their grandparents would have deemed possible for the richer classes of the older communities. He would find a plenitude of organized amusement, of organized culture and of cheap travel facilities. Had a modern Arthur Young conducted his tour of England in the black year of 1932 he would have been able to describe hunger marchers who marched in new boots with stout waterproof coats to a capital city which fed and housed them and sent certain contingents on a sight-seeing excursion in motor coaches before returning them by road and rail to their homes, so prepared for the return journey that discarded sandwiches littered the departure platforms.

The signs of absolute " want " are few : the signs of chaos are none. Some fifty million persons on islands adapted by nature to the support, in a frugal way, of but a quarter of that number enjoy food and raiment brought with regularity and ease from the ends of the earth. They move in townships of well paved, well lighted and ordered streets, with dwellings properly drained and fitted with running water and artificial lighting. These communities are guarded by trained experts in communal health, and are thus kept free from the plagues and epidemics which at a recent stage of our history swept periodically over the people. They are adorned with art collections that might be the envy of an ancient potentate. They have the use of ample open spaces for both sport and quiet recreation. They are linked by comfortable means of transport. For less than a halfpenny a day the inhabitants of any household can enjoy many hours of music and the exchange of ideas. In some of the smaller communities two empty jam-jars will procure visual access to the mock adulteries of experienced screen " stars ". Divorce is cheap and easy, and even a parent cannot now prohibit a marriage if appeal on certain grounds is made to the organized forces of the State.

If our touring Arthur Young were actually the returned Arthur Young of the eighteenth century he might well report that to his observation in the nineteen-thirties birth is eased, where it is not prevented, death is retarded, and living is cushioned by the paternal organization of a community too richly dowered, individually and collectively, with the material fruits of the earth. He could not in honesty report want in the midst of plenty or a chaos of capitalism.

But for all his observation of material betterment, the touring enquirer could not report in the community any great level of happiness. If he enlarged the terms of reference of his tour of inspection he would discern resentment and discontent. He would discover that the land he surveyed did not, with the founders of American independence, "hold these truths to be self-evident: That all men are created equal; that they are endowed by their Creator with certain unalienable rights; that among these are life, liberty, and the pursuit of happiness". He would find that with the successful endeavour to cushion life there was neither effective liberty nor the social arrangement conducive to a successful pursuit of happiness.

It is, of course, a debatable question whether the drafters of the Declaration of Independence were sound in their definition of self-evident truths. Many metaphysicians and theologians would deny that all men are, even in a spiritual sense, created equal. There are tenable theories of re-incarnation which would suggest that men, as they walk this earth, are created unequal, with varying deposits of previously acquired merit or demerit. There are theories which suggest that part of the Creator's plan hinges upon the inequality of his creatures. But whether created equal or not, men are but dubiously endowed with those " unalienable rights " of life, liberty and the pursuit of happiness.

The tenure of life to a physical animal is precarious. Far from being an unalienable right, it is a privilege secured by the exercise of certain virtues (and/or vices) against nature at large or certain competing creatures of nature. In so far as communal organization secures a long and personally peaceful tenure of life to the individual, it has succeeded in its first main task of supplanting a natural, and rude, mode of existence by a mode that, in comparison, may be called civilized. It is one of the characteristics of our own " civilization " that the expectation of life to the individual citizen steadily increases. (If any doubt this he may be reminded that the Municipality of Birmingham in one lustrum of the last century was able to reduce in one district the death rate from 53·2 per 1,000 to 21·3 per 1,000. Over the whole country the expectation of life of a newly born male infant in 1871 was 40·4 years ; in 1921 it was 55·5 years. That of a man of 35 in 1871 was 28·7 years ; in 1921 it was 33·3 years. A newly born female infant in 1871 might expect to live 43·5 years and a woman of 35 might expect to live 30·8 years, but in 1921 the infant had an expectation of 59·5 years and the woman of 35 had an expectation of 36·1 years. Expectations of life by census, it must be admitted, mean little to the individual expectant, but even the expectations of 1871 would have seemed Utopian to the citizen who was born into the pre-capitalist eras of the seventeenth and earlier centuries.) Contemporary civilization must be allowed its claim to have given its children more life, and to have given it more abundantly so far as material satisfactions and fulfilments are concerned.

The question is whether " life, liberty and the pursuit of happiness " are complementary or competitive " rights ". To prolong and pacify the tenure of life may imply—as Socialists, Communists, Fascists and High Tories think—the very negation of liberty. Liberty may or may not, according to the mind and temperament of the speculator, aid the pursuit of happiness. A community which takes collective steps to guard its collective health must circumscribe individual liberty. A man cannot have the benefit of a good sewage system and the liberty to evade his general rate payments. He cannot save his ankles from fracture and his person from assault by robbers by the use of a well laid, constantly repaired and properly lighted road with the liberty to use the gutter as a private cesspool, as his great-grandfather did, or to observe at will the habits of toads in the mud in the middle of a public thoroughfare. He cannot, obviously, have his children educated in elementary hygiene, and the smattering of *literae humaniores* necessary for the conduct of a civil life, with the liberty to keep them at home to wash doorsteps or help with a hawker's cart. Still less, perhaps, can he have the comfort of a domestic immunity from burglarious intrusion with the liberty to dispense with, or to withhold support from, a communal police force. To have life he must sacrifice liberty. The modern problem is at what point the successive sacrifices of liberty make life not worth having.

The conflict between life and liberty is hardly so apparent as the conflict between liberty and the pursuit of happiness. We shall later discuss in some philosophic detail what are the essentials of happiness and in what happiness consists. Here it is sufficient to say that, whatever may be essential to happiness, certain circumstances tend to make happiness a vain quest. A confirmed masochist may, for all one knows, be happy under perpetual tyranny showing itself in a series of petty irritations. A confirmed sadist might, for all one can say, be happy administering such a tyranny. The normal citizen would find either—and does find either—a role hardly conducive to happiness and certainly destructive to comfort.

In that much misconstrued work, *The Servile State*, Mr: Belloc has rightly insisted that slavery is not synonymous with unhappiness. It cannot be said of happiness, in the fullest sense, as of the Kingdom of God, that it is within you. Happiness, for most of us, is a hybrid of introversion and extraversion. If you cannot have a true republic without republicans, you certainly cannot have happy republicans without a republic. Slavery will be a state of unhappiness unless those enduring it are temperamentally slaves, just as, contrariwise, freedom will be a state of unhappiness to human beings so constituted. A psychological house divided against itself can stand, but it cannot stand happily. A race bred to a tradition of freedom cannot endure with ease a state of partial slavery. A race bred to servience cannot enjoy thoroughly a state of complete freedom, which means a state of self-reliance.

It is the peculiar misfortune of the English of our time that they live in a period of transition, when the casual tyrannies of more fortunate fellow-citizens are giving place to the organized tyrannies—beneficently intended—of the State and of the community in its various collective aspects. It is their added misfortune that they must confront such a period without the powerful aids of a strongly realized national tradition and an inherited ideal of communal relationships, for, as this book will strive to show, the inability of a few successive generations of national leaders to gauge the significance of abrupt additions to the economic armoury and of certain changes in political organization has confused the tradition and shattered the inheritance.

The sudden and unheralded access of productive power and command over distance which caused the " industrial revolution " did more than end the dominating fear of collective mankind which had persisted since history began, the fear of famine. It destroyed in the generations born into the productive era the datum of social comparison, and the incentive to conserve, which had governed the outlook of those whom we may, perhaps, however loosely, call the manual generations. When the word " want " meant want of the barest necessities of life, and not want of the means to maintain an accustomed standard of living still enjoyed by relatives and friends, and when the presence or absence of such want depended very largely and almost always upon the vagaries of nature ; when the word " plenty " connoted a sufficiency of a few necessaries and very few luxuries, and not a profusion of many varieties of material satisfactions and diversions—then progress was instinctively measured by the distance attained from a tribally remembered barbarism, and personal contentment was not disturbed by the obtrusion of visual comparisons, actual or cinematographic, with the more enviable lot of others. Experience confirmed what Holy Writ taught, that in the sweat of his brow man shall eat his bread, being born to sorrow as the sparks fly upwards.

When locally produced necessaries are at the mercy of the apparently irrational inflictions of some external Power operating through wind and rain, drought, plague and the descent of blight, and when imported necessaries are equally at the mercy of that Power operating through storm and tempest, organization for communal betterment very naturally takes the form of mass appeal under the leadership of a God-man, and the local overlord is saved from the recurrent wrath and discontent of his followers by either his own standing as a human being in some special sacerdotal relationship with the erratic Power or his obvious fellowship with the rest of the community in its trials and tribulations. In a primitive community hard times are less likely to produce revolt than good times, for in good times all men grow arrogant, but in bad times they grow humble and mutually consolatory.

But in less primitive communities a new psychological factor begins to operate. Once communal effort with the aid of contrivances achieves the levelling out of the incidence of natural vagaries, or supernatural visitations, by producing an overplus of necessaries and the means of safe storage, the wise and the less wise will be divided in motive. Wisdom will show itself as acquisitiveness. If the stored overplus is in the hands of a wise—that is, an acquisitive and powerful—few, the return of hard times will be an incentive not to conserve the communal unity but to disrupt it by expropriating the controllers of the stored goods.

Once a section of a community commands a supply of stored necessaries against an evil day when either production or distribution or exchange shall diminish or fail altogether, the "want" of the other sections will no longer be want of bare necessaries; it will be want of a larger share of the available wealth of the totality. The custodians of the storage, that is, the owners of the reserved wealth, will arouse the envy and even the enmity of the sections whose subsistence is too meagre to permit saving. It is a commonplace of modern wage bargaining that a minimum tends to become a maximum: with standards of living, the reverse is the case, and a maximum tends to become regarded as a rightful minimum. A community emerging from barbarism—which means a community emerging from hand-to-mouth, day-to-day living into a mode of life cushioned by reserved necessaries—will not make an even progress from enforced frugality to permissible prodigality, for those who welcome as a boon some temporary advance of standards will resent as an outrage any temporary retrogression. An army unit which has been contented with a ration of ten slices to a loaf of bread will accept gleefully an increase to a ration of seven slices to a loaf, and will be driven to insubordination by a return to the lesser portion, forgetting the days when that was the normal distribution.

The more complex the life of a community becomes, the easier does it seem to become for its members to falsify the time perspective as between present benefits and past lack of them. Thus, in our time, men whose childhood was spent in some wretched hovel ill lighted by poor candles, oil lamps or inefficient gasburners, supported by a dietetic régimen of little and unvaried food, maintained in a state of mental restriction and with a cultural education of the crudest, are capable of describing as a social chaos the conditions of their nonage wherein boys of similar social condition are bred in sanitary houses lighted by cheap electricity or incandescent gas, on a régimen of varied and sufficient food, with available facilities for a relatively high cultural education and varied amusements. Men whose boyhood was spent in garments contrived from the cast-off shoddy of a parent or elder brother are able in their maturity to describe as chaotic a state of society which clothes similar boys in garments new to the wearer and fashioned to more pleasing form from better materials brought from the world's ends. The word " distress " is applied not to a condition wherein the majority of the citizens are unable to preserve life, but to a condition wherein a number of citizens are compelled to return to a standard of living lower than they have once known but still incomparably higher than their fathers and grandfathers thought to be within the range of possibility at times of the greatest communal prosperity.

The essence of our present troubles, to any realist who can formulate it without any fear of an electoral vote mistaking his hard head for a hard heart, is not that men want in an age of plenty, but that we are producing more than we consume with our capacity for consumption far from sated. To put it into the homely examples of the rostrum, men are burning coffee for which other men would be grateful, men are throwing back into the sea catches of fish of which other men would be glad, men are restricting their production of tin, rubber, copper and various primary commodities while other men could find ample use for vastly increased supplies of these things. Men in one part of the world lack comforts which men in another part of the world could supply in exchange for comforts from the first group. Clothing workers would be glad to have motor cars and motor car makers would be glad to have more clothes, but both remain workless. Maltsters would like rubber floorings for their bathrooms and rubber producers would like more ale, but the two desires are not made coincident.

The machinery of exchange is not working to its maximum capacity, nor to its recent capacity, although its reduced working is sufficient to maintain a general standard of life surprisingly high in comparison with the general standard of a decade or two ago.

From the narrow viewpoint of economics, a country like Great Britain can well afford to maintain three or four millions of unemployed workers and still aspire to a general standard higher than that of the eighteen-nineties and far higher than that of seventy, eighty or a hundred years ago. But from the viewpoint of politics and sociology, Great Britain cannot afford to maintain a dissatisfied population in which new wants and desires have been created without applying to those creations the very obvious means for their satisfaction which now lie in partial idleness.

If the world as a whole cannot now afford to maintain in idleness vast masses of the population, then the term "labour-saving machinery" is a misnomer. If the world cannot employ all its people and its productive "labour-saving" machinery, and thus furnish life with adornments and fulfilments to everyone's desire, the human faculty for organization must be considered as having atrophied.

But what the world cannot do, and what Great Britain cannot do, is to survive if the benefit of productive machinery is so perverted that a portion of the population is compelled to spend twenty-four hours a day and seven days a week in idleness while the remainder works long hours and long weeks, for no increasing material personal benefit, because the fruits of such labour must be divided with the idle. Either labour-saving and labour-augmenting machinery mean greater leisure for all, or greater material comforts for all, or such a clash of interests that some form of internecine strife will end for ever the civilization which devised that machinery.

Man with "many inventions" has conquered the age-old fear of famine. Those very inventions are now so misapplied that the fear of famine returns. It returns, as far as Great Britain is concerned, in this way. The present "slump", as any pedant in any penny paper will tell you, has been caused by a catastrophic fall in world prices. In other words, it has not remained worth A's while to swop his goods with B through the mediation of C, D, E and F. The sudden diminution of trade showed itself as a rise in the number of the unemployed citizens at a moment when the national profit on trade was falling steeply. This led to the fear that Britain by attempting to sustain more persons than her means would allow would grow bankrupt. She was not, therefore, to be trusted. Monetary balances left with her were withdrawn. At the same moment that one motive for withdrawal operated, another even more powerful came into play. The diminution of trade hitting other countries created in their nationals the need to call home from London their deposited monetary resources. The symbol of this complex of factors was a flight from the pound—that phrase with which the man-in-the-street became so familiar in 1931. The flight from the pound led to Britain's abandonment of the gold standard.

Expressed at its simplest, though financial economics are never as simple as financial journalists care to pretend, nor so complicated as economists like to suppose, the abandonment of gold meant that a trader abroad could not count upon receiving if he wished a certain amount of gold in exchange for a given number of British pounds. Once divorced from gold, despite hastily devised financial machinery for supporting its value, the pound rapidly ceased to command its old return abroad. At the moment of writing the pound sterling in New York commands goods or services which would have been commanded a year and a half ago by 13s. 8½d. A dollar in England commands goods and services worth roughly 5s. 10d., whereas eighteen months ago it would have commanded goods and services worth only about 4s. 2d. Britain is not self-supporting. If the pound with which she must buy the bulk of her food supplies falls very low—if, let us say, for the sake of being thoroughly alarmist, it falls to an exchange value represented in the early part of 1931 by 5s.—the Briton for a unit of work represented by £1 will only receive in exchange goods worth the old unit of 5s., but he will for a present 5s. have to do a unit of work represented by the old unit of £1.

To earn the means of buying goods he, collectively, must find people willing to take the fruits of his own work. If he fails to find suppliers willing to exchange with him or if the maximum amount of his own produce in manufactured goods brings into his country an inadequate supply of food in exchange, famine is once again the immediate menace. It will be realized that when he tries to sell his manufactures on a devalued £ their apparent price abroad is low, since something worth to him, by his costing symbols, £1 is bought by the American for the equivalent of 5s.; but, on the other hand, the raw materials from which his manufactures have been wrought have cost four times as much as under the old fully valued pound, and wages will have advanced to enable the worker to buy the dear food which is still entering. Thus an article once quoted in sterling at £1 will have to be quoted much higher, and perhaps so much higher that the lower price abroad may not benefit the buyer; so, for example, an article priced at £1 is bought for the equivalent of 5s., but if costs force the price of that article up to £4, the new price abroad is still the old equivalent of £1.

The failure of imported food supplies to Great Britain is a matter of graver moment than the failure of food supplies to other countries. Britain has bred a specialist race of urban workers and has neglected her peasantry. She cannot by the utmost stretch of ingenuity and by the most marvellous aids of science quickly become self-supporting. A failure in supply means for her literal and actual famine.

A threatened famine, it is to be assumed, would be met by rationing. The imposition of short commons would itself weaken the stamina of the workers. The time might quickly arrive when there would not be enough to provide even short rations for all. That would mean a fight for what was available. If in London, with its seven or eight millions of dependent population, violent civic conflict arose, one effect would probably be the neglect of the essential public utility services. A London with neglected sewers, gas mains, underground railways and the like, would rapidly be a London swept by plague, and might be a London of collapsed buildings. Men would see the return of the rat.

The migration of men and the return of the rat in big cities and townships during a time of grave and desperate internecine warfare would be the return to barbarism, for there would be no wealthy neighbours able to provide for a disrupted Britain the aid that once went to a disrupted Central Europe.

It is to this possibility that the machines which conquered the fear of famine have brought us. Why? Because we have put our trust in pedants. Because we have elevated politicians and economists to the status of witch doctors and credited with an inhuman foresight men whose qualification was not an ability to direct the future but only to dissect the past.

Mankind, having lost the need, as Commander Kenworthy has forcibly said, for economists of the type of Joseph, whose wisdom was to fill the storehouses and barns, has reached the era of statesmen like Major Walter Elliot, whose remedy against possible famine is to prohibit the entry of foreign food so that the natives of the island may again learn to grow their own. But it is obvious to any clown in any country inn that the machines which once destroyed the fear of famine could, if the world were but properly organized, end the need for all men for arduous labour, giving to each a material standard of life and a cultural opportunity that would eventually make the earth a great and gracious habitat. It is obvious to any superficialist in a soup queue that when a machine will do the work of many agricultural labourers, and when the one agricultural worker who manages the machine needs not his old 5,000 calories of food per day but only some 3,500 calories, because of the reduced physical demand upon him, unemployment of labourers is inevitable, and is to be regarded as a boon and not a curse, for the amount of food produced by the one man and the machine is in excess of that once produced by the many, and their consumption demand is less. But there is no boon if the share-out of the product is not adjusted to the circumstances which have been created by the change of method.

It is the thesis of this book that the clown in the country inn and the superficialist in the soup queue, who are the true sociological realists, have proved in the past, and are proving now, better guides to the direction in which communal organization should tend than the professing economists, whether academic or Parliamentarian. It is the secondary argument of this book that the major fault of our time is that the ordinary man, reasoning as an empiricist in economics and as a human being with certain aspirations to personal happiness in politics, has been baulked of an effective control over his economic and political destiny. Even when he has had provided for him some democratic machinery bearing the appearance of an instrument of government he has been bedevilled by dons and bulldosed by caucus-bosses, whether political or trades union, until he has been rendered utterly unable to manipulate the instrument to his true desires.

The average citizen crying aloud that his feudal shoe pinches is fitted with the leg-irons of laissez-faire; protesting next that his fetters are more than he can bear, he is as promptly clapped into the iron boot of modern quasi-nationalization and monopoly. At each stage of his progress he is either told to be grateful that he is so well shod or he is offered as an alternative some equally menacing piece of foot-wear. Never is he permitted to fashion shoes to his liking or to go barefoot. He must limp as best he may in the handiwork of political patchers and economic cobblers.

Politico-economic systems, however, were made for man, and not man for the systems. The debt of a generation is to itself, and not to its posterity. In a recognition of these truisms lies the secret of communal organization for the old ideal of the greatest happiness of the greatest number, which by no means ruled out happiness for the minority. It is the third contention of this book that all " planned economy " is inimical to general happiness, since human psychology is such that it evades the economist as planner.

The doctrine to which the reader is asked to address himself, or invited with equal good-will to discard abruptly at this point, is that the solution to our present discontents must lie in conservation—the conservation of the common sense of the common man against the attacks made upon it by theorists, planners, currency reformers, dictators, propagandists of peculiar panaceas, and pedants.

CHAPTER II

THE RISE OF THE RICH

ONE of the most profound illusions of the human race is that communal happiness can be promoted by political reforms. Reform Bills that extend the franchise, popular education acts, repeals of fiscal laws—all these achieve but one thing, the creation of a new set of problems and irritations. The extension of the franchise into universal suffrage, far from giving to the community the benefits of democratic control, has merely deprived the individual vote of its value and thrust the electoral divisions into the hands of caucuses. Popular education has produced a race of semi-literates discontented with the conditions of craftsmanship but unable to find a sufficiency of lettered professions to absorb all who would enter. Free imports in Great Britain, attained after one of the most strenuous agitations in political history, have survived less than a century of rising criticism, to give place at last to a Protective system. The free press, for which persistent dialectical battle was once waged, is already again subject to legal censorship, partly by a law of libel so tortuous that fear of its unsuspected powers of retribution prevents the press from telling what its directors feel and know to be the truth, and partly by specific acts such as that which restricts divorce reports. The appeal to the legislature by organized bodies of workers for the supervision or fixing of contracts regarding wages and conditions has resulted in a triangular relationship between employers, employed and the political community which has perverted the collective bargaining to ensure which trade unions were formed; for the masses of workers it has rendered individual free contract an impossibility ; with the result that enterprise is fettered by standard rates, sometimes, as with the railways, affecting not only costs but revenue.

The further away from the individual citizen or the small group the business of readjusting irksome or unjust conditions has been taken, the less satisfactory has been the result. Of all forms of readjustment that undertaken by Parliament is likely, by its very nature, which will shortly be examined, to be the least satisfactory. Quite apart from any other flaws in Parliament as a machine for the adjustment of economic and social relationships, it labours under two major disadvantages—either it must fashion and make legal a change in relationships after the need for such change has become vocal, or it must adopt a change devised by energetic minds within its own walls and then proceed to impose it upon the community. In the first case, by the time the new law has become effective the community relationships will have changed, the need will have been met by some local expedient, and the reform, being belated, will act as a restriction. In the second case, the new form of relationship will be an imposition—that is, it will be something to which by an effort the community must adapt itself—and will in all probability be an imposition ill adapted to the temperament of the masses who must endure it, since it will have been devised by exceptional minds.

If this is the case in legislation which affects the social habits of the people, it is even more markedly so in legislation which affects their economic life. An enactment, designed to protect pedestrians and horsemen, that steam-rollers must be preceded by a footman with a red flag is barely on the Statute Book before it is a hindrance to the development of the internal-combustion engine. An eight-hour day is hardly made the legal minimum when it becomes a hindrance to those technocrats who desire to apply machinery to the giving of extended leisure through a six- or four-hour day. Licensing laws designed to prevent expenditure of time and money during a period of national emergency are almost immediately felt as irrational curbings of personal leisure or publicans' enterprise. Schemes of protection against unemployment impose upon entrepreneurs so many obligations that the cost of their fulfilment checks enterprise and causes the very unemployment which they were devised to prevent. Forms of registration multiply until they both add to costs and detract from enthusiasm. Dictated forms of conduct multiply until the entrepreneur, upon whom economic progress depends, is compelled before taking any new step, and sometimes before fulfilling even the routine duties of his business, to take expert opinion as to what will be demanded of him.

The constant interference of a political body eventually results in a new change in the psychology of the persons affected. The State ceases to be regarded as a central entity to which the community gives a certain amount of money for communal purposes, and to which the community turns for certain communal purposes which are of their nature the function of a central authority—such as the administration of justice, the conduct of foreign relations, the preparation of defence, and the like—and becomes regarded as an initiating body from which should come the incentives to and directions for enterprise. The individual citizen, the joint enterprise, and the organized locality no longer regard the responsibility for their economic support as resting upon themselves, but as resting upon the remote central authority. It is no longer the man who must find work, but some Ministerial body which must find work for the man. It is no longer the trader who must explore markets, but the Board of Trade. If the individual exerts his energy or his ingenuity he is probably confounded by some ordinance or rule or regulation. He therefore ceases to exert himself and awaits advice or direction from some bureau. He neither creates nor seizes opportunity, but waits for opportunity to be presented to him, bearing the National Mark or some other sign of official approval. In the picturesque exaggeration of the Rugger field, the individual citizen can neither seize the ball nor take a pass, but waits for it to be handed to him on a soup plate.

Individualism having been first hampered and then ended by Paternalism, the State, with its usual inability to move as quickly as the national psychology changes, then realizes that Paternalism is injuring national character, and returns to Individualism, managing with characteristic success to obtain the worst of both psychological worlds.

Ardent supporters of the existing political system are apt to talk as if man in these islands had steadily emerged from serfdom to self-government and had by a laborious process escaped from dictatorship to democracy. Ardent detractors of the system preach the contrary doctrine, that man from the relative freedoms of feudalism and the mediæval organization has been entrapped at last either into a bureaucratic tyranny, such as Lord Hewart has recently denounced, or into a democratic muddle, such as Sir Ernest Benn is never tired of denouncing, in which the bureaucratic method of Government by Committee is less a designed tyranny than a tragic confusion wherein inept ideologues are given freedom to fetter efficient practical men.

Neither school is, as I see it, a sound interpreter of history. Man has not emerged from serfdom ; he has merely changed masters and the conditions of his service. Man has not lost a primal freedom and been entrapped into tyranny ; he has merely changed the form of ill-ease and the type of his tyrant. Those who say there is a golden age behind us and those who say there is a golden age before us are equally deceiving themselves. There can be no political or economic golden age while there is psychological growth. You cannot satisfy an appetite which grows by what it feeds upon, whether it be an appetite for more freedom or an appetite for more discipline. Still less can you hope to satisfy a multitude in which some want extended freedom, some want more rigid discipline, and some want both at once. The best that can be hoped for is that some mode of organization may be devised under which neither appetite is completely neglected.

Such a mode will not be fashioned by experts ; it can only be fashioned by humanists. Leadership by a priestcraft must always have the defects of its qualities, whether the leaders be priests of a theological or of an economic system. The history of social and economic progress—progress meaning a going forward, and not necessarily, be it marked, a going forward from worse to better—consists in a series of failures on the part of a priestcraft to satisfy its laity in material affairs.

The economic history of the English is a tangled story, but it can be seen without overmuch distortion as a simple one. The remnants of Rome and the survivals of the Saxons took a new form under the Norman. Rome, it is true, remains in many of our civic distinctions and in the names of certain functionaries, but it is the Norman who gives its shape to what of our longest lasting economic and social organization survives after a century of industrialism. Despite the crowded changes of the last four generations, the modern economic man is still the recognizable child of the Norman manor.

The manor remained the outstanding feature of English social and industrial life through the eras of both Norman and Plantagenet kings. An understanding of the manorial system is the base and finale of all economic study. It is not, as some zealots suppose, a method of organization to which we can return, but neither is it, as some expositors would have us believe, a method from which we have even yet wholly departed.

The manor, as a rule, corresponded very roughly to the modern parish. The community which inhabited it was, to all intents, self-supporting. The lord who ruled it had his tenure from the Crown, either directly or indirectly, and the condition of lordship was military service. The original settlement of a community, in any place, at any time, has generally depended upon one of two factors: either the site has been strategically defensible or it has been that of a holy place. Defensibility implies the presence of the elementary factors of sustenance, water and cultivable land. The survival of a holy place almost wholly depends upon the same factors. The lord of a Norman manor very naturally dwelt in the most defensible spot of the area which he ruled. He had his castle, and about it spread the lands of the demesne from which the major sustenance of his household came. Most of the inhabitants lived in the village, a scattered collection of rude dwellings, near the centre of the manor, and occupied little land, although all, or nearly all, were cultivators.

Outside the demesne-lands stretched arable land, meadow land, a common pasturage and the waste of wood, scrub and marsh. The arable land was organized for the communal benefit. It was divided into half-acre strips—small allotments—distributed in such a way that the land of the individual cultivator might be scattered over the whole extent of the tract. A man with many strips would not control a self-contained area, for it might be that no two of his strips lay side by side.

After harvest the arable land, now stubble, was thrown open for grazing, and the next year saw a new partition of strips. Rotation of crops was achieved by dividing the arable into three fields, one for wheat, one for oats or barley, and one to lie fallow, the fallow being the next year devoted to wheat, and the wheat field to oats and barley. The meadow land was organized somewhat similarly, and thrown open to common pasture after the hay harvest. From the waste came sustenance for swine and the supply of wood for fires and implements. The manor also had certain closes which were not subject to an annual interchange. The community as a whole employed some herdsmen and shepherds to prevent cattle and sheep from straying and doing mischief.

The landlord held the land, but he did not in our modern sense own the land. Not only was he not the absolute master of the cultivators ; he was not his own master. He was subject to forfeiture if he did not render to the king those dues and services which were Cæsar's, but he could not inflict forfeiture upon the cultivators while they continued to render to him his own due. The lord had to provide protection and sustenance, through the means of sustenance, and the cultivator in return gave certain services and goods. Money did not complicate the relationship. The benevolent autocrat in the castle was paid in kind by the peasant proprietor. The cultivator in return for the right to cultivate his own holdings, gave certain days to the cultivation of his lord's land. Having laboured on his own behalf, he gave his labour to his lord. The exchange of services was simple, even if the sharing of the fruits of the combined services was unequal.

In practice, of course, this simplicity was far from Arcadian. Manners and customs were crude, and lords differed in their interpretation of the relation between them and the inhabitants of the manor. The standard of living was low, with little variety, but it was probably no lower and little less varied than that of the people of Zetland in Scott's *The Pirate*, many centuries later where against the sparse background of hard material living move men and women of deep emotional satisfactions and repressions. The dominant factor in communal relationships must have been the ever-present sense of interdependence combined with a common experience which gave a ready understanding of motives and actions. The community sense was strong. The dispensation of justice might be arbitrary, but it was understandable. The victim of the law could appreciate why he was so treated. The ordinary person was not baffled by the origin of restrictions upon conduct, however much he might be hurt by their operation. The sense of interdependence and of common understanding is what was lost during the centuries when the manor gave place to the town, the town to the city, the city to the industrial organization.

The growth of towns, or the growth of *a* town, was not rapid. The eighty towns of Domesday Book included many walled settlements that were by any measure of population and importance only defensible villages. In what towns there were the inhabitants were subject to much the same régime as the cultivators of a manorial holding. They were controlled by a lord, either the king or a manorial lord. They paid dues either for land or for trading liberties. But as towns grew in both number and size this control was loosened and lost. A charter of freedom could be bought either for a lump sum down, to ease the very present necessity of the Crown for gold, or by an annual payment. Towns became autonomous, and their burgesses replaced the central authority of a single man by a council of certain of their own number charged to maintain the liberties and to administer those affairs which were of necessity communal.

But behind all control, whether of the lord, the king, or the council, was a control which was at once a positive directing force and, as it were, a court of appeal or consolation. The ethic of the community, however disregarded on occasion, was not an empiric code of relationships devised from the experience of what would and what would not permit a community to flourish or to survive. It was a mystic code which dictated the relation of man to man and inferior to superior by the revealed code of relationship between all men and their Creator.

The Church was both visible and militant. It had power both spiritual and temporal. It formed the civilization of the known world and it unified the components of every unit of that civilization. Religion could hardly then be termed the " dope " of the workers, for everyone was an addict. " Priestcraft ", powerful as it was in certain phases of influence, was not a craft of supermen with supernatural delights that compensated in the onlookers' eyes for the natural deprivations of the office. When William conquered England, the parish priests whom he found, and who became attached to the manorial law, were no higher in status than the ordinary cultivator. In his *The Eleventh Century*, Vinogradoff says of them, " The parish priest with his virgate, half-hide or hide, appears as one of the villein shareholders of the township, though his tenement is held free of the common service on account of his special obligations." When the Popes introduced compulsory celibacy for the clergy it was not easily attained. The habits of the parish priest were the habits of the normal man, his tradition was the common tradition. The higher ranks of the Church, filled by the conquering Normans, were not of that ascetic metal which made continence easy. But discipline prevailed. The ordinary worker saw his priest denied the comforts of matrimony, and the sacrifice did not always tend to increase the respect of the parish for its incumbent.

The common need to force sustenance from a not too yielding earth with implements that were still crude, the common need to protect the community from maurauders, the common acceptance of local law, and the common adhesion to a mystical creed expounded and interpreted with sacramental rites by priests who, as persons, were low with the humble and, as ambassadors of an aloof Authority, were greater than the highest, gave a unity of interest and a unity of character so potent that it subdued very quickly the difference between Norman conqueror and Saxon conquered. Romantic history may make play with William's ravaging of the North, and with romantic rebels like Hereward the Wake or Robin Hood, but realistic history must see a mode of life rapidly toning both the racial temperaments into a common character. To recapitulate briefly, the manor was not a mere system but a mode of living, and the mode remoulded the men. The Normans were to the manor born, and the Saxons as its adopted children soon acquired its ways.

At that time the economics of life were supremely simple. It may be broadly said that no man pestered the throne or the people with economic theories, and that the accumulation of wealth was not a motive which greatly affected the people in the mass. Where accumulation was a motive, it was merely a motive of self-preservation against a coming shortage or against a feared attack. No villein strove to accumulate in order that he might buy his way into a superior social caste. Had he striven he could not have achieved, and had he achieved he could not have used his accumulation for such a purpose. The troubles of the time were not in our modern sense economic but personal. A man might strike against the king's deer and lose his hand, but he could not strike against his lord and lose his land. If the king—as the king on more than one occasion did—evicted men, he evicted them in the mass to make a hunting ground. He could not, nor could his deputy, the lord of the manor, evict them for caprice, as Naboth was evicted.

The villein was in many respects a slave. He was tied to the land on which he was littered. His freedom of action was severely circumscribed. He was made to work, and he could not do as he might wish even with his own family. But in other respects he was far from being a slave. The safeguards against injustice possessed by freemen were not his, but to protect him he had " the custom of the manor ", interpreted and enforced by the Manorial Court, which was an open court wherein both freemen and villeins shared the privilege and duty of acting as judges or assessors. The manorial lord might occasionally ride rough-shod over both manor and court, but against such tyrants there was always a very effective remedy, once applied with a certain melodrama against a king in the New Forest. Many a manorial lord had reason to " 'ware Red William's arrow ". None had any reason to fear an economic blockade.

But if in the individual cultivator or citizen wealth was not a motive, wealth grew. Barbarism was, in time, but a league behind the manor ; barbarism fringed it in space. Barbarism might well lie before it. But it escaped a return to barbarism because despite hard living, violent manners, superstition, and lack of culture, it had both discipline and a communal unity.

The development and progress of England under the manorial system has been succinctly described by G. E. Trevelyan :—

> No ancient system must be judged in the abstract, or by purely modern standards. The great merit of

> the manorial system in its day was this, that among men of primitive passions and violent habits, it promoted stability, certainty and law. A court that focussed public opinion and tradition, and that actually kept written records from the Thirteenth Century onwards, was established as part of the normal life of the English village. . . . During the centuries when this system flourished in England, wealth slowly accumulated ; more land came under the plough : flocks and herds multiplied in spite of frequent murrain ; and in spite of no less frequent famine and pestilence the population went up. . .

Agriculture and craftsmanship were both unscientific ; trade and exchange were matters of either natural and haphazard bargaining or easy expedients ; transport and communications were affairs of individual adventurings in a land that had all but lost the roads of Rome. Religion however divine in revelation, was received and practised as an organized superstition. The Faith had taught man neither to love his neighbour as himself nor to render unto Cæsar the things which were Cæsar's except within the confines of his own community. But the Faith had apparently, taught one thing supremely well—or to avoid undue contention, let us say that with the Faith flourished an older fetish—fairness. The test of manhood was not only virility, it was also fair dealing. Against unfair dealing the manorial customs and the manorial court were, in intent and largely in effect, a stout barrier and a redressant.

In the townships as they grew this sense of the necessity for fairness became more apparent and obvious. Not only "negative" means of redressing unfairness, but positive means of ensuring fairness were created and became important. The growth of wealth was at first unorganized. It was almost an unnoticed by-product of the mode of life embraced for the sake of stability. The aggregation of growing wealth into communal " pockets " —and personal pockets—and the increasing means of translating wealth into civic power changed gradually the surface psychology of the people. A king who by force of arms, military skill, and statecraft, could take and re-bestow land in return for armed service was eventually replaced by kings who would release vassals from armed service for a cash payment. Prowess in trade became more important than prowess in the tourney. The virtues of the mart became more valuable than martial virtues.

Nothing in conjectural history is more fascinating than the growth of a township after its earliest stages. Sited first for its strategical defensibility or command, a town attracts to it those non-militant inhabitants whose function is to feed and clothe the garrison either with necessaries or with the trumpery luxuries which fighting men relish. It attracts, also, a population of men and women either driven out from lonelier settlements or preferring the gregariousness and safety of the growing town to the uncertainty and loneliness of the village or hamlet. Once population in a town is sufficient to exercise a demand which shall give stimulus to the cultivators within a reasonable range of its own boundaries, it develops a double trade within its own community. Traders will come to provide the townsmen with their requirements and traders will come who see in the growing settlement a useful centre for operations over the surrounding and prospering areas. These will increase the prosperity of both the town and its local suppliers by buying their produce for transit to more distant places in exchange for locally desired commodities. The primary servitors of their fellows may soon be equalled and even outnumbered by the middlemen. In a primary exchange between simple producers values are known and appreciated, but once there intervenes into such exchanges a *tertium quid*, offering new and unfamiliar objects of exchange, values may, for the time being, become arbitrary until by a familiar economic process the worth of things exchanged finds a tradeable level.

At that point of intrusion by the middleman there enters cozening and sharp practice, advantages on exchange earned by nothing but the vendor's or purchaser's knowledge of the ignorance of his interlocutor. For a time the very valuable middleman who transforms a simple series of simple exchanges into a complexity of multiple bargains is, and probably must be, the assessor of his own value to those whom he serves. The known standard of " fair dealing " cannot cope with a new form of dealings in which one party is a person of unfamiliar methods and functions trading in commodities of as yet unascertained true value.

It was when this stage of development was reached that the townships growing with, and emerging from, the manors began to create their protections against unfairness. The Frith Gild came into being.

The rise of the gilds in English social and economic life began, it may very broadly be said, at a time of triple transition. Law was assuming a new shape. Manorial law and king's law and church law were mingling or refusing to mingle and bringing about that state of administration of justice which ended when Henry II achieved the most important step in the legal history of our people, of which more must be said later. The new language was forming itself from the double language which had been necessary to the early functionaries who were the go-betweens of the Norman lord and the Saxon villeins. Trade was beginning to usurp the domination of tillage, which meant that the material standards of life were rising with the rising possibility of variety.

All trade suffers from two ever-present dangers. There may be actions in restraint of trade, which prevent easy exchange, or there may be actions which destroy men's faith in trade. Credit, it must always be remembered, comes from the same root as *credo*, and without credit trade cannot expand. If belief in the fairness or honesty of a trader goes, if doubt is induced as to the worth of a commodity, if parties to a bargain are made to feel that some third intervener, no matter how useful his services, has taken more than his just share from either or both the main parties, trade languishes.

It is a characteristic of new and small communities that a man is seen whole. It is characteristic of large communities that a man is rarely seen whole. In a small community Mr. Bung may be, as in the children's card game, " Mr. Bung, the Brewer," but he is also Councillor Bung, and Bill Bung the bass soloist, and William Bung, P.M. P.P. Gd. St. Br., and Mr. Bung, Chairman of the Cottage Hospital or the Ratepayers' Association, and old Bung, the club bore. In a complex community he is too often seen in sections by sections, and Bung the Brewer, familiar to one suburb, is lost in Mr. Bung the sidesman of another suburb, and in Bung the ardent philatelist in yet another suburb, while in a remote town he is merely William Bung, the potential party candidate.

When communities in England were still small and self-contained the Frith Gild flourished, for the Frith Gild, was an association which embraced most of the interests of its members. It was partly religious, partly social, partly functional, partly political and wholly benevolent. Its tone was probably not unlike that of a modern Freemasons' lodge which confines its entrants to members of a particular profession, such as architects, actors, journalists, or lawyers, and the like. But as communities grew in numbers and complexity, the Frith Gild gave place to the Merchant Gild, which rapidly brought into existence the Craft and Trade Gilds. The interest of these new gilds was a specialized interest. They catered for the man *qua* merchant or *qua* craftsman, and not for the man *qua* citizen of earth and potential citizen of Heaven.

But the Frith Gild bequeathed to its successors its main purpose—the regulation of trading intercourse to ensure fair dealings. When the Merchant Gilds faded in power before growing Craft Gilds, both maintained the old ideal, that a specialized body with the duty of securing fair dealings has a responsibility both ways. A modern trade union has as one of its objects the prevention of the exploitation of the workers by the employers, either in direct contact and contract or through a State that may be too much the tool of an employing class. But the old Craft Gilds not only had this as their object, they also had the duty of seeing that the workers themselves acted fairly. Not only were the interests of the various producers—employers and employed, as we might call them—guarded, but the interest of the consumer was also protected. The gild dictated what tools might be used, the gild insisted upon a certain quality of raw materials, the gild insisted that no workman should for his private profit endanger the repute and good of his trade.

The strength of the gild was exactly the strength of the older local, manorial courts. It was the strength of focussed public opinion, which gained in strength when it was the opinion of a specialized opinion focussed within one section of the community. The purpose of the gild was the creation, preservation and regulation of a mode of life. It was not concerned with the accumulating of wealth. Like the manor, it rose to power by its ability to maintain a disciplined unity among its members. But, like the State of which it was a part, the gild grew rich, if not against its will, certainly against its original intention, as the Church was growing rich.

Possessions rather than status began to govern men's lives. The change was helped by the progress made in mechanical invention and growing skill in craft and cultivation, but it was helped much more by the growing craft and skill of the men of war. England as a nation warring with the French was something very different from a nation in arms. The king could not compel those liable to render military service to abide with his forces for periods long enough for his purposes, but he could hire men who would stay as long as he paid them. The services of the Manorial and town inhabitants were commuted for yearly payments in cash or kind, with the result that by the middle of the fourteenth century the whole social organization had altered, imperceptibly during the progress of the change, but quite definitely at the end of it. The lords were no longer the tied vassals of the Crown, the villeins were no longer the serfs of their lord. The methods of holding tenure having changed the methods of cultivation changed also. The small, half-acre strips were still allotted, but they were not regularly interchanged. The small landowner began to acquire strips that lay side by side in place of the strips that had been distributed about the general land of the Manor. The unified holdings began to be fenced off from each other. The modern farm appeared in embryo.

As this process went forward, war also had its usual effect of stimulating exchange between one land and another. The continent wanted more English wool. For the raising of more sheep the common pasturage and the " waste land " were brought into use, and, where it was possible, the arable land was diverted from corn.

Wool was enormously important. Its production and sale gave to the lords the means of paying their commuted dues to the king. So vital a trade did it become that it had to be regulated, and it was regulated by being passed through the " staples " of certain selected towns where a certain proportion of the export was taken by the king's officers for their master. These customs' officers were in a position of great but not ostensible power. They and the merchants, the middlemen, gradually obtained control of the trade of these staple towns, and became the merchants of the staple.

The merchants of the towns, the money-changers, the gilds, the Church, all grew rich. The Crown continued its wars abroad, an expensive hobby which threw the king more and more into the hands of those who found for him the means of prosecuting war. War itself changed its character. Gunpowder diminished personal domination in the field and heightened personal risk, for a cannon-ball knows no chivalry. Character and craftsmanship as the tests of a man's standing waned as wealth increased. The unity of small groups, of common levels of culture and aspiration, broke before the onslaught of new men and new modes from distant places. The towns were trading in more than commodities; they were trading in ideas. In the primitive pursuits, like agriculture, size of output became important. The urge was to increase holdings of land, which meant expropriation for some and a new relationship for all. The early feudal balance of duties and rights disappeared gradually, and left behind a new balance of masters who hired men and men who were hired by masters.

While the gilds were simple and strong, and the Church an organization combining temporal influence with spiritual power to bless or to ban, the balance gave a stable enough community through which change played like a wave. When the gilds waxed rich and became corrupt and the Church waxed rich and became corrupt, change ceased to play over the community like a wave and smote it like some disintegrating force.

To the Reformation, it may be said, the tendency was for the power of the old lords to diminish and for that of the workers, merchants and priests to increase. The king, as a factor in the State, passed from an erratic period when his power varied almost with each generation, to a period when he was a veritable potentate.

The turning point of English history, as every schoolgirl realizes, was the time of the Tudors. Henry VII and Henry VIII were children of the Renaissance. If the elder Henry turned miser in old age, the younger presented to the gaze of his subjects an example of material magnificence which could not have been sustained had not the general comparative standard of living been rising rapidly. The increase in facilities of transport, the more constant intermingling with the home-staying populations of itinerants from far countries, the growing specialization of avocation to meet a wider ranging market for goods and services were not confined to these islands. Feudalism died soft or died hard in different portions of the world, but it was dead or dying when the revival of learning changed the mentality of mankind in the mass. Men began to eat voraciously of the tree of knowledge, and the forbidden fruit left them with no stomach for the Faith as their fathers had known and kept it.

Whichever of the many causes advanced for the trend of the Reformation be the dominating cause we need not argue here. It is certain that the despoiling of the monasteries would not have been possible had the masses of the people not been ready to see brought down the institution which the Church Visible seemed to them to have become. The monasteries had suffered in men's minds that degradation that in our own time has afflicted Parliament. A venerated institution had become first a tolerated relic of a past age, next a refuge for ambitionists, and finally a thing of mockery that was disliked because it was still powerful to work discomfort either by exactions or by interferences.

The same process had affected the gilds. In a word, wealth had transformed the defenders of the poor into their scourge. The monastic bodies and the gilds might irk the king and his rich and powerful friends, but they racked the people. Both Church and gilds, having fallen too largely under the sway of avaricious men activated by the desire to demonstrate the petty qualities of statecraft, invited the antagonism and received the attack of avaricious statesmen who had chosen a different instrument. The general mass of the population, in as far as it understood the matter, did not care which gang of rich men bested which, but it probably had a hopeful feeling that when tyrants and parasites fell out honest tradesmen might come to their own.

The hope was vain. The aggregations of wealth which the monasteries and the gilds had accumulated might have furnished the Throne with such economic power that it could have re-instituted a modernized and reformed feudalism, having in it a place for a purged Church and a purified system of gilds. Those aggregations were, by a syphilitic king whose will power had waned at the moment of its most forceful exercise, dissipated among his sycophants. The desire of the king to legitimize the children of Anne Boleyn made possible the maraudings of Thomas Cromwell, but neither consolidated the economic power of the Crown. A new disciplined unity, which for a moment was possible, was thwarted. The reign of the rich men began.

CHAPTER III

THE TYRANNY OF TRADE

IT is an interesting, but a fruitless speculation how far the Reformation would have been possible had it not been for a purely natural catastrophe which hastened the end of the feudal relationship. That catastrophe is a landmark in both social and economic history. It was the Black Death. Before it, the English village was a self-sufficing entity whose major problem was sustenance but not unemployment. After it, the whole face of England was changed. The Black Death came out of the East and halved the population of these islands. Early populations are always matters for hot, and even embittered, controversy, but if we assume that what had been a nation of some four million people before the onslaught of the plague was after that onslaught a population of less than three millions, and perhaps less than two and a half millions, we shall not err gravely.

The Black Death made its appearance in 1348 and was stayed in the winter of the following year. Its effects were manifold, and economically the chief of them was that much land had fallen into disuse, owing to the diminution in both producers and consumers, and labour had doubled in value. Labour has never been slow to press upon the community its minimum worth. After the Black Death the claim for higher returns from labour became so forceful and exacting that law was needed to regulate the matter. The Statute of Labourers in 1351 fixed a minimum wage and compelled the worker to remain during the summer in the service of the same place where he had worked in the winter. But the regulation of the rate of hire and the place of employment did not mend the actual shortage of workers. An attempt to remedy the many disadvantages of this shortage lives in history as the precursor of the Peasants' Revolt—for the remedy was the attempted imposition of decayed feudal rights and a poll-tax, and these together led to Wat Tyler's revolt.

That revolt would not have been possible had not the teachings of the Lollards sunk deep into men's minds. Hinds had come to believe that they had a right to work where they might please, and though Wat Tyler was slain, and the revolt burked, the doctrine remained. The conquerors of the revolters remembered that there had been a revolt to conquer, and that a man with a scythe or a bill-hook in his hand might under careful agitation and leadership be more than an agricultural labourer. It was a lesson that France was to learn again and more terribly four hundred years later.

With Wat Tyler there entered into the national composition something which was not, perhaps, new as a concept and a dull, dumb feeling, but was new as an active factor in social relationships, something which to-day we recognize as class-consciousness, which is a very different thing from mere recognition of the existence of social classes. Class-consciousness grew with the spread of free labour, and the disappearance of the villein.

The growth of free labour made ready the background for the Renaissance, which, as all know, owed its rise to the incident of the sack of Constantinople by the Turks. Had the terrible Turk not driven the scholars of Stamboul from their seclusion, the homes of wealthy traders in North Europe would not have given shelter to new tutors. The thirst for learning would not have grown, and printing would not have had the importance which all recognized on its invention.

Labour was for the first time relatively fluid; the Crown had overcome the danger of too powerful lords; townships had grown in number and size; the old and new worlds were causing a quick expansion in trade, with all that that implies of change in social habits and standards; and King Henry sacked the monasteries and despoiled the gilds and distributed the loot among his lackeys. But in the two hundred years between the Statute of Labourers of 1351 and the Statute of Treasons of 1534 unemployment had become a problem, which it had never been in the manorial years. The Statute of Labourers ordered that unemployed persons should not refuse work when it was offered and that the lord of the manor was to have preference; that no higher wages were to be asked or given than had been customary in and before 1346; that no labourer could leave his employ before the specified time; and that all victuals and necessaries were to be retailed at reasonable prices. This Statute had given place to subsequent Acts which gave the justices of the peace power to fix wages, according to the price of provisions, at a maximum beyond which they could not rise. As early as Richard II the State was forced to take steps to deal with both "sturdy vagrants" and the impotent poor. The legislation of 1388 made the distinction between these two categories very clearly. The vagrant was subject to harsh physical penalties—imprisonment, branding, whipping—but the genuine poor were merely ordered to stay where they were if the town could support them, and, if not, to return to the places of their birth.

In this distinction we may see the first shadowy promise of the Means Test, but although the State organized those in want, it did not provide for them. That was left to charity, and mainly to the Church and its monasteries. The sturdy beggars, who still in the nursery rhyme "come to town ", were recruited largely from the riff-raff and scum of the Wars of the Roses. The impotent poor were the victims of the swiftly changing economics of their time.

The dissolution of the monasteries destroyed one very active and valuable source of relief. The " free inn " of the poor man had gone, not to return. The unemployment problem had taken a new turn. This was met by a law of 1536 which endeavoured to organize charities with the double object of finding work and giving relief, a duality of aim with which 1933 is still very familiar. In 1552 a firmer step was taken, for it was ordered that each parish should appoint two collectors " to gently ask and demand " a sum from each man and woman each week. Those who did not respond to the gentle demand were brought before the Bishop and admonished to do their duty. In 1563 these passive resisters of the demand were subject to a law which enabled them to be taken before a magistrate and assessed for a contribution to the needs of their unemployed fellow parishioners.

It is of some interest in passing to note that James Gairdner in the Cambridge Modern History cites Chapuys in support of the belief that although it is not altogether easy to estimate the precise effect of the fall of the monasteries upon pauperism, there is no doubt that it was the immediate cause of bitter penury.

> Altogether no such sweeping changes had been known for centuries. As regards the land some of the new results may have been in the end for good. But problems were raised which were new in kind. . . . The King's high-handed proceedings, alike as regards the Church, the monasteries, and the coinage lowered the moral tone of the whole community. Men lost faith in their religion. Greedy

> courtiers sprang up eager for grants of abbey lands. A new nobility was raised out of the money-getting middle classes, and a host of placemen enriched themselves by continual peculation. Covetousness and fraud reigned in the highest places.

Before returning upon our present track to look at Henry's action with regard to the coinage, stressed by Gairdner, and the rise of that money-getting middle class, we may pursue a little further the treatment of the unemployed.

The Statute of Labourers marked a change from a localized regulation of trade and labour to a national control, but that change was hardly effective, or even real, until after the gilds had been despoiled. Under Elizabeth the law of apprenticeship became a State matter, under the Statute of Artificers. The provision for the poor became definitely a matter of civic obligation upon the citizen. "The chief agents of this statutory control of the nation's economic life," says Trevelyan in a very significant passage, "as also of its political and judicial life, were the unpaid Justices of the Peace appointed by the Crown, who formed the link between the views of the central authority and the facts of local administration. They performed as servants of the State many functions which the feudal baron had performed in his own personal right." These unpaid magistrates were, of course, of the classes grown newly rich from the despoliation of the gilds and monasteries and of the money-getting middle classes.

It will be seen that the Tudors made final the transition of the Norman system. Once the local power had shifted from a personality with a special obligation upon him for the conduct of his lordship, and with the check of ecclesiastical displeasure before him, to an unpaid magistrate able to hold office because of the place bought for him in the community with wealth largely obtained from trade remote from his immediate fellows—when it was not the result of his maraudings or his sycophancy to the actual marauders—there could be no going back. When in the future any expansion of men's knowledge, whether of the arts or crafts or of the extension of the world, needed financing or staffing, these new rich were in a position to command the benefit. At one end of the social scale were men living in flamboyant extravagance and enjoying a wide and refreshing new culture: at the other end were the impotent poor and the sturdy vagabonds.

In the middle sections were merchants and usurers in very comfortable circumstances and workers with their lives increasingly regulated by State enactments. The tendency of the comfortably circumstanced was towards closer alliance with the rich. The tendency of the hired workers, men landless, and with no claims on any manor for support in times of general or individual distress, was to drift into antagonism to the rich save when their economic resentments were overcome by some other emotion, such as that of nationalism or sentimental love, hatred of the Spaniard or affection for Gloriana.

There had, in short, been created the Two Nations which Disraeli was to discern in the nineteenth century after the industrial revolution had hardened and emphasized their differing characteristics.

During the long age of transition from the Black Death to the Elizabethan Statute of Artificers a double gestation was taking place. There were being shaped the monetary system and the theory of economics, the one a necessary corollary to the other. The history of money is so familiar that it needs no rehearsal here. The development from barter to an agreed standard of value in a medium of exchange—the selection of a precious metal because of its qualities of desirability, portability, malleability, divisibility and indestructibility—the change from units of weight to units of named and guaranteed value—these stages had been passed before the coming of the Normans and the foundations of the manorial system. But money played a small part in the life of the manor. It was only when trade began to expand, wealth to increase, and townships to grow that money as a circulating medium began to end payments in kind, which had sometimes been regulated on a money value and sometimes not.

Expanding trade means the growing need for credit, and at times credit implies money. If, for example, a merchant could not persuade a manufacturer to supply goods for a delayed payment—if, that is, the manufacturer demanded money and refused credit—the merchant would have to borrow money, which means that instead of using his credit with the manufacturer he would use it with some third person. Since trade involves risk and money is precious, no money-owner lightly lends the one to stimulate the other. If he does lend his money he requires, very naturally, compensation for the loss of the profit which he personally might have made on it. Even if a merchant does not require credit in an absolute sense, he may require it in a particular place. A merchant who might be trusted by manufacturers or producers in Appleby, might have no means of impressing his probity on manufacturers or producers in Antwerp. A man whose honour was trusted at Chester might be without standing at Manchester. Any third party to his trade who had standing in both places would be worthy of his hire to complete a deal.

In the lending of money in modern times it is not really difficult to compute what compensation is just for its enforced idleness in the hands of the actual owner through its absence on loan. That computation was not so easy in the Middle Ages. It is not easy to-day in a gold-mining rush. Between two men of honour it is not really difficult to say what share of the profits of a bargain, or series of bargains, should go to the actual inceptor and conductor of the trade and what share to the useful intervener who has made it possible by lending his cash or credit. Between two men of different standards of honour, the division may involve dispute. Again, some owners of money may be prepared to lend it on the promise of an agreed proportion of gain, others may not. Simon may assist in fitting out the *Golden Vanity* on the promise that he shall have a tenth of whatever the *Golden Vanity* brings home from the Spanish Main, but Isaac of York may only be prepared to find money for the venture on condition that he is paid a certain return no matter what may be the fortunes of the argosy. Money may be in great demand or small demand, and its cost will differ accordingly. These factors greatly affect modern trading, but they much more greatly affected mediæval trading.

A man with command of money may lend a hundred crowns willingly if he knows that under agreement he will, after a certain space, receive again a hundred and ten crowns each of the same value as those he lent. His ardour is a little damped if he realizes that there is a strong chance that the hundred and ten crowns that come back to him may have been clipped of some of their value either by private or crowned rogues. Conversely, a man may be extremely unwilling to lend his money if he can keep it securely, but quite ready to lend it to some responsible borrower if he has no means of safeguard. An Elizabethan citizen, for example, might have an ingrained distrust of goldsmiths, but a greater distrust of the power of his own shop and residence to resist thieves, and would therefore deposit his wealth with a goldsmith. The original goldsmiths, as we know, took in wealth to guard; the later goldsmiths took in wealth to lend, well knowing that all their depositors would not at one and the same moment demand their possessions back again.

Borrowing from a professional lender of money has one great advantage over borrowing from private lenders—the money is there to be borrowed when it is most wanted. The squire may be willing to finance a harvest this year, but next year may himself be in need of funds at the vital moment. The professional financier is always ready, for it is his business so to be. The squire, finding himself in an unexpectedly awkward situation, may want his money again at an inconvenient moment. The professional financier will not worry until the agreed time of repayment, and even then, for a consideration, will renew the loan. The squire may be able to lend the money but not able to assist in its transmission to a distant creditor, but the professional financier will arrange to lend the money in one country and actually deliver it—for a consideration—in another.

All these points, which are part of the history of banking and credit, are commonplaces to our generation. The men of the Middle Ages had to discover them as their trade expanded and their customers and suppliers spread from a locality to a nation, from a nation to a continent, from a continent to a vast new world. Their money, supposed to be both a standard of value and a medium of exchange, was extremely unreliable, for in addition to the ordinary fluctuations, which they little understood, its purchasing power was liable, as we have seen, to arbitrary diminution at the hands of manipulators. Their price levels were affected by events not only out of their control but out of their cognizance. It is no wonder that two types of man grew powerful in relation to the producers—the trader and the money-lender, who were sometimes the same person.

The rising domination of these types, it may be said, was largely due, in Gairdner's words, to the fact that the age did not understand economic laws. It is an understanding after which we still painfully toil. It was also due to the associated fact that the controllers of the social and economic life were activated by motives which were individually selfish. The pursuit of glory or women by despots is never an occupation governed by economic insight or restraints. When the powerful become, either by will or by force, the pimps of a potentate, the primary producers must suffer, for they in the last resort pay the piper to whom the king " capers nimbly in a lady's chamber to the lascivious pleasing of a lute " or " rides in triumph through Persepolis ". A central authority demanding funds and prepared to extract them by tyrannical means affects trade directly and immediately. Men with the means of credit, knowing that they may at any moment be the victims of exaction without return, do one of two things ; they husband their resources and do not lend, or they lend more feverishly but at higher rates.

When Henry attacked the Church he did two things which in combination bred most, if not all, of our present discontents four hundred years after him. As Mr. Belloc has so often and so forcibly insisted, he destroyed what had previously been a triple balance of wealth, consisting of the Crown, the Church and the gilds, and, by dissipating the loot, created the beginning of a plutocracy. He also caused the change from an ethical motive in dealings to a non-ethical motive, and this he did before economists became effectively articulate. The evidence of Professor Cannan will hardly be suspect of any prejudice other than a liking for the truth. In opening his *Review of Economic Theory*, he writes :

> The fact is that these ancient philosophers [Plato, Aristotle] were not and could not be economists in our sense of persons who are interested in and think and perhaps talk and write about the material welfare of mankind. They professed to be concerned with higher things, and if they were not always so in fact, it was because they thought of themselves rather than because they thought of their fellow men. Their State, of which they made so much, covered a contemptible little district with one small town in it and a population of which the great majority were not citizens but slaves. It was impossible for economics to develop in such an environment. . . . The European Middle Ages show some progress. Economic matters came under the consideration of theologians who had to decide what actions were allowable and praiseworthy to a Christian man.

Professor Cannan is an economist and no propagandist for the Church which Henry smote. Sir Norman Angel is in the same category. He has recently written, in *The Story of Money* :

> One of the greatest events in the story of money is the change of ethical attitude in reference to loans, and interest thereon, and all that ecclesiastical ruling on such a matter implies. We find it difficult to-day to realize that for long ages nearly all the great moralists and teachers, nearly all the great religious bodies, including the Roman Catholic Church, condemned the charging of interest as a vile crime comparable only to murder. It was no casual or incidental condemnation with which the Church—and for centuries the secular State as well—visited

this offence. Its heinousness has been the subject of a vast literature ; of disputations carried on ardently from generation to generation, and age to age.

The denunciation of usury was based on no simple principle, or, perhaps, it is more accurate to say that it was based on a simple principle that was fallacious. *Pecunia pecuniam non parere potest,* said the men of the Renaissance. But money is not essentially unproductive, and to believe so is to confuse the symbol with the thing symbolized. Money is, after all, in one of its aspects, only a call upon certain goods and services. Goods and services are undoubtedly productive if properly used. Usury means not the exacting of interest for money lent, but for money lent for an unproductive purpose.

To return for a moment to the simple example of the elementary text-books on economics : If, having two ploughs, I lend one to my neighbour, I am at least entitled to ask that he shall return to me a plough, and not the worn-out remnants of a plough. If I lend him money that is the equivalent of a plough, I am entitled to a return of that money. But his use of the plough has prevented my making it productive in my service and has enabled him to make it productive in his service. Am I not, then, entitled to some compensation for my loss which shall take the form of some share of his profit ? Between friends and in certain circumstances I may forgo that compensation. In a communal society I may gain my compensation indirectly through the lack of need to support my neighbour by my own use of two ploughs. But to demand from a stranger that from the gain which he has made by my plough some compensation for my own loss through my non-use of that plough shall be paid is to ask, surely, nothing unjust. The end of the transaction leaves us in the same relative position as that which we occupied when it was entered upon. But if I demand a return upon a loan which has not been, and cannot have been, productive, I change the relationship. My loan has not enriched but impoverished the borrower. He or some part of his possessions passes into my power.

It is obvious that in small communities trading internally where men are not professional, but only incidental and casual lenders, it is simple to distinguish between a productive and an unproductive loan. In complex communities where trade is partly internal and partly external and where some men are professionally employed gathering together the means of lenders to re-lend to borrowers, no lender can tell to what use his loan is put. When I am in credit with the joint stock bank which manages my account, my money may be lent for legitimate interest on a productive transaction or it may be lent at usury. When I contrive an overdraft the money of the depositors upon which I draw may be used for a productive or non-productive purpose, but I pay the interest whether it be usurious or non-usurious, for it is not the rate of interest but its legitimacy which determines usury.[1]

The rise of the professional moneylenders as trade expanded through the Middle Ages meant inevitably that the lenders of money to those who lent it again were thus divorced from any inspection of or concern with its use. They ceased to " decide what actions were allowable and praiseworthy to a Christian man " and lent money for the mere sake of the return upon it. We shall not be considered guilty of mere empty anti-Semitism in marking as significant the fact that the traffic in money was at first largely conducted by Jews, who were men outside the tradition of the Church which in manorial times dictated the ethic under which trade was conducted.

[1] The view of the Catholic Church is discussed at length in the essay on usury in *Essays of a Catholic*, by H. Belloc.

Once the general communal motive shifted from an organized desire to ensure fair dealings, and the two powerful checks of the Church's metaphysical ban against the sin of avarice and the gilds' insistence upon definite standards of material and craftsmanship were removed, social life changed rapidly into a scramble for material benefit and advancement, not for the community as a whole but for the individual. It should be noted that the earlier motive implied nothing of what to-day we call communism. Any family which is not abnormally constituted is actuated by a desire for the material benefit of its totality, but it is far from being a commune. It is generally an uneasy despotism, where it is not a matriarchy. There is no communism in an army, but the general as opposed to the individual benefit is the actuating motive of the General commanding it.

With and after Henry VIII it was not, as ancient historians ingenuously imagined, politics which shaped the life of the community, but the life of the community which shaped politics. The new "aristocracy" of the money-getting middle classes aided by the host of placemen and assisted by the great incursions of wealth which began to pour in from the New World had neither concern with theological niceties about what was permissible to Christian men, but equally they had little or no interest in theories of Government. They were intent upon the maintenance of the monarchical and caste system, partly because it was an inheritance which had served them well, but mainly because they could conceive no other system. For the most part their interest no longer lay with a small section of the community whose relationship with the rest of the world was their own relationship, but with the whole of the community as a producing and consuming entity.

The change was not, of course, abrupt or clear-cut. The squire remained a squire in the sense of being something like a Norman manorial lord long enough to see the industrial revolution well under weigh and to complete the work of the Tudor despoilers by enclosing what was left of the common lands. But his power was changed and his outlook was changed, and his personal focus of responsibility was changed. He was less the subject of laws directed against his possible rapacity than the instigator of laws designed to protect and forward his interests against those of the other sections of the State. Two quite representative types of the new ruler may be studied in Cecil, Elizabeth's Minister, and George Heriot, the goldsmith to James I.

Another change which followed the break-up of the monasteries and the gilds was that change in what may be called the youth's ladder of ambition. The Church in pre-Reformation times, as in Ireland to this day, offered a way of escape to the boy of special gifts from his original environment. It opened a way to such men as Wolsey. The gilds provided the " horizontal " complement to the Church. Through the Church a boy might rise to great power of statecraft and scholarship. Through the gild he might grow to completion as a master craftsman, sure of his eventual status. After the Reformation the ladder of ambition was wealth, and the way to wealth was not by remaining a craftsman.

Successful ambition under Henry VIII might be Wolsey, but under Elizabeth successful ambition was personified in Thomas Gresham. Heriot visited James, it may almost be said, because Elizabeth had so freely visited Gresham. The link between the Crown and the counting-house was both narrow and firm, as it could not have been a hundred years earlier. A Church which had whipped Henry to the tomb of Becket no longer existed to whip the money-changers from " The Temple ", where the laws of England were conceived and administered.

The complete revolution in relationships had a psychological effect on both of " the two nations ". The difference in habits of life between the trading rich and their henchmen and the producing poor was more than a difference of material standards. It was a difference in culture. In the early Middle Ages any selected community in the British Isles would be not unlike the Duke and his court in the forest of Arden ; by the sixteenth century it would be more like Prospero and Caliban. In the early days the physical life and the mental background would be shared by all. At the table all dined together with the same table manners, and all heard the same ballad-monger or story-teller. In the later days the physical life and mental background of the money-getting middle classes was something entirely different from that of the labouring classes. Disraeli's categories were, in fact, an understatement, for there were in England not merely two nations growing up side by side, but two races.

The dominance of the money-getting middle classes towards the end of the eighteenth century changed the whole course of the machine age. It affected first the financing of the machines and next the fluidity with which men who grew rich by the machines permeated the political and social governing castes. But long before the industrial revolution had dawned, the diagnosing economist had become a factor in the direction of national life. The theologians having been shouldered from the rostrum by the philosophers, theories of the State were discussed which involved theories of property and contracts. John Locke, producing *Two Treatises of Government*, inoculated economic thought with a theory of value that, like all economic theories, had its day and ceased to be. But the economist as more than an aspect of the philosopher did not appear as a portent until the opening of the seventeenth century. The nations continued to grow richer as they grew more belligerent, and more belligerent as they grew richer. Nationalism was like a heady wine which drove kings to excesses for which trade *had* to pay.

Money was the symbol of wealth. A person with a fixed income seeing his money flow out naturally grows alarmed, for the inflow is fixed. A sophisticated trader is not alarmed when his money flows out, for that may only mean a broadening of the whole basis of his profit-making business. But a sophisticated trader is quite definitely alarmed if, over an extended period of operations, more money flows out than flows in. With money as the symbol of wealth and a population largely unlearned in the significances of its movements, a situation is created wherein the passing of coin, or the metal from which coin is made, from one nation to another becomes a matter of alarm. So great was this alarm in the Middle Ages that history is sprinkled with attempts to prevent the export of either coin or bullion. Such prohibition to a trader is fatal. The interest of the merchant classes was, therefore, against the prevailing fear of the courts.

It was silver—destined to be always the most mischievous of metals—which caused the empiricists who traded with the East Indies to turn theorists. Silver was produced in the Western world and was in constant demand by the Eastern world. The merchants trading with the East naturally desired perfect freedom in its export. The bare fact that money was passing out of the country—or the bullion from which coins could be minted—frightened the court, but it did not frighten the trader. What frightened him was the obvious folly of a theory of prohibition which hampered his prosperity. The export of bullion could not itself be bad. What, then, was the fault?

Looking at the state of the nation the merchant observed that it had neither silver nor gold in its own lands. The more silver and gold it had in its possession, the richer it was. The aim, then, was to import more silver and gold than was exported, and thus to accumulate an ever rising balance for the military and economic war chests. Merely prohibiting export was hopeless, for that, where it was not skilfully evaded, caused a diminution of trade, and trade gave the nation claims to more and more symbols of wealth. The great need was to conduct trade in such a way that the nation sold more goods other than gold and silver than it bought, and the foreigner would then settle the difference by sending gold and silver to redress the balance.

This diagnosis of the needs of the nation found a most convincing enunciator in the person of Thomas Mun who produced a truly epoch-making work entitled *England's Treasure by Forraign Trade, or the Ballance of our forraign Trade is the Rule of our Treasure.* This work Mun, who was a director of the East India Company, wrote in the early-mid years of the seventeenth century, but its publication was delayed until 1664. It founded a principle of economy which was to govern not England only but the whole trading world until the appearance of the now more famous *Wealth of Nations* destroyed its power for over a century. It arose from its ashes again in 1931.

The effect of the mercantile theory of Thomas Mun we shall discuss in a later chapter of this book. It is necessary to mention him at this stage, for his effect was to set the minds of those controlling affairs into a channel which was violently changed by Adam Smith, who in turn became an influence who very potently affected the directional trend of national life in ways later to be as violently criticized.

While Mun and his mercantile theory worked on the minds of those who either had or were about to have the main directional power, the status of the workers in the mass was steadily changing as the mode of industry and exchange altered. In their admirable *Economic History of Europe* Professors Knight, Barnes and Flugel write :

> The emphasis upon commercial and financial development between 1500 and 1750 should not be allowed to obscure the fact that industry had grown enormously. This growth had carried with it considerable changes in organization and technique. In the Low Countries many industries had spread from the towns to the countryside, where by the sixteenth century they had undergone a degree of capitalistic organization by " merchant-manufacturers ". . . . The rural artisan produced on a small scale, and usually marketed through a middleman or entrepreneur. Oftentimes this " merchant-manufacturer " or " clothier " also furnished the raw material. As fully developed during the two centuries just before 1750, with the various processes divided among different households, coming together in the clothier and reaching the market through him, this was called the " putting-out " system. It was very common in the textile industries of England . . .

The growth of the " putter-out " was by no means universal, for

> . . . there was a great deal of really independent rural industry in the English county of Yorkshire clear into the nineteenth century. The artizan was free to buy his own wool and to sell his finished cloth in the markets of Bradford, Leeds, Halifax, or Wakefield. Under such conditions, where the independent artizan might and could compete with the clothiers, or where the industrial capitalist did not exist at all,

> life under the domestic system was often quite attractive. It was in many cases a mere adjunct to agriculture, carried on by renters (or even owners) on rainy days or in seasons of little farm work.
>
> Rural industry expanded in other regions for quite different reasons. Where the soil was rich, proprietors were particularly tempted to apply capitalistic methods to agriculture. The social prestige of land-holding led many men who had made fortunes in commerce to purchase estates, and there was a certain carry-over of their earlier methods into their later activities. Many peasants and small renters increased their holdings.

Farming was becoming more technically efficient. Holdings were being consolidated. Roads and transport systems were subject to an improvement that, while it left them still poor, was a marked advance to the successive generations affected. Some industries and avocations were drawing men from the rural areas to the towns and some were attracting men back from the towns to the countryside. The major result was the steady growth of a propertyless class.

Even before machinery with a power drive had been devised, there was a growing tendency, where it was practicable, to group various processes of manufacture under one roof, although the tendency was checked by the many obstacles which often outweighed the saving in transport costs and the increased efficiency which came from closer supervision and co-ordination. The old village was in its death throes, although it was an unconscionable time a-dying. Our three American professors remark with penetration :

> Perhaps the most important changes which had taken place were in the realm of ideas, beliefs, and

> incentives—where nobody but a very simple-minded person will use scales or a measuring-stick with any confidence. . . . Once the medieval hierarchy of the "spiritual" over the "temporal" was overturned, competition unfettered, and the acquisition of wealth made respectable, a stupendous force was unchained.

Against that force the religious instinct and tradition existing in the mass of men fought both vainly and bewilderedly in a scattered battle, whose story has recently been re-told in R. H. Tawney's *Religion and the Rise of Capitalism*. The new force could hardly do other than hold, consolidate and increase its gains, for religion after the Tudors was no longer centralized.[1] It fought by divided battalions with sectarian *francs-tireurs* operating on all flanks. It was then it became—by a change of metaphor—the "dope" of the baffled workers whose intelligences and organization confronted the industrial revolution with cloudy understanding and ineffectual opposition.

The history of the industrial revolution is so familiar that even the barest remembrancer of its outlines would be an affront. It had two chief qualities at its beginning. The machines needed capitalization, but the machines did not need much capital or need that little long. The possessors of wealth were placed in an initial advantage which was quickly shared by the possessors of acumen. In the coarser sections of the textile industry the new machines were of especial benefit. Coarse grades are more adaptable to mechanical manufacture—or were in the

[1] It is, perhaps, necessary to emphasize the fact that in noting the disappearance of a unified and authoritative religion, and its effects, no approval, tacit or other, is implied of the tenets of that religion. In noting the rise and dominance of the money-getting middle class no moral condemnation is, at the moment, implied. These immediate pages are not concerned to discuss whether a change was good or bad, but merely to record that such a change happened.

eighteenth century—and the market for them is wider. Once a start on machine-making had been made, profits returned quickly in some volume, and experience led the way to further improvements. To the original wealth-owners, who could capitalize the new machines, was quickly added a stream of recruits to their economic and social class drawn from the successful entrepreneurs of the new modes of manufacture. To phrase it simply, the proportion of masters to men, of property-owners to hired workers, increased with some rapidity.

The advantages of wealth and an aristocratic status are summed up in the possession of a spaciousness of both time and means to secure a broad culture. This culture is symbolized by a courteousness of manner which masks and excuses selfishness and tyranny. The character in Dickens who preferred being knocked down by a man with blood to being picked up by a man without was a novelist's expansion of the old adage that an Englishman loves a lord, but the snob was not such an empty fool as he seems. It is said, for example, that many foreign and Imperial statesmen would prefer being snubbed once more by the late Lord Curzon to being smitten genially on the back by Jimmy Thomas. The psychological reason is obvious. There is a sense of gratification in being the object of the attention of a superior being, and he who has an obviously greater command of those mental assets which give a mastery of life—a deeper comprehension of cause and effect, a wider knowledge of significances—is quite definitely a superior being. A "brave" with two scalps at his belt is superior to the "brave" with but one. The master is superior to the entered apprentice. The wife with a fur coat is superior to the wife without a fur coat.

What the industrial revolution did, and did suddenly, was to give mastery to men who were quite obviously beings not superior in anything but their possession of luck and low cunning. The old landlords did not go down before the new industrialists in the sense that they were driven from their position and power as the governing caste, but they went down in the sense that the new type of wealthy man gradually usurped the place held by the old type. Intermarriage, and social acceptance, gradually changed the kind of political master under whom England laboured. The direction of England's diplomacy for commercial ends was as old as Walpole, but the direction of England's diplomacy by commercial men really began fitfully with Peel and quite definitely with Gladstone. The change was foreshadowed by the emergence early in the nineteenth century of statesmen like Huskisson, and was complete early in the twentieth century when governments were composed of representative industrialists like Alfred Moritz Mond, Stanley Baldwin and Philip Cunliffe-Lister, with a sprinkling of commercial lawyers or lawyers-turned-company-directors like Lord Reading, the late Lord Birkenhead and the late Lord Brentford.

The factory system, before the invention of power-driven machines, made but slow progress, and was spasmodic in its appearance. The machines made the old home crafts and the putting-out system obsolete. The owners of the machines obtained a mastery over the destinies of their workers more absolute, but far less obvious, than that wielded by any other master-class in industrial history. Propertyless men without an equality of weapons are helpless in the face of men who own both the means of existence and the means of exerting force. The thoughtless, and in some cases ruthless, organization of machine industry by the masters, and the abrupt new contrasts which were created between wealth allied to power and poverty allied to impotence, very naturally stirred the subdued mass of workers to sullen revolt, which very occasionally flamed into action, as when the Luddites—those early technocrats—took to frame-breaking or the Chartists tore up the railings of a public park. For the most part, however, the workers endured and either grumbled ineffectually or told their Maker about it at the meetings of their sects.

Attempts to organize the workers against the employers were either met legally by the application of laws against conspiracy or by the assurance—not without truth—that the tyranny of a trade union would be worse than the tyranny of the master. *Vis-à-vis* the master, the worker had, of course, some freedom. He could leave his work and his master if he did not mind starving or would face the pains and trials of migration. He could, and did, keep his economic plight and his political opinions in mental compartments and cheer for the same man politically that he damned industrially. An early trade union was far more restrictive.

Popular education was late in arriving. When it came in 1870 the generation which was about to be made literate was faced by an interwoven political, social and economic system which lent itself readily to illusion. There was the illusion that man had deliberately chosen to live under what was called the Capitalist System. There was the illusion that this system had somehow caused the lot of the worker to be materially worse and the illusion that it had caused the lot of the worker to be spiritually better.

Actually, as the Hammonds rather belatedly caused men to realize, the horrors of the industrial era were only horrible when compared with later possibilities. They were often improvements on what had gone before. The industrial labourer in a new northern town living in a jerry-built, back-to-back house was poorly served compared with the petty bourgeois of thirty years later, but he was materially very much better off than the agricultural worker of thirty years earlier. The employment of children in factories and coal-pits was shocking to the conscience of the later nineteenth century, but it was by no means shocking to men who had seen the plight of similar children before warm factories took them from the health-blasting employments and environments of the countryside.

But whatever the illusions about the effects of the Capitalist system, the master-illusion was that it was a system, for the chief characteristic of the years between, roughly, 1790 and 1890, was a complete lack of systematization.

It is no exaggeration to say that every accretion of mechanical power was a complete surprise to the industrialists who gained from it and was treated as if it were a permanent thing which would not be superseded. England, for example, was covered with a haphazard network of unorganized railway systems which had barely been retrieved from their early competitive muddles when the internal combustion engine rendered them potentially obsolete. Towns and cities were laid out in inconvenient tramway lines, and the consequent muddle of local financing was not thoroughly straightened out until the lines had to be, or should have been, torn up for the much more convenient omnibus. It is folly to blame the early entrepreneurs for this lack of foresight. They did well by their generations. The point is that the social complex which resulted from their well-meant efforts was not a thing created by a system.

When men talk of the capitalist system, of course, they mean no more than that method of financing enterprise which relies upon capital supplied by private owners who take a private profit from the fruits of the enterprise. Their objection to " the Capitalistic system " is that such a method as applied in European history did not make it easy for many men to acquire sufficient capital to assist in financing for profit. The original owners or acquirers of capital, in other words, were avaricious and not generous.

The defenders of the system very rightly point out that financing from private capital cannot continue if the capital owner is generous, and that in many cases generosity is not even possible. If a man with his capital employs one thousand men at £100 a year each, he must pay them £100,000 in wages. If the enterprise makes a net gain of £10,000 on the year, after the wages have been paid, and the generous capitalizer decides to distribute it all, the addition to each worker is about 3s. 10½d. a week, but the capitalizer has had nothing for his skill, trouble and risk. He could have done much better by leaving his capital elsewhere to make a return for him while he enjoyed a sweet idleness. If the enterprise only made £1,000 net the gain per worker by a total distribution would be so small on the year as to be almost unnoticeable. To say, therefore, that the capital provider is a parasite because he takes for himself ten times the amount of the average worker's remuneration is really a grotesque inversion of what really happens—that each worker contributes a few coppers a week to employ the capitalizer to create and maintain the joint enterprise.

Neither the early critics nor the early defenders of the Capitalist system after the industrial revolution saw the matter in either light. For quite a long time the capitalist was the master almost in the old feudal sense. He was a man who knew the business wherein his capital was employed and who worked at that business. Only as the enterprises grew (with the growth of markets and the development of machinery) and the day to day intercourse of master and men was interrupted as the body of interveners, the foremen and overlookers and the like, also grew, did the capital provider begin to assume his parasitical aspect. But as enterprises grew the capital for their inception and maintenance ceased to be the contribution of one man or of a local group. It was gathered from many providers and from far afield. Eventually the men who directed the enterprise were almost as divorced from the ownership of its capital as the men who served it in the meanest capacity.

The thoughtless rapacity of the masters and the awakening consciousness of the workers caused the death of the old individual bargain for service between employer and worker. The trade union became the instrument with which all the workers collectively bargained with the employer, and, later, with similarly organized employers. The working time of the worker was sold by an official to his master. In order that the collective bargain might be effective it was necessary that any disputes under it should be regarded as general to all affected by it. The worker sold his right to remain at work to his officials in return for the benefit of the collective bargaining instrument. The manufacturers and the merchants eventually possessed themselves of the effective power of the legislature, by the process of absorption and inter-marriage of which we have spoken above, and in the intervals of dealing with political questions applied their power to industrial and economic matters. The workers, finding that Parliament appeared to work against their aspirations, or worked but slowly in favour of them, did not proceed to scrap the inefficient instrument, but to clamour for a hand in its operation.

That muddle-headed blunder was to be the prolific father of many of our present discontents.

Chapter IV

THE DEGRADATION OF PARLIAMENT

To regard Parliament as a steady development of the old "folk-moots" and "shire-moots", as most children are taught to do, is to misread history. The Anglo-Saxon representative gatherings which were overthrown by the Norman Conquest did come to some kind of resurrection in the "Common Council", but that council was not the ancestor of Parliament as the people knew it in the nineteenth century.

When Simon de Montfort in revolt against Henry III summoned a national assembly to Lewes, and included in his writ of summons both knights of the shire and representatives of the burgesses, he created a precedent upon which Parliament later stood, but even the gathering of 1265 was not the parent to which our Parliament can really trace its origins. After 1265 representatives of the shires and boroughs were summoned again in 1275 and to the "model Parliament" of Edward I in 1295, but whether or not the Edwardian assembly was a model Parliament it was certainly not the model of a modern Parliament. Those assemblies set the precedent of the method of summons—and the ostensible field of representation—which survives to our own time, but they were so different in motive and power as to be hardly recognizable as an early form of our present instrument of government.

The greatest difference, perhaps, between the early gatherings which sentimentalists regard as the forerunners of Parliament and the gatherings which bore the name of Parliament at and after the industrial revolution was the attitude of the people towards the summons. To quote the most easily accessible commentator, Hugh Chisholm :

> . . . the Commons, unconscious of their future power, took their humble place in the great council of the realm. The knights of the shire, as lesser barons or landowners of good social standing could sit beside the magnates of the land without constraint ; but modest traders from the towns were overawed by the power and dignity of their new associates. They knew that they were summoned for no other purpose than the taxing of themselves and their fellow townsmen ; their attendance was irksome ; it interrupted their own business ; and their journeys exposed them to many hardships and dangers. It is not surprising that they should have shrunk from the exercise of so doubtful a privilege. Considerable numbers absented themselves from a thankless service ; and their constituents, far from exacting the attendance of their members, as in modern times, begrudged the sorry stipend of 2s. a day, paid to their representatives while on duty, and strove to evade the burden imposed upon them by the crown. Some even purchased charters, withdrawing franchises which they had not yet learned to value. Nor, in truth, did the representation of the towns at this period afford much protection to the rights and interests of the people.

Certain characteristics differentiate those early Parliaments from the modern assemblies under that name. The representatives attended for the most part with reluctance and on behalf of reluctant constituents ; they attended for one purpose, to grant money ; and they were sent by a community which was definitely opposed to new laws as such. The history of England for long generations is that of a people resentful of added enactments. Again to quote Chisholm :

> It must never be forgotten that in these early times, and indeed long after, the making of new laws is as abhorrent as it is rare. The cry of the nation, so often expressed in the charters, is not for the making of a new law but for the preservation of old ones, while the levying of taxes is almost unknown except for purposes of national defence.

With Edward I Parliament assumed the aspects of a settled and permanent institution. It became not only a meeting-place for representatives of the various classes of the people who enjoyed (or resented) a writ of summons, but a court. It not only made laws but redressed grievances and heard petitions. Under Edward III two significant developments occurred. The knights of the shires, who had earlier been drawn towards the barons by all social ties, allied themselves with the citizens and burgesses, and the House of Commons began to sit as such. Secondly, the king, being in constant and not fitful need of funds, summoned Parliament every year, with the consequence that its early function of granting taxation was extended. It began to discuss matters of State theretofore left to the king and his great council.

Historians are uncertain whether at any earlier time the whole assembly had ever voted as one chamber, and the balance of historical probability is against it, but under Edward III the procedure quite certainly was for the three estates to meet together, to separate, and afterwards to deliver a collective answer to the king. Convenience dictated that the Commons should have a room of their own, and they took possession of the chapter house of the Abbot of Westminster. With the attachment of the knights of the shire to the citizen representatives, and the habit of deliberating in the chapter house apart from the barons, there came into being, not by accident but certainly not by careful constitutional forethought, the two Houses —Lords and Commons.

It is vital to an understanding of the failure of Parliament in the nineteenth and twentieth centuries to conduct successfully the economic life of the nation to grasp two facts about it. One is that its original purpose was simple —it was a body which assembled (with extreme reluctance, as we have seen) to grant money to the king. The king did not impose taxation in the sense of saying that his needs were such and such and would be raised in this way and that. He virtually consulted the Parliament and laid before it the extent of his needs, leaving the deliberators to say what amount would be given and leaving them to determine the method of its collection. The second vital point is that with the Reformation Parliament was transformed. The Saxon moots and the pre-Tudor assemblies, despite their similarity of form and even of ceremony, were different in kind from the Parliaments that assembled from Henry VIII onwards. Of that difference two signs were discernible. The gradual extension of function from finance to other matters of State, which began under Edward III, made a sudden forward leap, and Parliament developed a technique of interference with the life of the people which it had not earlier possessed. The power of Parliament passed into the hands of the new class which had waxed fat on the double dispoliation. Large landowners and great merchants possessed it. The Commons became an aristocratic House, and the master of the king.

An aristocrat, it need hardly be said, is not a man with a title, or a man tracing his descent from some remote ancestor through a long line of specially powerful, wealthy or cultured progenitors. These meanings are given to the word largely through the sentimentality which attributes—very rightly—glamour to these characteristics. Aristocracy in our own sense of the word does not even mean what the word originally implied—a government of the best. The Aristocratic State which arose from the Reformation meant what Belloc, in *The House of Commons and Monarchy*, has called it, " a State governed by an Oligarchy indeed, but by an Oligarchy which received the permanent and carefully preserved respect of its fellow-citizens ".

The aristocracy which arose with the Tudors was, indeed, a deliberate creation replacing an earlier aristocracy which had long lineage as its characteristic. " The exclusion of the aristocracy remained a first principle of Tudor statecraft," says Trevelyan, and the first Parliament of Elizabeth made it known that " the wanton bringing up and ignorance of the nobility forces the Prince to advance new men that can serve ". The men that could serve were, of course, the extortioners of Henry VIII, and those who advanced most rapidly were such as Cecil, who had come from trading stock to the status of a country gentleman.

By a complex of circumstances the new aristocracy not only possessed itself of the power of Parliament, but of certain other powers also. Because the people, through tradition, resented high taxation to the point of revolt, the Tudors had perforce to be thrifty. Because the people were armed and the Crown had no overmastering forces, the king could not create a network of agents to govern the people in local matters, for such agents would have needed a sanction of arms if their work was resented. The effect from these two causes was the great extension of the power and duties of the unpaid functionaries—the justices of the peace. Henry VII had first relied on his magistrates, and the growing power of the Commission of the Peace suited excellently well the individual and collective ambitions of his son's and grand-daughter's advancing " men who were able to serve ". In London, as a member of Parliament, and out of London, as a magistrate, the country gentleman became almost all-powerful. The rule of the gentry had begun.

The historical diagnosis of any existing discontent is open always to a grave liability to error. Looking back upon a vanished caste, as upon a dead despot, one finds that prejudice is apt to colour an examination of its significance. Those who adulate the energy and glamour of Napoleon will find a different significance in the Napoleonic régime from those who dislike the Corsican's personal characteristics. Charles the Martyr is, of necessity, a very different historical influence from " the man, Charles Stewart ". But it is possible that what in the very long run of several generations develops to the mind as a bad régime may have been composed of very good men. The gentry as a type of contemporary culture was a good caste. The gentleman, before he degenerated into a self-conscious nitwit wearing an old school tie, was a very creditable product of civilization. He had not, as the Disraelian novelists like to believe, an identity with the knights of ancient chivalry, but he was in many respects the better man. If the gentry were no paladins, the paladins were no gentlemen.

The self-imposed limitations and fetishes of the two castes were very different. Certain conventions were common to both, notably a highly specialized and artificial code of conduct towards women. Wife-beating, for example, has been the failing of all generations of boors. The hind might legally beat his wife with a stick no thicker than his thumb, and the Gilbertian costermonger was expected to spend part of his time jumping on his mother, or on the mother of his children. But neither the ancient knights nor the later gentry beat their wives. They preferred politely to break their hearts, as the heart of Amy Robsart was broken.

This digression is necessary because it has become fashionable in certain circles to ascribe to the gentry a malignity and a deliberation in the " exploitation " of the workers which was never theirs. The gentry of any age, whether of the age of the Tudors or that of Victoria, were no more conscious of exploiting the workers than any Tudor or Victorian parent was conscious of tyrannizing over his children. There was ample exploitation, as there was, and is, ample household tyranny, but it was unconscious. To carry Hibernianism to the extreme, the typical gentleman was class-conscious, but only unconsciously so. When he, as a caste, took power through Parliament and the local bench, he did it for the best of reasons, that he felt himself the right person to have power. None but he was capable of good government. The nobility was debilitated ; the masses were ignorant ; the Crown was dangerous.

But having taken power, the gentry—being but human even in their inhumanity—used it to shape a State that would most advantage their caste. Their attitude was not that of the army phrase, " *I'm* all right : —— you ! " It was rather that of the comfortably assured person who says, " That's all right, my boy, you leave it to me ; I'll see that you don't suffer."

For an aristocratic government there is everything to be said for as long as those governed will tolerate it. It ensures, for example, that those who exercise the functions of government will be trained in government. Successive generations of aristocratic rulers are not only steeped in the technique by being bred in places where government is discussed perpetually and casually, but they are almost always trained in addition by having a model state either under their own hands or under their eyes. The faculty which comes to the use of the State is developed on the estate.

In addition to his other advantages the governing aristocrat has—until his caste falls into decadence—a code of manners and conduct which pleases, even though it may also irk, those governed. His manner, while conveying without arrogance that he is not as other men are, creates the impression that he is as other men would like to be. Tradition gives him an eptitude which prevents his being abashed by life. He has assurance—and it is, indeed, that assurance for which men most envy and hate him.

Under the Norman system the ostensible handlers of power were the king and his lords, and the king was a sacramental man. The Church was the overlord of lords and the king of kings. As the Norman system waned, the Church, through its own power to sway the superstitious and by its communication of a peculiar ethic of relationships to the gilds, maintained its power. Whatever might be the visible authority of the temporal State, men felt, and knew, that the ultimate power was with the Church. The priest as the adviser of the Crown persisted until the Reformation, and then gave place to the aristocrat, who was the money-getting middle-class man brought to a new phase of development. With his ascendancy to power, Parliament as we still know it came into being.

Through Parliament and by Parliament the new aristocrats governed. Through Parliament and by Parliament the new aristocrats, reinforced by such recruits to their ranks as Cromwell, broke for ever the superstition of the sacramental man, for they took him and slew him, and no outraged God smote them for their iniquity. Through Parliament and by Parliament they eventually restored the son of the slain man to the Throne, but not to kingship. After Cromwell's Protectorate the King of England was a civil servant, a bureaucrat.

Just as the first Cromwell smashed for ever a triple balance of repositories of wealth, the second Cromwell smashed for ever a triple balance of repositories of power. King and people could not again menace the lords, for the king was a nonentity in power, and the lords were transcendent in both the Houses of Parliament.

Having had the power of Parliament demonstrated in such a way, the people very naturally assumed Parliament to be all-powerful. It was that tradition which caused the blunder of the new economic masses in the nineteenth century.

Not only the tone but the scope of Parliament widened with Elizabeth. The discussions of such matters as the succession to the Crown, the Queen's matrimonial prospects, ecclesiastical abuses and the granting of monopolies—which Parliament condemned—gave warning of a clash between the monarch and the commons which actually became the clash of arms under Charles. With the Restoration the exercises of Parliamentary power increased. New laws were passed in relative profusion. The revolution of 1688 and the incoming of William III were Parliamentary achievements. Not until the time of George III was the oligarchy of comfortable, and comfortably corrupt, gentry seriously perturbed by any intrusion of popular agitation for better representation. We can, for convenience, date the beginning of the industrial revolution in the 1760's—Kay's flying shuttle was invented as early as 1738—and throughout the decade from 1760 to 1770 there was ample public agitation through press and platform and an insistence upon the right of petition. In 1771 the publication of Parliamentary debates caused a profound psychological change in the political consciousness of the country.

With the industrial revolution began that era of reform bills which lasted until after the Great War with its abrupt extension of the franchise to manhood suffrage and the later Tory Act which gave votes to women on the same terms as men. The vote became an object of abject superstition. It was elevated from its obvious significance as a civic function into a mystic right. Even after the various extensions of the franchise had quietened the clamour of the working men for a share in the task of choosing their political governors, advocates of female suffrage were still able to draw tumultuous applause by applying to their cause a Gladstonian remark that " Ireland shall have Home Rule, not because she wants it but because it is her right, and the right must prevail." The workers had secured the vote, and women were to have the vote—not necessarily because they wanted it but because it was their "right", and the right must prevail.

The vote, as all know, was gradually extended with a fine show of reluctance. The opponents of wider suffrage like Robert Lowe, were as mistaken as the advocates in their estimates of what the power of the vote might mean. Phrases which have passed into familiar political idiom were used in all seriousness—men talked of "a leap in the dark" and of "educating our masters". The workers having painfully organized themselves into trade unions for collective bargaining, transformed those unions into vast political machines for securing the return to Parliament of Labour members. The purpose of a trade union being to secure justice from the so-called "capitalist system", of which it was an integral part, the trade union leaders, with complete and utter blindness to the contradiction, began to use them as propaganda machines for Socialism.

This reliance upon Parliament as an instrument for reforming maladjustments which were essentially economic was in more than one way stupid. Even had Parliament been adapted to the new uses to which it began in the nineteenth century to be increasingly put, what mattered was not the right to vote for representatives, but to choose the representatives who solicited votes. The controllers of Parliamentary life were far too astute to permit an increase in electors to affect such a matter. They were advantaged by the fact that issues of broad political import are far more attractive to the popular imagination than those of close economic import. Until a decade or two decades after eighteen-seventy even the economic issues had to be presented as broad and sweeping political issues.

In a working community of a few thousand people it was felt as a hardship that the effectual choice of a representative at the hustings fell to a mere handful of voters. The candidate of the Buffs and the candidate of the Blues struggled and bribed for the determining handful of votes, where those votes were not already " in the pocket " of some powerful local gentleman. From the viewpoint of the growing masses, had they but " seen straight ", the Buff man and the Blue man were the same man, since each was the chosen fugleman of a particular oligarchy which commanded the Parliamentary machine, but it eased resentment when the victor was chosen before his opponent not by a handful of citizens but by a mass of them. Throughout the vital years when what really mattered to England was the organization of the capitalization and conduct of her swiftly expanding industries, including, necessarily, the adjustment of the eventual share-out of profits between capital, labour and the new factor, management, what the increasing mass of enfranchised men voted upon was no question affecting industry, but such issues as Disestablishment, Home Rule, Armenian pogroms, " forward " foreign policies and the like, all of which were vastly important to the nation but none of which was within the mental comprehension of the average new voter. Even when great new constituencies, like Birmingham, were organized on what was really a basis of class-consciousness born of economic dissatisfaction, it was by the lure of some question such as religious freedom in education. It was, in fact, from the ashes of an " Education League " directed to the ends of religious nonconformity that the famous Chamberlain caucus rose to work for the " three F's " of Free Church, Free Schools and Free Land.

The workers and the lower middle classes—that is, the mass of propertyless men—thus for years wasted their political energies to secure the return of some chosen spokesman of the propertied classes to a Parliament which was so intent upon the wide category of political issues that matters of urgent economic adjustment received but scant attention, and when given that attention too often reached the form of an Act without the implications of the new legislation being properly realized. The important example of this, as we shall shortly see, was the legalization of limited liability.

(It is again necessary at this point to reiterate the fact that in discussing the background of the past in an endeavour to get into a true perspective the discontents of the present, I am not taking a side. In saying that propertyless men grew excited over the question of which of two spokesmen of a propertied class should represent them in Parliament I am, for example, not preaching " class hatred " as a sound political doctrine. There is an admirable case to be made for the belief that property owners alone should make the laws of the country : I refrain from making it. The consideration at the moment is that the workers, who are the majority of the nation, at the period of early and mid-industrialization turned to Parliament as an organizing machine, and have suffered, do suffer, and will suffer from that mistaken confidence in it.)

The oligarchy of Parliament was originally an aristocratic oligarchy, and the instrument which it shaped under its hand was for the purpose of conducting the affairs of a State under aristocratic rule. As the industrial revolution gathered force, that rule by aristocracy waned and was eventually supplanted by a rule of a plutocracy. When the Thackerayan Nabobs returned from the East with their hoards of personal wealth, they were easily absorbed into the governing caste. When landowners who had turned to banking turned later to industry, they, too, were easily absorbed.

But there came a time when the prevailing type which grew rich by the new industry could not be so absorbed. There were too many of him and his traditions were not those of the oligarchy which he joined. Peel and Gladstone, with their conventional school and university backgrounds, were only too much akin to those whose councils they joined, but Cobden and Fowler, Forster and Jackson were not akin. They were a new type to Parliament. When the ruling oligarchy was joined by an occasional exotic, like Cobbett or Disraeli or even George Canning, it could use him either in office or opposition, but when it was joined by a relative mass of newly moneyed men representing a new governing caste it could neither use nor absorb; it had itself to be virtually absorbed.

Cobden, of course, was the real portent. He wanted cheap labour, which implied cheap food. He caught the public support on the cry of cheap bread and by his attack on the older gentry. Not for years after his death did the people to whom his cheap bread was offered as an electoral bait realize that Codlin, the manufacturer, was no more the friend than Short, the landlord. But even so, the pathetic faith in the Parliamentary instrument was maintained, and the genuine controls of the economic destinies of the masses which non-Parliamentary methods offered were ignored, because they were not realized.

With the spread of the franchise the aristocratic machine, which was badly functioning as the instrument of a new plutocracy, began to be regarded as a genuine instrument of a democracy. Working men in the North, offered the choice of a Chancery lawyer from London or a retired Colonel from Worthing to be their representative, felt that they were actually helping to govern their country.[1]

The illusion could not last. Labour candidates began to appear as the representatives of the trade union organization. These were countered in some cases by working-men candidates of the other parties, such as the unfortunate Mr. Tom Smith, who as a Tory working man fought a succession of Lancashire elections, and, failing to win a seat, lost his wits under the strain. The Labour candidates were returned in growing numbers as attachés to the Liberal Party. Eventually, as all know, there came into being a definite Labour Party with its own imitation of the normal Parliamentary discipline. This change of attitude coinciding with the Tory landslide of 1906, and the ascendancy of the reforming Liberal Party, made

[1] In case this seems a wilful exaggeration I place on record the fact that my first personal experience of political elections in a West Lancashire division saw the following choices of caucus candidates: 1906. Edward Marshall Hall, K.C., versus John Astbury, K.C. 1910. Major Godfrey Dalrymple White, D.S.O., versus the Baron de Forest (a naturalized Austrian). 1910. Major Godfrey Dalrymple White, D.S.O., versus H. Drysdale Woodcock, Barrister-at-Law. None was native to the county. The constituency had never been a "safe" party seat, so that none of these estimable gentlemen was merely winning his spurs by fighting a forlorn hope.

certain a reform for which many had long agitated—the payment of members of Parliament.

With the return in some numbers of trade unionists as Labour members and the institution of a salary for all members, the prestige of Parliament, which had been so glamorous that it had distracted the attention of the nation from its obvious inability to cope with the new problems set by industrialization, crumpled and fell away. And this was due to two causes. The theory of representation in Parliament had always been that the men who came there to speak came to speak for a district, a locality. When a worker was sent to Parliament by the financial aid of his fellows in union, he was of necessity the servant of his paymasters. He spoke not as the representative of a district, although he was called such, but as the delegate of a function. He was not the Member for Crewe in anything but name : he was the railway workers' delegate.

That was the first cause of the decay of prestige which the House suffered. The second was that it ceased ostensibly, as it had long ceased actually, to be an assembly of " gentlemen ". It became the gathering-place of professional politicians. It may be said that great lawyers like Asquith and adventurers like Bottomley, who sat in the Commons before payment of members was introduced, were obviously not of the gentry in the old sense, and that would be true. But Asquith was the spokesman of the old régime and pursued their interests, and Bottomley, although he aped the attributes of a tribune of the people, was actually a city man who could be expected to watch that nothing spoilt the freedom of the city, in the wrong sense of that honoured phrase. It may also be said that the appearance of trade union delegates cannot have been so great a change, since there had been since time immemorial men who, elected for a locality, actually spoke and acted for certain " capitalist " interests—they were shipowners' delegates or brewers' delegates. That also would be true, but those who sat in such a capacity were skilfully camouflaged to the eyes of the unsophisticated electorate, and shared the glamour of the old aristocratic-cum-plutocratic member.

For a brief interval the payment of members threatened to have a wholesome effect. It made things easier for the carpet-bagger, and there might have been a serious disturbance of the caucus arrangements by the intrusion of sincere persons at nomination day. This, however, was soon amended. By laying down that any candidate must deposit in cash a large sum before seeking the franchises of his fellows the way to election was barred to any moneyless person, however gifted, however sincere, who had not the backing of some moneyed person or organization. Judas, who carried the bag, might be nominated, but not Jesus.

The deposit system had, and has, another disadvantage. Before payment of members was the rule every unmoneyed aspirant to membership of the Commons had to be sure of some kind of income upon which to live. He reached the Commons by spending his best years making sufficient capital to give him a competence, by obtaining the patronage of some rich man or rich organization, by following a profession—law and journalism were the most frequent—which would not prohibit his attention to his Parliamentary duties, or by plunging into debt. He had, of course, always the assurance that his status as a member would throw into his way means of making a livelihood, some honourable, some not so honourable, and some positively corrupt. Payment of members, although the amount of the pay is inadequate even to meet some members' expenses, might have eased the way for younger men desirous of practising statecraft in their earlier and more vigorous years without dependence upon paymasters or the sale of their honour. The need for a deposit now means that the aspirant must practise the same unworthy strategems before election that he once had to practise afterwards.

But, in any event, what most people saw in payment of members was an invitation to " professional politicians " to enter the Commons, and the oligarchy which had so long maintained the prestige of the machine by cultivating the respect, and sometimes the positive adoration, of the electors, was no longer regarded as the main body of membership.

The declining prestige of Parliament just when the workers were assured that they were gaining command of it was hastened by a series of scandals affecting the honour of certain members. Whether these scandals were the effects of causes associated with the general change in Parliamentary standing or merely coincidental we need not enquire. They were of two kinds. There was the discovery that some active member was a rogue. Jabez Balfour and Horatio Bottomley both left the green benches for the plank bed, and certain others, about whom a finicky law of libel dictates the old adage " no names, no pack-drill ", had narrow escapes. There was also the other and more deadly kind of scandal, which consisted in the accusation that ministers and members of power had used their positions for personal or sectional gain. Even where these accusations were not proved, the vigour and sincerity with which they were made reflected a general distrust in current governmental morality. The silver scandal, the Marconi scandal, the dope scandal, the nickel scandal were such accusations from which those accused emerged with honour, but from which Parliamentary prestige emerged greatly shaken.

The more numerically powerful the workers' avowed representatives became in the House of Commons, the more did the power of the House to command respect wane. In addition to the scandals, there arose a general feeling, openly voiced, that the politicians were but the puppets of some mysterious " money power " which kept itself hidden from the public gaze. In the years immediately preceding the Great War the impotence of Parliament to provide the community at large with a life tolerably free from economic and social irritations was explained very largely by the existence of a bogey-man called " the International Financier ", and the two older political parties were increasingly derided as expedients of this hidden controller whereby a game of " ins and outs " might keep the uneasy masses from paying too much attention to the true source of their troubles.

Even so, it was always to Parliament that the general eye turned for easement in the contemporary inflictions. Organized Labour and the unorganized middle classes who had missed the money-tide of the nineteenth century both imagined that in the intervals of wrangling about Irish Home Rule, the tangled politics of Central Europe, Education Bills and Licensing Bills, the bewildered representatives and delegates sent to Westminster to work an antiquated legislative machine would somehow bring to good the ill-defined, half-misunderstood economic forces that were working upon social relationships.

The Parliament of the early twentieth century was bound to assume in all its debates and actions that the fiction of a political democracy was true. It had to assume that before the law one man was as good as another and that in ordinary communal relationships one man was as good as another. It was upon that theory that the wide franchise was based. In industrial and social life the too obtrusive fact was that this theoretical equality was an imaginary one, save in the cynical sense of Anatole France's remark that " the law, in its majestic equality, forbids the rich as well as the poor to sleep under bridges, to beg in the streets, and to steal bread ".

It is arguable that a state of society in which the mass of men and women are slaves and the minority, highly cultivated and specially trained for the functions of government, rule from a cultural oasis to which the mob is denied admission is the best form of society both for rulers and slaves, but such a society must be consistent to endure. It must train the masses for servitude as surely as it trains the minority for rulership. Towards the end of the first century of industrialism, however, society had reached a stage in which half its activities were founded upon the necessity for servitude and half upon the theory that all men were free. Those whose energy was necessary at a low level of subsistence to work the mechanized industries had no slaves' claim for permanent support; upon those who employed or overlooked them they were encouraged to widen their mental outlook by the provision of free schools, cheap books, local libraries and the like, and they were given the right to cast a vote for representatives to a governing body which was recommended to them as the most democratic institution in the world, although its internal organization was plutocratic and its capacity for business, by reason of its methods, was grossly inadequate to the needs of a congested democracy.

The inevitable happened. Trust was withdrawn from the contemporary repository of authority. The political leader who had replaced the sacramental man as the people's leader and director ceased to command confidence. Before, however, this withdrawal of trust could take shape in vigorous action, the failure of the statesman-as-witch-doctor to gauge and control the economic forces at work on the world resulted in the Great War of 1914. For a time Parliament as the necessary instrument of re-adjustment to changing conditions recovered and almost retained its authority. When the war ended and before the peace was shaped, the statesman had drawn to his aid a new witch-doctor, whose characteristics—as a type—rendered him eminently suitable to capture the confidence of a generation which had learned after half a century of popular education and twenty-one years of expanding secondary and " university " education to adulate without comprehending academic distinction in exposition, and which was blissfully ready to believe that a learned expositor must be a skilful inaugurator or administrator.

The day of the *Expert* had dawned, and while the statesman still occupied the forefront of the perspective it was the economist upon whom he leaned and to whom he pointed for justification when his actions were challenged. In the Field of the Cloth of Shoddy at Paris, Maynard Keynes was cast to play Wolsey to the Henry of Lloyd George. Unfortunately—or fortunately—the drama was given a modern American tempo. The denouement was " speeded up ". Hardly had the economist presented himself as the saviour of society than monarch and adviser quarrelled violently and publicly, with the consequence that the people at large were for over a decade to be taught that their salvation lay with the economists, only to find that on all vital matters where authoritative guidance was needed the economists were speaking with divided voices, until eventually a bewildered nation looking up were fed over the State-controlled wireless by cross-talks between famous economists adopting the very jargon of music hall nigger-minstrels. In an alleged democracy there was no Nero to fiddle while the economic Rome burned, but as Mick and Mack Sir Josiah Stamp and Mr. Keynes could at least maintain the Neronian attitude by a light-hearted exchange of wisecracks. The only objection which the ordinary citizen might raise to their performance was that from their cross-talk no guidance emerged, and the wise-cracks were hardly so good as those provided by the professional comedians, Alexander and Mose, or even by the great protagonists' pale shadows, Maxwell and Benn.

A College of Cardinals advising a king at least spoke with unanimity; a Cabinet of statesmen leading an aristocratic House of Commons at least took care to follow the wisdom of Melbourne, and " all said the same thing "; but a collection of economists proposing to lead a supposed democracy through economic chaos to a new and more glorious order could only present itself as an adjunct to crazy variety.

CHAPTER V

THE ECONOMIST EMERGES

THE rise of the economist as a national witch-doctor was not so abrupt as the rapid survey of the last chapter assumes. He had had his minutes of great power even when the oligarchy of statesmen was at its most powerful and arrogant self-sufficiency. That great man, William Pitt the younger, almost dramatically avowed his dependence upon Adam Smith, and in 1903 the sudden obtrusion upon the consciousness of an economically illiterate electorate of what was known as " Tariff Reform " gave the professional and academic economist a share in the spotlight—if such a metaphor may be permitted—which at times threatened to deprive of their due the leading political figures of the electoral battle which ensued.[1]

At the risk of further tedium we must return to a quick survey of history and resume our dealings with Thomas Mun, whom we left so abruptly in Chapter III and with an earlier person of equal importance, Sir Thomas Gresham.

Writing in 1873 Walter Bagehot said, " The briefest and truest way of describing Lombard Street is to say that it is by far the greatest combination of economical power and economical delicacy that the world has ever seen. Of the greatness of the power there will be no doubt. Money is economical power." The repository of power is only tolerable to those who suffer or endure its exercise when there is allied to it a palpable recognition of responsibility and duty. Power is irksome to those controlled when it is both arbitrary and erratic, and is the

[1] The ensuing electoral battle was not, actually, fought on tariff reform. See for a discussion of this period the author's *This Tariff Question* (1931).

more irksome when the seat of its direction is unknown, and its method of exercise obscure. It is for this reason that government by a plutocracy almost inevitably causes discontent. The personality of a monarchy or the personnel of an aristocracy is known. That of a plutocracy is unknown, partly because the wielders of power do not reveal themselves as such, but work through agents, and partly because the personnel changes without announcement.

No sooner had Bagehot described the power of Lombard Street than he noted its decadence.

> [The] increasingly democratic structure of English commerce is very unpopular in many quarters, and its effects are no doubt exceedingly mixed. On the one hand, it prevents the long duration of great families of merchant princes, such as those of Venice and Genoa, who inherited nice cultivation as well as great wealth, and who, to some extent, combined the tastes of an aristocracy with the insight and verve of men of business. These are pushed out, so to say, by the dirty crowd of little men. After a generation or two they retire into idle luxury. Upon their immense capital they can only obtain low profits, and these they do not think enough to compensate them for the rough companions and rude manners they must meet in business. This constant levelling of our commercial houses is, too, unfavourable to commercial morality. Great firms, with a reputation which they wish to transmit to the future, cannot be guilty of small frauds. They live by *continuity* of trade, which detected fraud would spoil. When we scrutinize the reason of the impaired reputation of English goods, we find it is the fault of new men with little money of their own, created by bank " discounts ". These men want business at once, and

> they produce an inferior article to get it. They rely on cheapness, and rely successfully.

Bagehot's picture of the greatest combination of economical power that the world has ever seen was, thus, a picture of a society in which the worst elements tended to conquer and drive out the better. He had indicated, but he had not exactly formulated, a law—that under the financial and economic system of his time bad men drove out the good.

Three hundred years before Walter Bagehot wrote, Thomas Gresham had actually formulated the same law as to money. It was Gresham who, more than any other, had helped to make the Lombard Street in which he lived, and which Bagehot was so brilliantly to describe, the greatest economical power. It is Gresham who may be taken as a symbolical figure of the great change which was wrought in English life by the Tudors. It was Gresham who might almost have antedated Pitt in paraphase with the declaration that " England, having transformed herself by her exertions, will, as I trust, transform Europe by her example ", for certainly Europe was effectually transformed by the internationalism of Gresham and his like.

It may be said that before the end of the gilds those who assisted the king with money did so reluctantly, while after the end of the gilds they did so with enthusiasm. The generalization, like all such, is not literally true, but it is true enough to enable a long transition to be reduced to a comprehensive simplicity. Old Isaac of York and the victims of the ingenious Morton were parted from their surplus wealth under pressure which they could not with comfort or security withstand, but when Thomas Gresham aided the Crown with funds he did so with the utmost willingness, for the transaction meant to him not loss but profit.

Gresham, as all know, was the son and nephew of men who were well established as London merchants. His family was not of the type whose sons marry their masters' daughters, but of the type whose daughters marry the apprentices. The Gresham business in the years between 1544 and 1570 took him much abroad to the trading capitals of Europe. In 1551 he became royal agent, with the significant title of " king's merchant ", and took up residence in Antwerp. His chief duty was to negotiate loans for the Crown from and through the rich traders of Germany and the Netherlands, to supply the Crown with such amiable foreign products as gunpowder, saltpetre and arms, and to keep the Privy Council informed of all matters of importance passing abroad. The source of his wealth was a middleman's traffic and the source of his power was also a middleman's traffic, and it is hard to say, surveying his mid-career, whether the wealth more greatly increased the power or the power the wealth. He had, of course, his ups and downs of personal fortune. The changing favourites at Court affected his own standing there, as he, in his quiet way, affected the fortunes of those favourites. But when he had returned to residence in London and had founded the Royal Exchange, as a place where his fellow-merchants might come in out of the rain, the Queen delighted to do him honour and the ironists and satirists of his day were quick to detect the significance of his rise to a political and social standing rare in a man not actively engaged in high politics.

The opening of new worlds of trade, the influx into England of Lombards and Flemings and other alien craftsmen, the rise of the middleman from a producer's convenience to a producer's essential, culminated as a phase in English social and economic life in this remarkable man who had learnt, or had been born with, the secret of waxing fat upon every turn of the national fortunes.

War and the fear of war were to him as valuable as peace and the prosperity of peace, for both needed a traffic of commodities and both needed the arrangement of finance.

The foolish, of course, see in a functionary of the Gresham kind only a parasite on the producers of wealth. The wise cannot fail to realize that, far from being a parasite, the type is a germinator. All increases in wealth take their rise from a coincidence of wants—a coincidence which at its simplest is but the desire of two men to " swop " temporarily unwanted possessions at the moment of their meeting. The function of the merchant and the financier, and Gresham and his like were both, is to contrive interchanges which shall make coincident those wants which would not be so without the middleman's intervention. Such a labourer is worthy of his hire, and it is only when the extent of that hire is unrealized, or is left entirely to the fixation of the middleman himself, that the functionary becomes dangerous to the happiness and settlement of all parties to the transactions which he arranges and conducts. It is when the lubricant becomes of greater cost than the propellant that the machine which needs both begins to seem uneconomic to the user.

Gresham's initiative in founding the Royal Exchange, an addition to the amenities of London which had often been discussed before his time, was of far greater importance than he could realize. It had a significance which is probably not realized to this day by most of those who flourish on activities still conducted in the vicinity of its site. In the earlier days of England's expanding trade the local " fair " (or " feast " as it was called in some parts of the country) retained its importance. The buyers and sellers, the direct producers and direct consumers as well as the middlemen, gathered together at certain times in approved places to conduct their business. They were, so to speak, the welcome guests of a community. Whether the fair remained a periodic interruption into the usual monotony of the community's life, or whether it was a weekly—or even daily—market, did not affect the relationship. The traders came to the community. With the growing habit of self-segregation into localities of certain types of trader, and finally with the erection of a noble bourse (the Royal Exchange was " the burse " to most of its first frequenters) wherein merchants would be always together with their allied functionaries, the financiers who traded in nothing but money and credit, the relationship changed. The middlemen became not the functionaries who went, in person or by agents, to the producing and consuming communities, but a community to which producers and consumers came.

The Royal Exchange and its neighbourhood, widely known after the marks of Royal favour to be the haunt of men honoured and powerful, and not merely of men rich by unrespected means, assumed a new importance. The development of " the burse " would not have been possible had not the City long enjoyed special privileges and immunities, but once the Royal Exchange had taken its place in the national relationships, the City itself gained a new strength from this veritable " central keep " of economic power. From the viewpoint of the normal citizen between Vectis and the Wall—that old Roman sweep of dominance—it meant that the realized attachment of the subject to his governor had not only shifted from a local lord or a local council, but had shifted to an unknown focal point.

The Crown and Parliament were still ostensibly the seats of power, but the city had attained to an influence sometimes quite unsuspected and always underrated. The king might still sit on the throne where the Parliament-men had placed him, but the final arbiters of the nation's destiny were behind the arras. Those who control the finance and munitioning of war, control the final sanction of action.

In our time we have come to look on war as a wasteful and ghastly interruption of peace. The habit is quite modern. Older generations saw peace as a restful interlude in a life of war. When the more primitive communities were not preparing themselves against possible famine, they were preparing themselves against probable rapine. When, with expanding world trade and the new energy of the merchants, the fear of famine grew remote, the fear and love of war remained. War coloured the thoughts of men like Gresham and war dictated the mental trends of men like Thomas Mun, who was born some eight years before Gresham's death in time to grow into a representative type of the post-Gresham expansion of the city.

Gresham as a merchant had been what one may call an empirical economist. He had not traded blindly from bargain to bargain. He had studied and analysed the forces and influences which affected his trading, and which he, as a trader, affected. He had formulated at least one enduring truism about money—that strange new factor in the forming of national life—that bad money drives out good. He had left a legacy to his more intellectual fellow traders. Thomas Mun was himself a merchant. The Gresham example of theoretic investigation into practical trade he greatly bettered. He was obsessed, inevitably, by the thought of the national treasure, for the national treasure—that is the nation's wealth—was to him and his contemporaries nothing more or less than a potential war chest. All things for war, from gunpowder to mercenaries, were to be bought by gold and silver, for gold and silver were desired of all men. It was obvious that the politicians' idea that neither gold nor silver should leave the nation was somehow wrong, for gold and silver were but the means of commanding other commodities, which meant that other commodities were the means of commanding gold and silver. A good bargain was obviously a bargain wherein the seller received greater value than he sold. The nation's trade was, after all, the sum of the trade of its people. The nation's profit was the sum of the innumerable small profits of its traders.

Thinking on these simple lines Mun arrived at an historic formulation which was to found a school of economists:

> Although a Kingdom may be enriched by gifts received or by purchase taken from some other Nations, yet these are things uncertain and of small consideration when they happen. The ordinary means therefore to increase our wealth and treasure is by *Forraign Trade*, wherein wee must ever observe this rule; to sell more to strangers yearly than wee consume of theirs in value. For suppose that when this Kingdom is plentifully served with the Cloth, Lead, Tinn, Iron, Fish and other native commodities, wee doe yearly export the overplus to forraign Countries to the value of twenty-two hundred thousand pounds; by which means we are enabled beyond the Seas to buy and bring in forraign wares for our use and Consumptions, to the value of twenty hundred thousand pounds; by this order duly kept in our trading, wee may rest assured that the Kingdom shall be enriched yearly two hundred thousand pounds, which must be brought to us in so much Treasure; because that part of our stock which is not returned to us in wares must necessarily be brought home in Treasure.

Mun drove his arguments home with simple analogies. To suggest that the "Exportation of our Moneys in Trade of Merchandise " was not a means to increase " our Treasure " was to him as foolish as to look on the actions of a husbandman in the seed-time.

> When he casteth away much good corn into the ground, wee will rather accompt him a mad man than a husband-man ; but when wee consider his labours in the harvest which is the end of his endeavours, wee find the worth and plentiful encrease of his actions.

Mun's " balance of trade " theory found immediate acceptance with the merchants, for he was but voicing what all of them felt about their own trade. Nor was the theory unsound. As Professor Cannan says of it in his *Review of Economic Theory* :

> In itself and without the erroneous corollaries which were attached to it, the balance of trade theory was and is perfectly correct. A country which does not itself produce gold and silver and which is not in a position to compel other countries to give it gold and silver for nothing, must either go without those metals or give other commodities or services for as much of them as it wants. It is true, of course, that the sum of the value of all exported goods other than gold or silver at the national frontier (even if correctly recorded by the custom house), minus the sum of the value of imported goods other than gold or silver, will not give the value of the net imports of gold and silver unless allowance is made for freight and various other things dealt with in the modern text-books.

Mun was a practical merchant and was acutely aware of Professor Cannan's point as to the adjustment of the balance, although he did not talk of invisible exports and imports in the words we now use. The trouble of which his theory was the begetter arose not from the unsoundness of his theory, or from the blindness of Mun and his disciples to the adjustments which had to be made in practice to its bare formulation. The trouble arose from two causes, that the merchants and their entourages who read Mun with approval mistook the object of getting a favourable balance of payments for the object of procuring increasing stores of money, and that the politicians, whom the merchants so greatly influenced, felt the urge to aid the trading community in achieving Mun's economic policy.

What happened was later summarized by Adam Smith :

> Some of the best English writers upon commerce set out with observing, that the wealth of a country consists, not in its gold and silver only, but in its lands, houses and consumable goods of all different kinds. In the course of their reasoning, however, the lands, houses, and consumable goods seem to slip out of their memory, and the strain of their argument frequently supposes that all wealth consists in gold and silver, and that to multiply those metals is the great object of national industry and commerce.

But the best English writers on commerce, with their supporting claque of merchants, had the statesmen in tow. Unfettered trade could not be trusted to secure the requisite " treasure ", because unfettered trade meant the exchanging of all kinds of commodities. What was needed was to prevent people from importing and to encourage them to export. The whole trading world was conceived as a rivalry—a kind of round game—in which the object of each national unit was to get more gold and silver than its neighbours and rivals. The function of the State was that of a handicapper. It had to devise means whereby the importer was, so to speak, bunkered. Those means consisted in duties, bounties, and all manner of regulations.

The critics of Mun, from Adam Smith onwards, have never been quite fair to him and his contemporaries. History showed the world as a great rivalry to obtain the largest war chest of " treasure ", and the solvent of the impossible situation which was created by the attempt of all to sell more than they bought had been war, when the contents of the chests were dispersed before the game began again. It was not the fault of Mun that just as his diagnosis was promulgated the relationship of the world began to change. It was not the fault of Mun that just as his diagnosis was promulgated the very relationship of other commodities to gold and silver was about to change. *The fault was in the readiness of the State to accept blindly the advice of the economist as a guide to the future, when it could be but an exploration of the past and a commentary on a very fleeting present.*

Duties, bounties and regulations for their success demand either a static form of industry or great elasticity. If the form of industry is to be static, population must not greatly vary. The consumption demand must not violently outstrip production nor production suddenly outleap the growth of consumption demand. If either of these things happens, the regulations made for the benefit of the nation become malign in their effect. Hardly had Mun pronounced his doctrine and the State adopted it than both these things happened. Consumption and production began a game of see-saw which has not since ceased, and in which the duration of the upwards and downwards swing has grotesquely lengthened.

It did not take long for a new diagnostician to arise. Mun had prescribed for an infant trading community a régimen which ill suited its adolescence. Adam Smith, with his authoritative bedside manner, took the adolescent in hand and subjected the patient to a new clinical examination. The splints and bandages of Mun were condemned. Trade needed no coddling; it needed exercise and fresh air. If we can overstrain the metaphor, where Dr. Mun had concentrated upon stimulating the blood content and flow, Dr. Smith concentrated upon muscular development. The life-blood of trade might be gold and silver, but, after all, blood pressure is itself a disease. The patient needed variety of diet, which Dr. Mun's assistants had so carefully forbidden.

It is quite certain that Mun as a doctrinaire would have been politically ineffective had his doctrine not been immediately acceptable to those in power. Despite the adherence of Pitt, Adam Smith was doomed to be politically ineffective until those to whom *his* doctrine was materially congenial had become the persons in power. Neither Mun nor Smith, let it be remarked in passing, was wholly master of the mind of the State. Just as the Holy Roman Church recognizes "unconscious Catholics", so the student of economic history must recognize unconscious disciples of certain schools of thought, who follow the creed though they neither name nor formulate it.

In France a school of political economy arose, known by the name of "Cameralists"[1] whose chief concern was not the wealth of the nation as such, but the health of the State revenue—a very different thing from a short viewpoint. The unconscious Cameralists in England have always been many. Their viewpoint may be said to cut athwart both Mun and Adam Smith. They do not, with the Mercantilists who sprang from Mun, concentrate too intensely upon gold and silver as the desired result of a trade balance, but, on the other hand, they would not

[1] "The name Cameralist", says Professor Cannan, "is derived from *Camera*, the King's chamber, in which he was thought to spend his time discussing with his Ministers the ever-present problem of how to make ends meet. It is the counting-house of the old rhyme, 'The king was in his counting-house, counting out his money.'"

have trade freed from all regulations to find its own means of increasing the wealth of the people.

It is quite obvious that when the effective power in a State lies with traders who combine the functions of merchants with those of money-lenders, who are, that is, merchant-bankers, the trend of State policy towards trade will be very different from the trend when the effective power lies with men who are primarily merchants or primarily money-lenders, and even more different if the power lies with men who are producers. (The term " money-lender ", it ought, perhaps, to be said, is intended to carry no savour of contempt. There is nothing derogatory in its application as the name of a function.) The growth of industrialism helped to quicken the splitting of the once twin functions of merchanting and banking, and created a new and wider community of wealthy men who were solely producers, and merchanted only in the narrower sense of selling their one range of products to middlemen for further disposal.

To these new men free trade was a vital necessity. Not only was the machine improving to such an extent that production, from one local aspect, outleapt consumption, but the growth of communities of workers about the factories was such that, from another local aspect, consumption was outleaping production. These incompatibles actually seemed to be happening together, because " production " in the local sense only meant the deposit of goods at the point of consumption. To keep the machines occupied, export had to increase. To finance export and to feed the workers, imports had to increase also.

State artificialities designed either to ensure the correct over-plus of gold and silver (for the Mercantilists of Mun) or to ensure that the King's counting-house had an adequate supply of money for him to count (for the

Cameralists) were alike fatal to the new producers. Not only had there to be a generous flow of imports—for the double reason just stated—but the commodities imported had to be cheap, for if they were not cheap, costs would rise. Cheap raw material and cheap labour were the needs of the industrialists of the machine age, and both demanded the shoring away of the restrictions and imposts of the Mercantilists. Adam Smith " rationalized "—as we should say in our contemporary jargon—the quite selfish and almost instinctive clamours of the machine owners, and when these began to enjoy more and more Parliamentary power, Adam Smith became the recognized doctor of the State.

Between the publication of *The Wealth of Nations* in 1776 and the Budget of 1853, Pitt, Peel and Gladstone managed to implement the Adam Smith doctrine. Peel and Gladstone were both of the merchant class, the one the son of a northern manufacturer, the other the son of a wine vendor, and they had about them, exercising a steady pressure both in Parliament and about the country, perfect types of the new manufacturers in Cobden and Bright. The interests which flourished on the work of financing trade were obviously on the side of those whose political object was to swell trade by taking off its fiscal fetters. Manufacturer, merchant, ship-owner, and banker—each was, so to speak, a natural Adam-Smithian. They had no difficulty in taking the power of Parliament.

There were two sections of the community, however, which were affrighted, if not affronted, by the reign of Adam Smith. The new masses of industrial workers suspected the " cheap labour " motive—it is significant that the Corn Law League was antipathetic to the point of physical clash to the Chartists—and the agriculturists saw at once that floods of cheaply imported grain meant ruin to them. Not only did it mean ruin to the agriculturists as such, but it might mean ruin to the nation. Cobden—the International Man as he was well called—was a pacifist, not in the sense that he wanted peace at any price, but in the sense that he could not understand sane men consenting to interrupt the beneficent spread of trade by war. To him the mutual interdependence of nations consequent upon flowing and free trade could only mean less and less cause for war. He actually spoke of the abolition of tariffs as God's own way of cementing the friendship of nations, with something of the ingenuousness that led persons like the late Marie Corelli to speak of God's own time as opposed to Summer Time.

But less optimistic observers foresaw that war would not be abolished by freer trade, and the prospect of some twenty to forty millions of people on a group of islands that could not provide them with bread to withstand a wartime blockade was not cheering. To them, it was useless to advance the argument that it could no longer be in men's self-interest to go to war. It was no longer in men's self-interest to become dipsomaniacs or to contract venereal diseases, but men did both. They were prepared to admit that given the existence everywhere of a being called " the economic man " the doctrines of the disciples of Adam Smith were irrefutable—only they denied the existence anywhere of that economic man.

But although the workers in the mass might doubt the disinterestedness of those who followed the economic teachings of Smith and the agriculturists might prophesy dire doom to what had long been England's largest and most important industry—agriculture—Free Trade remained the talisman by which statesmen conjured away all criticism of the economic organization of the nation. They were singularly blind. If Free Trade meant anything, it meant Free Trade, but what was acclaimed as Free Trade was a system of trade whereby imports into

Britain were free but her exports into the lands of her customers were still subject to rising duties and more stringent regulations, a system whereby the selling of goods was freed from certain State restrictions but their manufacture was increasingly subject to more and more restraint, sometimes by the insistence of the trade unions and sometimes by the intervention of the State.

The humanity of the nation under the powerful " drive " of Shaftesbury began to impose conditions upon the employment of child and female labour. The unions were eventually able to impose conditions upon the employment of male labour. The ideal of cheap labour which was among manufacturers the main cause of the enthusiasm for cheap food was thwarted to a growing degree by these new restrictions and regulations. The trade unions themselves quickly reached the stage where they prevented the competition of cheap English labour with their own work, but supported the free importation of goods made by cheap foreign labour.

For cheap labour to remain cheap, it must be plentiful. The existence of a mass of unemployed in an unrestricted labour market is an assurance that competition for work will keep wages down. The remedy against this competition was organization, but organization took time. Conversely, if the mass of unemployed becomes too great the social and civic quietude is threatened. A surplus population must not grow too big. A growing population must have about it a growing industry.

As all know, the happy accident of Britain's geographical position and mineral resources made her at the opening of the machine age the workshop of the world. She could survey her growing population with equanimity, even with approval. The fact that population was massing in certain districts—round particular ports or in areas where certain minerals were mined—did not perturb her.

Overseas was an expanding market and at home the masses represented a consuming market. The urge was to export and to export and to export. What was exported mattered little.

So it came about that while some men were exporting goods, others were exporting the machines which made those goods, and the nation was exporting technicians to train competitors in the use of those machines. It seemed, for perhaps a quarter of a century, that consumption demand the world over must continue to expand and that Britain would always be the centre from which the main production would be drawn and the centre which would finance all developments. The surplus wealth which was resulting from the first fine careless rapture of industrialism was being used to enable peoples at the other end of the world to buy British goods. Mines, railways, waterworks, manufactories, in America, Asia, Africa and Australasia, were all created by an outflow of British loan capital, with the hearty approval of the contemporary economists.

This trend had several results which were far from happy. The division of wealth was unequal and the possession of wealth was erratic. The rich grew richer and the poor seemed to be growing poorer—" seemed " to be growing poorer because the emphasis of attention was directed to the unemployed or sweated surplus labour. The great mass of the poor was actually growing richer than it had ever been, although its standard of comparison was no longer the hard times of an earlier generation but the flaunting riches of a large population which surrounded it. The cotton operative saw new " masters " suddenly endowed with both wealth and power, and read of Jew comedians, like the Barnato Brothers, who had returned from the Colonies with millions to apply either to social display or political intrigue.

There was throughout the whole period of machine development growing unrest and discontent. The money masters of the new age were divorced from any trace of the old feudal responsibility, and that increased the resentment at their riches. They were so divorced largely because of the paternalism of the State which had divorced the ruin of a man's enterprise from the ruin of the man himself.

In the early phases of the machine age men who risked their wealth in new ventures were still the "gentlemen adventurers" who had financed the opening up of the new worlds—that is to say, they placed their possessions at stake in the enterprise and if the enterprise failed, they were personally ruined because the creditors of the venture could demand personal satisfaction. As enterprise grew and spread the manner of financing it also grew and spread. A small group of personal friends or a small community of acquaintances was no longer a sufficient "pool" from which to draw capital. Shares in enterprises were offered and taken far afield from the seat of the venture. The owners were out of personal touch with the directors, to whom they looked only for a return on their investment. It was quite early realized that this relationship was dangerous to the suppliers of capital, and in the 'fifties of the nineteenth century the law recognized the principle of "limited liability" by which the responsibility of the contributor of capital was limited to the amount of capital he contributed or (in the case of partly paid shares) proposed to contribute.

The recognition of that change in the law had surprisingly little effect until 1878 when the failure of the City of Glasgow Bank spread a ruin so wide and so abrupt that the moral was forced home to the consciousness of all who had capital invested or to invest. That dramatic failure brought to penury even persons who, as beneficiaries under trusts, had not even realized that their fortunes, to the last rag of personal possession, were dependent upon the prosperity of the bank. The benefits of limited liability once generally realized concealed its hidden dangers.

Growing markets and unfettered competition demand a steady cheapening of costs allied to a steady increase in production. With machine production the two go naturally together. Large aggregations of machines using large volumes of power demand large capital. Large staffs of supernumeraries, in the shape of sales staffs, distributors, advertising experts and the like, also demand large capital. The monster capitals of the later aggregations of machines and plant of the nineteenth and early twentieth centuries were drawn from an ever-increasing mass of small savers.

To the small saver this development had two aspects. One was that he was enabled and in many cases invited pressingly to participate in ventures to which in an earlier day he would have been denied access and was enabled to do so without risk of much personal loss. His natural view of the enterprise into which he placed his savings was that it said to him, " Heads, you win heavily ; and tails, you can't lose much." He was attracted to the rival claimants for his small portion of capital by one consideration only, that of generous returns with little risk. The enterprise which offered the highest return with the lowest risk could command unlimited means, for its purpose was but a secondary consideration to the great mass of capital owners.

The second aspect which appealed to the normal small saver was that in the new conditions he need not worry unduly about his venture once it was decided upon. Kindly experts took away from him all cares of management. If a small tradesman lent his savings as a sleeping partner to another small tradesman in his own community, the direction of his money was an ever-present factor in his daily life. Should the user begin to trade stupidly or evilly, the lender was immediately aware of it. But if a small tradesman lent, in the form of share capital, his money to some enterprise situated many miles from his own habitation and conducting a business of which the lender was ignorant, this ever-present awareness was no longer possible. John Jones in Manchester might know that Thomas Smith in Stockport was sweating the workers whom they jointly employed, but John Jones in Manchester could not be expected to know that Smith, Limited, was slaughtering niggers at the far side of the earth in order to produce dividends. He could not even be expected to know that Smith, Limited, was sweating women and children two counties away. If he did know, and developed moral scruples on the question, he could but sell his shares, or, at some expense and trouble, travel to an annual meeting of proprietors at which the agenda and the skill of the chairman ruled into silence or ineffectuality his moral protests.

The need was for large and widespread capital contributions to enable large and wide-flung markets and sources of supply to be exploited by expensive plant and manifold departments of man-power. Limited liability catered for this need, but created a growing divorcement between the owners of an enterprise and its direction. It also changed the attitude of those owners towards the enterprise, for it concealed responsibility. Estimable men and women could engage in dubious businesses or businesses conducted in a dubious way without their knowing it, and without their neighbours knowing it. The stigma of dishonourable trading was not upon them. To give an extreme example, the wife of a Nonconforming minister who would have died rather than help to finance a brothel in her own township, might draw dividends without shame from some remote property enterprise which made its high returns from renting apartments to bawds or harlots in distant towns, or even in her own town.

As the great labour organizations grew in numbers and power they naturally accumulated surplus funds which they were storing against some desperate need. Those funds they could not leave idle. The effect of limited liability having been to expand enormously the number of companies and to extend enormously the number of investors, the Stock Exchange was naturally the focal point for the attention of trade union officials charged with the duty of wisely placing the surplus funds until they were wanted. The active market in shares assured the placers of immediate liquidity when the need for other use arose, and also promised a reasonable income on the invested funds. The motive of those officials in investing the money was very rightly the usual commingled motive of a desire for a return and a desire for safety. There thus came a time when the money of one union was invested in the enterprises to forward which men of other unions laboured. This created a very ironical state of relationships.

The directors of an enterprise, knowing that its power to attract new capital for further expansion depended upon their showing an attractive return to the capital already invested, thought first of profit, and in making a profit costing is all-important. A vital factor in costs being labour costs, the directorial endeavour was of necessity to keep wages low. If adequate dividends were not paid, the shares of the enterprise would fall in the open market, and holders would sell before their losses became greater. This would prevent the raising of further capital on reasonable terms. The members of the great and small unions and the small savers who had invested thus became the instrument of oppressing their fellow-workers in other industries. It could even happen that a trade union member was all unwittingly one of the factors making for the sweating of himself.

The contemporary economists were too busy assuring the industrialists and the statesmen that the secret of success was to buy in the cheapest and to sell in the dearest market to sound any warning that from economic success might grow social disaster. The trade unionists were too much occupied with fighting for that marvellous thing called " recognition ", and for the acquisition of some Parliamentary power, to analyse their own significance in the changing social and economic complex. Nobody, with the possible exception of Walter Bagehot, had managed to convey to the general apprehension of the nation exactly how important, even how sinister, the old area of Gresham was becoming. Nobody, in short, had realized that the day-to-day life of the ordinary citizen was more affected by what happened between one end of Threadneedle Street and the far end of Throgmorton Street than by what was discussed at Westminster and in the controlling offices of the industrialists.

This sweeping statement deserves a little expansion. An astute man of business, realizing that in some undeveloped portion of the world the provision of transport facilities would cause an immediate stimulation of progress, would turn naturally to the City of London for the necessary finance which his proposal required. Obtaining funds from those able to provide them, and satisfied with the prospects of future profit or present interest proffered by the borrower, he would begin the work of constructing a railway system. That would start a wide train of effects. The demand for iron, wood, upholstery, wire, tools, and some labour would stimulate prosperity in several districts of England. That stimulation would draw population to those centres. The completion of the railway would cause the trade along its tracks to increase not only greatly but suddenly. That in turn would draw population to the new trading areas and would make a consuming market stimulating to centres at home, again drawing population to new centres. The increased export and import of the area opened up would cause extra shipping facilities to be required with all the associated facilities of communication. Again population would be affected. Eventually the prosperity of the new area would attract the attention of avaricious men, not wisely considering what further facilities were needed but considering only how soon they could jump in and take a share of the new wealth. Others, seeing certain home industries enjoying unusual prosperity from the opening of the new and growing market, would turn a similar attention to those industries. The familiar cycle would result—a period of under-provision followed by a period of over-provision, resulting in a changing incidence of prosperity as between the competing caterers and exploiters, this resulting again in a fluctuation of population.

Not only would such an event change the locality of many citizens, but it would change the vocation of many citizens. It would change the proportion of vocations one to another.

If the astute man, instead of seeing that new transport facilities would yield new wealth saw, instead, that wealth was to be made for him and his associates by providing a district with a manufactory for goods which it at present imported, these effects would be intensified. At its simplest—the erection of factories to make garments in South Africa would stimulate the textile machinery makers and depress the wholesale clothiers, but the stimulation of the machinery makers would be under the distant menace that some day what this man had done for local garment-making some other man would do for textile-machinery-making. A specialized industrial country could not hope for ever to sell both cotton goods and the machines for making cotton goods, but neither could it expect for ever to sell either the one or the other without its market being sooner or later invaded.

What undoubtedly enabled the industrialized England of the nineteenth century to exploit the opportunities of wealth in the great world which was expanding both in the sense of providing new trading territories and in the other sense of discovering and applying new technical means of production and transport, was not so much the fortunate coincidence of geographical position and appropriate mineral deposits. It was the presence in the capital city of the country of a free capital market. That free capital market was adequate to the demands upon it because of the existence of the method of financing enterprise by limited liability. The thrifty Scot could be tempted to lend his money to a group of Lancashire men to provide machines for Germans or rails for niggers, not because the Lancashire men had themselves assured the Scot of the merits of the enterprise, but because in London there existed a machine for the express purpose of linking idle capital to projected enterprise without danger of complete total ruin if the enterprise went awry. What determined the direction of both capital and enterprise was the judgement of the men controlling that machine.

It is of more than casual interest to realize what the professed economists were discussing while this dominance of the banks and the Stock Exchange was being effected.

Chapter VI

THE MEANING OF MARXISM

It is significant that the word " economics " was not in use until the late years of the eighteen-seventies. The old usage was " political economy ", and when the British Association for the Advancement of Science—the Mudfog Association of Dickens' satire—decided in 1856 to extend the scope of the existing section devoted to statistics it cautiously used the term " economic science ".

The first use of " economics " appears to have been by the American Sturtevant, but the word was given a more definite paternity by Marshall, who in his *Economics for Industry* in 1879 advised the abandonment of the term " political economy " on the ground that the adjective was misleading, since " political interests generally mean the interest of some part or parts of the nation ". Jevons in the same year discarded the old term on the grounds of verbal convenience. The change from the old term to the new was only slowly accomplished; it was not general, even among those who approved it, until the eighteen-nineties.

In 1755 Richard Cantillon published in Paris his *Essai sur la nature du commerce en général.*[1] This essay was destined to have a marked effect on the thought of economists after a long period of neglect. Exactly how deep was its penetration into contemporary thought it is difficult to say with certainty. The work opened with a chapter of about 150 words headed " Of Wealth ", which read:

[1] It was made available in English translation with accompanying French text in 1931 by Macmillan & Co., acting as publishers for the Royal Economic Society.

> The land is the Source of Matter from whence all Wealth is produced. The Labour of man is the Form which produces it: and Wealth in itself is nothing but the Maintenance, Conveniences, and Superfluities of Life.
>
> Land produces Herbage, Roots, Corn, Flax, Cotton, Hemp, Shrubs and Timber of several kinds, with divers sorts of Fruits, Bark, and Foliage like that of the Mulbery-tree for Silkworms; it supplies Mines and Minerals. To all this the Labour of man gives the form of Wealth.
>
> Rivers and Seas supply Fish for the food of man, and many other things for his enjoyment. But these Seas and Rivers belong to adjacent Lands or are common to all, and the Labour of man extracts from them the Fish and other advantages.

Having thus noted the source of all wealth, the good Cantillon opened his second chapter with the dogmatic assertion that

> Which way soever a Society of Men is formed the ownership of the Land they inhabit will necessarily belong to a small number among them,

and proceeded to prove succinctly and forcibly that no matter how land might originally be distributed, it would very quickly fall into the hands of a small minority. The famous Liberal marching song "God gave the land to the People" would have stirred nothing but a pitying contempt in his bosom; he was a realist. The private ownership of property was to him a necessary base of society, and private ownership of property meant that ownership of land would tend by a natural force to fall into selected hands.

Now, although Cantillon's work was published in French, its author was a British merchant who later carried on the business of a banker in Paris. His heredity, environment and breeding should have made him a good temperamental Mercantilist ; his mind made him perhaps the most formidable critic of that system. In 1881 Stanley Jevons brought him, after many years of neglect, into the notice of economists by an article in the *Contemporary Review*[1] in which he said :

> The opening sentence of the first chapter, " De la Richesse," is especially remarkable. . . . This sentence strikes the keynote, or rather the leading chord of the science of economics. It reminds us at once of the phrase " land and labour of the country " upon which Adam Smith is so frequently harping. Yet it holds the balance between the elements of production more evenly than almost any subsequent treatise. Quesnay attributed undue weight to some other remarks of Cantillon, and produced an entirely one-sided system of economics depending on land alone ; Smith struck off rather on the other track, and took " the annual labour of every nation " as the fund which supplies it with all the necessaries and conveniences of life.

It will be seen that the contemporary thought of the eighteenth century agreed that Mercantilism was wrong, but was divided as to where it was wrong, and what theory of economics was right. Mun, the merchant, had misled his followers, but the followers of Cantillon, the merchant banker, were not certain where he led, and, in Jevons' colloquial phrase, " struck off " on different tracks.

The Quesnay of Jevons' remark was a French Court physician. He and de Gournay in the mid-years of the

[1] Reprinted in the edition of the *Essai* previously mentioned, from which all quotations in this work are taken. This valuable edition also contains a short biography of Cantillon by Mr. Henry Higgs, its editor, and the editor of Jevons' *Principles of Economics.*

eighteenth century reached a common set of conclusions from different angles of approach. Quesnay was bred of landowners and farmers, and had an agricultural experience as the background of his thought. De Gournay thought as a trader and financier. They founded a school which is known in economic history as that of the Physiocrats, but was called by its contemporaries that of the " économistes ". The essence of the teaching of that school has been distilled into a paragraph by Professor Othmar Spann.

> To the question, what activity of the individual regulates the economic machinery, and upon what foundation the well-being of economic life depends, Quesnay answers: upon the natural economic activities, namely the agricultural; and consequently upon the exclusive foundation of the primal productive activity, above all upon the tilling of the soil, whereon the production of other goods and therewith the economy of the division of labour are upbuilded. " L'agriculture est la source de toutes les richesses de l'état." Not money, trade, traffic, and industry are the true founts of public welfare, but the tilling of the soil. The former activities merely transform matter and move it from place to place; they are nowise creative. The husbandman renders them possible by nourishing those who engage in them, and he supplies the raw materials without which they cannot be undertaken. Commerce, industry, and transport are to be considered as forming a " dépendance de l'agriculture ".*

The " other track " on which Adam Smith " struck off " was a very different avenue. To him the wealth of a nation did not depend, as with Mun, on the balance of

* *Types of Economic Theory*, Allen & Unwin.

trade or the quantity of money within its borders, nor did it depend, as with the Physiocrats, upon agricultural labour. It depended with him upon the annual labour of every nation.

> The annual labour of every nation is the fund which originally supplies it with all the necessaries and conveniences of life which it annually consumes, and which consist always either in the immediate produce of labour or in what is purchased with that produce from other nations.

He remarked that labour devoted to things not permanently of use or having an exchange value was unproductive. The wealth of a nation, therefore, was, as he taught, greater according to the proportion of those in it who engaged upon productive labour to the idlers and decorators whose services were not productive. This proportion turned upon the amount of capital devoted to the employment of workers and the fruitfulness of labour. Labour was most fruitful when divided into specialized groups, each aided by its natural advantages. To borrow again from Professor Spann's always fair and always penetrating exposition :

> The fruitfulness of labour is increased mainly by the division of labour. Consequently, the division of labour is the chief cause of enhanced prosperity. The further the division of labour is pushed, the more is production carried on with an eye to the market. Now for the purposes of the market there must develop a general means of exchange or instrument of trade, namely, money. Commodities are exchanged in the market through the instrumentality of money, as the medium of exchange, and there thus originates an exchange-value or price of goods as contrasted with their use value. We see, then, that

> the division of labour is the starting point of the whole economic process and its development! It is the cause of the exchange of goods. . . . But the exchange is effected in accordance with exchange-value (price); and the formation of exchange-value is therefore decisive: (a) for the distribution of goods, since it settles the question who can buy them; and (b) for their production, inasmuch as this is guided by the expectation of the price to be realized.
>
> Upon these considerations Adam Smith builds up his economic system; and so do all the individualist schools that follow in his footsteps. The laws that regulate the formation of exchange-value are held to be also the laws in accordance with which the wealth of nations comes into being; they are, in fact, the laws of political economy, the primary laws of economic motion.

It will be seen that the vital difference between economic thought under Smith and economic thought under Mun and Quesnay was this—the mercantilists and the physiocrats had made productive circulation the basis of their reasoning; Smith inaugurated the study of the laws of exchange-value. From Smith forward the economists were to concern themselves chiefly with the theory of value and the theory of prices.

The broader aspect of Smith's teaching was, of course, that which seized the general imagination. Enlightened self-interest as the motivation of all economic activity was the major chord to which the hearts of his political and industrial disciples responded. "Laissez-faire, laissez-passer," was the phrase of power. If economic activities are left severely alone, are freed from all fetters, checks and restraints, they will develop harmoniously. Competition will work to the benefit and betterment of all. Admit the selfishness of each unit, as part of original sin, and the propellant of self-interest will receive sufficient " braking " from that aspect of self-interest which makes a man watch his neighbour closely. Consumers will have the best goods at the lowest prices, producers will be able to give vent to their energy and enterprise, and workers can seek work at the highest wages.

But, alas, an entrepreneur giving vent to his energy and enterprise is himself a consumer, and the " goods " he consumes include labour. Competition in supply means low prices, and the law holds good for human work as for the products of human work.

Laissez-faire, it will be seen, at once set working in each man two opposing sets of motives. There had been a a time when a man's environment and tradition taught him to aspire to be a fair tradesman or a competent craftsman. The environment of laissez-faire and the tradition of Adam Smith taught him to be sometimes a competing producer and sometimes a competing consumer, but always a competitor. The new temptation was not to get a fair share of a good bargain, but to make the best of a bad bargain. It was no longer easy to see the trading relationship steadily and to see it whole ; men saw its two shifting aspects alternately. They were, so to speak, cross-eyed and grew cross-tempered, particularly in the labour relationship. For employers to force down wages by encouraging competition for jobs was good business, but for workmen to try to force up wages by combining to refuse a low figure was conspiracy and a dastardly attempt to ruin England by forcing up costs.

Division of labour meant the congregation in certain spots of certain groups of workers. Laissez-faire meant competition in labour. But the congregation of groups of workers in certain spots and the resistance to low wages meant combinations of such groups to thwart the apparent plan of exploiting them by ensuring the existence of local groups of unemployed. These combinations, despite the disapproving eye of the Legislature, grew powerful.

Again two conflicting forces began to work in opposition to each other. The accepted economic doctrine of the day taught that the secret of wealth was freedom in trade —that a district fitted to produce a certain commodity should produce it freely—which implied that population should be fluid, and able to congregate easily where expanding opportunities of work offered themselves. But the need to combine in groups of self-protective craftsmen against the menace of a surplus inflow of labour when such opportunities attracted workers implied a check to this fluidity. The rapid development of new industries and the expansion of old industries implied the need for an adequate supply of trainees; but the fear of over-crowding an industry with skilled workers—again, the menace of the surplus labour pool—implied a need to restrict entrants.

Workers at home were succeeding in enforcing a collective wage bargain on employers; humanists of the Shaftesbury mould were successful in prohibiting the labour of young children and pregnant women and in securing a reasonable—or by contemporary standards, reasonable—amount of leisure. Laissez-faire was throughout the whole of the nineteenth and early twentieth century being subjected to checks and reservations. But abroad such checks were not operative among producers, and the children of Adam Smith in high places insisted that imports should not be artificially checked. The surplus labour pool at home was of quickly decreasing value in forcing wages and costs down for the benefit of the employer and the capital providers, but unchecked imports permitted to secure the lowest prices to the consumer were, from the aspect of the workers, doing exactly what that pool had once done—enabling the consumer to buy goods made at the lowest wage-cost.

Incidentally, of course, the Smithian free flow of trade was lop-sided. In theory Britain was developing those commodities which she was by nature fitted to produce and was freely exchanging them for commodities as fittingly produced in other countries. In practice other countries were carefully protecting their workers against imports from Britain and behind artificial restrictions were quickly building up industries to compete with those of Britain. The producer, whether employer or employed, was a natural free trader, since he wanted cheap raw material, and also a natural protectionist, since he wanted all the advantages, natural or artificial, that he could secure for his goods in the market. The consumer was wholly a free trader—he wanted the cheapest goods.

The wise statesman on questions of economics is always an expedientist. His attitude is, broadly stated, " Here *qua* consumer you must suffer that you may benefit *qua* producer ; here you must endure an economic loss to attain a political gain ; in this piping time of peace you must forgo a possible benefit in order that in a drumming time of war you may not lack certain essentials when they cannot be imported for you." But the economist can, and perhaps should, despise such expediency. It is very certain that the economists of the Smithian school did so when their influence over statesmen was most potent. The result was a further bedevilment of the citizen's mind.

It is glorious to be allowed to sing heartily, " Oh, the roast beef of old England, and, oh, the old English roast beef ! ", but it is a little disconcerting when the singing is over and the chairman has introduced the principal speaker to be told that God and sanity have laid it down that the rightful course is to import your beef from the Argentine. It is still more disconcerting and confusing to be told that God and sanity have laid it down that beef from one part of the continent of America is to have acting rank as the roast beef of old England, but that beef from another part of that continent is to be denied the honour. The normal person either buys the best beef his purse will afford or he buys the best beef he can get within a trading circle where he has certain palpable, if unformulated, obligations to be a customer to his customers.

It was not that the economists were at fault in their economic reasoning. It was that they were economists and not psychologists. A man may very fairly say, " It is not economically sound for that man to carve his lawful wedded wife into small pieces, which under reasonable division of labour is a surgeon's job, to make her a grave under the concrete flooring of his cellar, which is a job for the builders, and to book passages, which he cannot afford, for himself and his mistress to a land where his own profession is in little demand." Having fairly said that the commentator goes beyond his province if he adds, " Ergo—that man will never perform that series of operations." Similarly a man may fairly demonstrate, as Bloch and Norman Angell demonstrated, that economically and strategically warfare must be indecisive and as ruinous to the victor as to the loser, but he goes beyond his province if he adds that, this being proven, nations will not again go to war. Yet again—economists may debate the precise identity and value of each factor in a theory of values and present their conclusions with an easy professional conscience, but they go beyond their function if they say " because this is the rational method of testing values, legislation should be based upon it ", for in certain sections of the community, or in the case of certain specialized commodities, the measure of testing values may be wholly irrational owing to the introduction into the exchange of some impalpable sentimental or emotional factor.

To take a foolish example, when a man exacts a shilling from some reveller for a balloon rationally worth a penny, he is not selling merely a contraption of rubber, air and string ; he is selling a key whereby the reveller can unlock a certain store of emotions. He is selling a means of self-expression, though the expression may consist only in the foolish waving of coloured inflated rubber and the self may only be that of a muddled toper. The exchange value of fruit out of season is by no means governed only by considerations of labour-content or " rent " ; it is also governed by an unassessable content of subjective pride in the purchaser.

To phrase it another way, with every material import into the store of a man's possessions there enters an invisible import, and that invisible import is the concern not so much of the economist as of the psychologist or the moralist. On any economic standard of value a copy of *Lady Chatterley's Lover* is worth probably three and sixpence ; on a psychological standard it may be worth what it at present fetches, three guineas. The same consideration applies to a pair of imitation crocodile-skin shoes in a community of clog wearers. At the same time, on some other and contemporarily operative psychological standard, neither *Lady Chatterley* nor the shoes may be worth more than pulping value.

Throughout the whole period of the first phases of the industrialization of Britain—roughly to the end of the eighteen-eighties—the economists were intent upon this very analysis of values. Ricardo and Mill, Marshall and Jevons, and a host of lesser men argued and expounded. " Pure labour " theories contended with theories of " utility ".

A strange, elderly gentleman with an inconvenient knowledge of the Middle Ages even tried to expound in the

Cornhill Magazine a theory that was suspiciously like a theory of pure righteousness, but they soon stopped that by refusing his further articles, and leaving Mr. Ruskin with yet another grievance against his age.

Systems waxed and waned, but the characteristic of each of them was, that that aspect of it which appealed to the empiricism of the industrialists both in and out of the legislature was roundly applauded and more or less aptly applied. The hard-headed Englishman was a little misled. Metaphysicians he could deride and ridicule as self-styled " thinkers " who quarrelled among themselves about their preposterous systems constructed from abstractions, but men who quarrelled about their systems which were not constructed from abstractions but from homely realities, such as the price of corn, rates of wages, imports and exports, could not be derided. And, most impressively, whatever else they quarrelled about, these profound gentlemen seemed unanimous in advising that no political artificialities should interfere with the free and natural flow of trade which came from unfettered competition.

And then, in the eighteen-eighties, it became apparent that the very industrialists who applauded the orthodox economists most loudly were behaving like heretics. A grocer from that home of Adam-Smithian doctrine, West Lancashire, grew suddenly rich first by applying the true milk of the word and having soap boiled by specialized workmen and next by recanting the word and working with all his shrewdness to end competition. The bracing air of Adam Smith was being artificially warmed for a host of small capitalists by the Sunlight of William Lever. The simple faith of laissez-faire was being conquered by the complex Trust of the new capitalism.

Rings, Mergers, and Amalgamations ended for many industries any pretence of free trade as Cobden had understood it, for, scorning the protection of State Tariffs, producers erected invisible tariffs of their own by the formation of allotted territories and sales agreements. The whole trend might, academically, be uneconomic, but it paid. Lip service had still to be rendered to the good old doctrines. Electors had still to be told that the whole duty of trading man was to buy in the cheapest market, even though the candidate who addressed them had committed his industry to a price level fixed by agreement and himself to buying from nobody but a particular ring of suppliers. Protection as an outworn shibboleth was still to be condemned, even though every department of industry was increasing its Protection through trade union agreements, buying-and-selling agreements and price-fixing agreements.

While the mart hummed with the activities of men intent upon thwarting free imports by cartel agreements, and the trade union lodges devised new methods of making a monopoly of each section of labour, the lecture rooms still echoed to the expositions of the Ricardian theory of land-rent, the fiscal doctrines of List, the wage theories of Thünen, and the attempt of Marshall to formulate a " law " that the value of goods fixes itself at the intersection between their utility and the " disagreeables " attendant upon the labour of producing them.

Those many millions who had not the privilege of attending the lecture rooms were even more concerned with the " disagreeables " than the economists. They were perpetually aware that the more disagreeable the labour, the lower the reward. They were, for example, acutely aware that a pluralist Chairman of a public utility company received more for a few minutes' work a month than the actual key-labourers in the enterprise received for a year of hard working days. It was of little interest to them what effect the " disagreeables " had upon the value of goods; it was enough that whatever the value of the goods in terms of profits the share-out was a little illogical.

The tendency of the governing classes—if one may use the term with no party political connotation in mind—had always been to extract from academic economists those parts of their teaching which either matched the empirical conclusions of the practical trader or landowner or promised to justify and further the aims of the possessive classes. After the spread of literacy inaugurated by popular education in 1870, the tendency of the non-governing classes was to do exactly the same thing. The persons who stood most to benefit from free competition in goods and services found their justifiers. The persons who stood most to benefit from certain sets of communal restrictions found *their* justifiers. Nietzsche somewhere makes the point that man acts by instinct and then calls in his reason to justify his actions. The "wealth-gathering middle class" first embraced as a policy of action unfettered competition, and next a policy of agreed co-operation between allied interests. The lower and middle classes, which had not been able to gather wealth, first embraced a metaphysical doctrine that their ill-luck in the scramble would be to their benefit in some future compensatory life, and next a very material doctrine that if the existing system had prevented them from gathering wealth the fault was not in them nor in the good God, but in the system. It was the very tolerance of private ownership of capital that was to blame. The evil thing must end. Economists were not found wanting to justify this new credo. Karl Marx was the prophet of the new evangel.

Marxism actually contained more fallacies than the official teachings of the orthodox Capitalistic economists. It was summed up for political purposes in the slogan, "workers of the world unite! You have nothing to lose but your chains!!" This was seriously said at a time when the material benefits of the worker from his industry were at a standard never before reached, and were yearly increasing, and at a time when the possibility of overcoming the innate nationalism of the workers was remote indeed. The workers of the world had been busy for a century slitting each other's weasands in Europe and worshipping leaders like Garibaldi, Bismarck, Napoleon le Petit, and equally busy blowing each other to pieces in Asia and Africa. There was a far more instant temperamental response to Chamberlain's Protectionist slogan of " Tax the Foreigner " than to the injunction of the Marxists.

In short, the economists upon whose teachings the new Socialism and the new Communism were to be reared were even more oblivious to the psychological factor in economics than those whom they challenged had been. They did, however, unsettle large sections of the masses, and caused all workers to challenge, either silently or vocally, the old social values which had for generations affected men's response to economic values. More important still, they provided an answer in the right jargon to the economic justifications which were offered for the various social, and sociological, injustices which still existed too obviously for the Parliament-men to deny. To a nation which had cheerfully sung for generations, " Britons never, never, *never* shall be slaves," they did present the possibility that slavery had more than one form. This service—if it was a service—had the defect of its quality. Many a man had found comfort in his economic and social servitude by metrically declaring himself to be free, but under the new teaching men as free as any civilized men are ever likely to be found a new ill-ease in declaring themselves to be wage-slaves.

Karl Marx as a thinker was the spiritual child of Hegel. Hegel's philosophy of history taught that the history of mankind is real only as a history of ideas. Each idea affirmed as truth calls into being its own negation. The conflict between the two creates new and higher ideas, which become embattled in turn. Marx saw history as a similar battle between economic forces, fought between the social classes which are the products of those forces. A particular class created by a particular set of economic forces rises to power and moulds the State to its liking, but its very success brings into being an antagonist class which does not like that mould. As Mr. G. D. H. Cole has described it:

> Thus, modern capitalism cannot develop its powers without calling into being a proletariat—a working class depending solely on its wages as a means of life. This proletariat, moreover, must be gathered together in factory and mine, and organized into a co-operative force labouring to produce wealth for the capitalist. Thus concentrated and organized, it becomes a power, and develops a will of its own, contrary to the will of its capitalist masters. In time, it develops far enough to be able to dispense with these masters, and organize the changing and ever-expanding forces of production in a new way. It turns upon its masters, and in the fulness of time overthrows them, and sets up a new social and political superstructure corresponding to the new needs of the productive forces.

Although Marx has been derided and deified above his demerits and merits by empiricists whom his gospel outrages or to whom it strongly appeals, he was an economist at least worthy to rank with the greatest of the orthodox schools. Ricardo had taught that the value of commodities depends on the amount of labour involved in their production as finished products. From this teaching the early Socialists wrested the conclusion that the workers, therefore, had a right to the whole produce of their labour. Rent, interest on capital, and profits were extracted from the worker by no right but by the accident of power in the landlord, the capital provider or the employer. Marx seized upon the theory of " surplus value ", which, at its briefest, is that the labourer by his work produces a surplus over and above what is needed to keep him and his family alive. A worker working a twelve-hour day may need the products of six of those hours for his subsistence ; the other six give a fund from which the " exploiter " takes his various exactions. There is then a surplus value of 100 per cent of the labourer's wage and 50 per cent of the total product.

Labour, Marx admits, is not always of equal value. The skilled worker, producing more value than the unskilled worker, receives more wages. This is governed by the difference in cost in producing and maintaining the skilled and the unskilled workers. The labour of a skilled worker may in an hour produce as much value as two or three hours of the labour of an unskilled worker. The difference is to be measured by the relative cost of producing the different types of labour. The " labour " which is the measure of value is not the simple, straightforward manpower-time which produces the commodity, but a more complex " labour "—" an abstract, undifferentiated human labour "—of which skilled labour is a multiple. Again, all labour is not useful, and some labour is slower in operation than other labour. Marx admits a category to cover these variations, that of " socially necessary labour ".

Where Marx differed from the earlier Socialist economists was in his treatment of the right of the worker to his product. It is not the labourer who has that right but the whole mass of labourers. The economic system is one and indivisable ; its products belong to all the value producers in the system. That was a doctrine not unpalatable to labour busy organizing itself into " brotherhood ".

Any competent student of economics can discern the flaws in every one of Marx's theories, but the early adherents of Marxism were not competent economists. They were disgruntled workmen who saw and felt that certain members of society were taking more than a just share of the growing increase in national wealth, and justifying the injustice by skilful dialectics into which was woven a mystagogic jargon. This new prophet of the mysteries seemed, in a very satisfying way, to be on the workers' side and had an even more satisfying jargon for dialectical use. The whole age, it must be remembered, was permeated by a kind of pseudo-science. Huxley, valiantly declaring that he " would not plaster the fair face of truth with the ghastly cosmetic of rhetoric ", was effective in teaching his generation to plaster the foul face of fallacy with the ghastly cosmetic of mock-scientific terminology.

With such a vogue at its height it was obviously more satisfying to describe oneself as a proletarian than as " an honest British working man ", and to regard the " old Guv'nor " as an exploiter rather than as " the gaffer ". It was in some way gratifying to sit in a six-roomed house, with water laid on and a little garden attached, with a tea-table garnished by exotics from the ends of the earth, and with the children newly home from a day's schooling in the elements of culture, and to speak hotly of striking off one's chains. It was somehow comforting to rage against exploitation in the intervals of pigeon-flying or whippet racing. These things could be done with an easy, and even a glowing conscience, because the new jargon removed any personal direction from one's wrath. It was not the old Guv'nor as such who was being denounced as a slave driver, but an impersonal being—the exploiter. It was not one's own actual circumstances which were being degraded as so many chains, but an abstract set of circumstances conveniently summed up as " the system ". The Tennysonian lady who could murmur " And that good man, the clergyman, has told me words of peace ", represented the old revolt against science. The contemporary trade union official who could shout, " And that good man, the expounder of the materialist conception of history, has told us words of war," was the representative of the new revolt against anything that was not science, whatever science might be.

The workers, in short, did not reason thus: These economists with their wranglings about values and balances of trade have led us into a mess of discomforts, let us have no more of them. They rather reasoned: These economists with their wranglings about values and balances of trade are obviously " gaffer's men ". They have led us into a mess of discomforts. But let us have men about us who will wrangle about values and balances of trade as workers' men, and all will be well with us. Instead of crying, " Suffer not the old King, under any name," they cried instead, " Down with King Log; up, with King Stork ! "

Marx, of course, was not the first economist to denounce the wage system of contemporary capitalism. That had been done very effectively by no less a person than John Stuart Mill in the late eighteen-forties. He foresaw the discontent which Marx, in his own word, was to exploit.

> To work at the bidding and for the profit of another (wrote Mill) without any interest in the work—the price of their labour being adjusted by hostile competition, one side demanding as much and the other paying as little as possible—is not, even when wages

> are high, a satisfactory state to human beings of educated intelligence who have ceased to think themselves naturally inferior to those whom they serve.

A decade later he wrote:

> It will sooner or later become insupportable to the employing classes to live in close and hourly contact with persons whose interests and feelings are in hostility to them. Capitalists are almost as much interested as labourers in placing the operations of industry on such a footing that those who labour for them may feel the same interest in the work which is felt by those who labour on their own account.

It will be seen that Mill and Marx—and nearly all writers on politics and economics—deal generously in generalizations. The employing classes—the working classes—the exploiters—the proletariat—who are they?—how are they to be recognized? The general manager of a great insurance company or a large railway system with a salary of many thousands of pounds a year—is he of the employing class or the working class?—is he exploited or does he exploit? A hundred operatives with shares in the mill at which they work—an enterprising fellow making bicycles or wireless accessories in a shed with the help of three neighbours—a grocer with two assistants and one apprentice—a grocer with a hundred chain stores and many hundreds of employees—the Chairman of the Liverpool Gas Company—the manager of the Birmingham gas department—Mr. Jack Hylton, the conductor—the conductor-manager of the Southport Corporation Band—the members of the Rochdale Provident Co-operative Society—the shareholders of the International Tea Stores—into how many and different categories do these fall?

A labourer employed by a public utility company if exploited by the shareholders is no less exploited when that company is taken over by the local municipality in which he is himself a rate-payer. A telephone girl under the National Telephone Company becomes a telephone girl under the General Post Office—is she still exploited, and if so is she consoled for her feeling of being exploited by the warming thought that she is a martyr to the communal needs of the taxpayers? Is a worker who enjoys high wages and good conditions under a private capitalist less happy than a worker who enjoys low wages and poor conditions—at the same work—under a communal body? Is there, indeed, such a being as a "worker" or an "employer"—or do there only exist Tom Smith, Molly Brown, Sir John Jones, and their fellows, to whom the terms and conditions of working life, in whatever capacity, will appear differently as personal idiosyncracy, temperament, private relationships, dictate their mental reception?

The employers of the period of laissez-faire and its later transition were bitterly upbraided for considering their human employees as "hands". But the conventional term "hands wanted" meant precisely what it said. The employer did not want complete human beings; he only wanted their hands. Marx, however, could not separate the hands from the man, for he foresaw that a time was rapidly coming when most employers would be under the same disability. He snatched, as it were, the private lives of his followers in theory because he foresaw that men like Lord Leverhulme, Mr. Henry Ford, Mr. Cadbury and others would snatch them in practice, either by controlling their social activities in compounds called model towns or garden cities or by limiting through legislation, such as the Fourteenth Amendment, their power to satisfy their private tastes in the spending of their leisure.

CHAPTER VII

THE LESSON OF MALTHUS

LIKE all other economists, Karl Marx was a day or two behind the fair. The moment when he drove home to the consciousness of the workers the inevitability of class warfare was the moment when class was rapidly losing its old force in social and political life. The spread of industry and the rise of mechanical invention had done two things—it had brought into being a new type of man whose personal power and personal comfort were governed entirely by his wealth, and it had made the transition of any ingenuous and forceful fellow from one social category to another a matter of comparative ease.

Certain class distinctions in dress lingered late into the nineteenth century, like the paper cap of Lewis Carroll's carpenter, but before the twentieth century had well advanced these had gone. Personal taste alone dictated distinctive garbs by the time the Great War of 1914-18 was ended. Costermongers no longer wear pearlies, mill girls no longer wear clogs and shawls, newsboys no longer wear rags. Between the sporting dress of the Prince of Wales, with its combination of violently coloured pull-over and foreign beret, and that of any draper's assistant riding a second-hand motor cycle there is no difference save in quality. Between the evening amusement of a sprig of the aristocracy, taking some girl to a West-end cinema-show or dancing to broadcast music, and that of a labourer, taking some girl to a cinema-show or dancing to broadcast music, there is no difference at all in kind, though there may be in quality. Between the son of a miner aspiring to a political career and the son of a Duke aspiring to a political career there is no difference of technique—each must cultivate the men who control a party organization, each must have some aptitude for platform speaking, each must be able to mouth the fashionable economic jargon of the day. The son of the miner may have to serve an apprenticeship in administration as the official of a trade union, but the son of the Duke probably serves a similar apprenticeship either on an estate or in the employment of a city house.

Even the possessing classes against which the proletariat was to revolt were no longer classes in the old sense. Everybody in some way or another did, or could, or might, belong to them. As we have seen, the trade unionist, *qua* collective investor, was in the ranks of the exploiters against whom, *qua* political agitator, he fulminated. The ostensible master against whom his discontent *qua* worker should have been directed was by the late nineteenth century probably himself an exploited member of the salariat. If the exploited proletarian wanted to kick the exploiting capitalist he found himself about to kick either his old mother, his cousin Jim, a trade union secretary or a mere manager. True, some obvious capitalists existed —and still exist—upon whom wrath could be centred. The first Lord Leverhulme, one of the most significant figures in modern social and industrial history, Lord Northcliffe, Sir Alfred Mond, Andrew Carnegie, were such figures ; but they had without exception risen in a single lifetime from circumstances very far removed from those in which they stood when the accusing Marxist pointed them out as objects of sinister import to men who for a lifetime had regarded them as brave exemplars of self-help and dogged pluck and the old virtues of individualism. These, in some cases, were the very men whom political constituencies were returning with very comfortable majorities to speak for Labour in the Commons, and who were dowering upon their employees all manner of comforts outside the mere wage bargains made with trade unions. It was impossible to regard them as men lacking sympathy with the workers, lacking understanding of workers, or in class antagonism to the workers.

The disciples of Marx preached that production for profit was wrong, but they had as audience vast numbers of men and women who knew that production for profit had brought into existence the very means whereby they earned their livelihoods, and that without a profit incentive those means would not have been created or involved. Some of the largest enterprises at the end of the nineteenth century had been the wildest and most risky ventures forty years before, enterprises so foolhardy that no representative official of a community would have dared to embark upon them. They had been nursed very often through their infant years by men prepared to devote laborious days and forced energy to their nurture, which no bureaucratic official of a community would have either wished or been allowed to do. It was all very well to denounce greed as a motive or vanity as a motive or lust of power as a motive, but these motives had undoubtedly been beneficent in their results. And it was rather bewildering to be told by sincere men that an economic system which was opening up all kinds of once-closed avenues of ambition to the workers, which was improving their habitations and enriching their cuisine, which was providing just those things for which the Chartists of an earlier day had hopelessly clamoured, was nothing but a chaos and an outrage upon those who were compelled to serve it.

While ardent Socialist Parliamentarians, like the now all-but-forgotten Mr. Victor Grayson, interrupted debates to protest against a system which allowed men to starve upon the Thames Embankment, older men could not but remember that this very system had at least provided the embankment upon which men starved, instead of the mud flats and stenchridden fever-pits where the previous generation had starved in far greater numbers. While certain spokesmen of the new economics cried aloud for a complete conversion of the system from private enterprise to communal ownerships, certain of their constituents were only too painfully aware that communal ownership in municipalities seemed to have made no difference either to the workers thereunder or to the users of the services locally owned, except that the communally owned enterprise was distinguished by a more peremptory manner in its officers and a greater delay in its operations. It was also a little bewildering for those who had been trained to fear the tyranny of monopolies to regard the prospect of all services being under one great monopoly as a vista to be looked upon with equanimity.

The growth of what became known as " big business " which limited liability had made possible brought into being a new category of functionary, a servant of the enterprise, generally, but not always, a " hired man ", who can best be described as the organizer. In the days of limited operations the single owner or the small group of owners of a business could organize it successfully by very minor delegations of duty. In the days of widely extended operations when the ownership was also spread, delegation had perforce to increase. In addition to the nominal directors there had to be not only the older fashioned departmental managers, but new specialists—sales managers, staff managers, and the like. It was charged against these that they renewed the old fault, and treated the human beings engaged in the enterprise as mere " hands "—worse, they treated them as machines.

To some extent the charge was true, but if the workers came to be treated like machines they were treated with the same care as machines. It pays no entrepreneur to own machines or to hire machines which constantly break down and fail in their functions. The wise entrepreneur therefore cares for the machines and employs mechanics who can repair them. " Big business " studied the psychology of the workers and provided mechanics who could not only repair them but also prevent them from needing repair. The morning cup of cocoa, the free dental clinic, the works canteen, the rest room, the holiday on pay, the scientifically adjusted working shift, the educational adjuncts, the sports club—all these were added to the workers' lives, not from any sense of humanity in the organizers but from a sound sense of the value of a well-kept human machine. It was vain for the hater of the system of private enterprise to cry that these things were but the bedecking of the chains with roses, for the wearers of the chains liked the roses and had a shrewd conviction that some kind of chain, in the form of labour, would have to be worn whatever system operated.

Similarly, with the growth of the personnel of each enterprise there arose—except in very exceptional cases—an *esprit de corps* which showed itself in various forms, as pride in the achievements of the works dramatic society or football club, or as pride in a long service medal. It might be true to say that these things were emotional sops to the wage slaves, but the wage slaves liked both the wages and the sops. The revolt of the proletariat in disgust with the system which was exploiting them receded in the mental perspective of most workers and was overshadowed by more immediate pre-occupations, including, very often, the winning of small monetary rewards for suggestions dropped into a box whereby one enterprise in the existing system might be improved.

As the Parliamentary power of Socialism grew, its menace to those who preferred private enterprise as a national system waned. However sound Marx might have been in his economic teaching, or however unsound, it was soon apparent that his psychology had been altogether at fault.

Even had Marxian psychology been sound, the effect of the industrial revolution on the national psychology was such that it changed rapidly between generation and generation. Every mechanical invention ministered to that change. Perhaps the most staring example of such change was this—that the family remained the unit of social life, but for the majority of the people the old tradition of the homestead disappeared. There was lost, probably for ever, continuity in personal environment.

The statement just made is, palpably, a sweeping generalization to which ample contradiction can be adduced. There are to-day many hundreds of families living in the same township or village which housed their remote ancestors. There are many thousands of families engaged for the most part in trades and occupations which were the avocations of their predecessors. But for the majority, the coming of the machine age meant the end of local continuity.

It is said, I know not with what authority, that a Londoner of three generations is very rare. Contrariwise, in townships like Bradford, Leeds, Wigan, Bolton, Blackburn, Pudsey, Heckmondwike, Newcastle and Claygate, families persist without uprooting themselves. But even in such settlements, the aggregation of population as the local factories flourished did not consist only in natural growth. The immigrants were many. As old or infant industries decayed, workers migrated. The scouring of the southern workhouses for child labourers was an extreme example in the early days, as the migration departments of modern Labour Exchanges in our own time are an indication to-day, of the existence in England of a nomadism which was not a factor in the eighteenth century.

English tradition, of course, is filled by an adventurous spirit which drove Englishmen over seas, either on military crusades or naval occasions or to colonize distant lands, but it is not filled with a tradition of restlessness within the nation's own borders. When a delineator of the type of Smollett draws his contemporary England, the wanderers are the exceptions. The old lady in *David Copperfield* who has such an aversion to people who go meandering about the earth is a commonplace type of her time. The agricultural counties of to-day preserve still the feeling that an incomer from a neighbouring county is a foreigner. But in the streets of houses which were built to house the workers of the industrial age wanderers and meanderers and "foreigners" were commonplace inhabitants, for it was the need of the age that labour should above all things else be fluid, not as the old journeyman was fluid, but in quite a new sense. The old journeyman was what his name implied. The new nomad left a home for a new home. He did not continue to journey; he uprooted himself only to find a new settlement, and, very often, a new trade.

This change in social habit had effects which—as far as I am aware—have never yet been properly analysed. The attitude of the unpaid magistracy, for example, was affected. The bench was no longer in many cases dealing with local delinquents whose habits and motives were familiar, but with strangers to whom the magistracy was a body of penologists and little more. In the incomers loyalty to local tradition was non-existent, for they had not absorbed local tradition. On the other hand, loyalty to their original local tradition was purposeless, for they were no longer among friends. To take this at its simplest manifestation, a man's personal conduct among people to all of whom he and his family are known differs from his conduct among strangers. His choice of a bride will be governed by other factors than adolescent love or temporary convenience, and when he has children he and their mother will inculcate in them a common inheritance of manners and morals. It is not so with a man among strangers. He will comport himself with either greater reserve or greater freedom from reserve, and he will woo without any of the inhibitions or stimulants that come from a close knowledge of a girl's personality and environment. Children will be brought up in the atmosphere of two different traditions, even though the difference is slight. They will be bred apart from other children from the same stock; they will lack a sense of cousinship. The family as a unit will not be a large congregation of kinsmen; it will be a small unit. The place once taken by the kin of the man and woman must, perforce, be taken by neighbours, and those neighbours will for a time be untested neighbours. The result of this will be to increase the dependence of the worker upon his fellow workers; it will be an incentive to unity even outside the working hours.

It was in such circumstances that "friendly societies" first flourished, and with them "burial clubs" and the like. To a working family a death may be a crushing economic disaster. Even if some tradition does not dictate a costly funeral, a funeral there must be, and coffins and graves take more money than the average worker saves without aid against sudden demand. When such an event happens, it means much to be one of a large family in a community of much inter-marriage. If there is no such family, one must be created artificially, and it is not without significance that most of the friendly societies were named "brotherhoods" or used "brother" as a formal mode of address in their rituals.

A proletariat which has fashioned for itself friendly societies which serve the emotional and economic purpose of family associations, which is deriving a living that improves in standard with each generation, which finds its demands for political representation and control granted grudgingly, perhaps, but still granted ; which is itself admitted to the magistracy ; which is freed from the danger of an iniquitous wage bargain by powerful unions of its own creation ; which in its working life is provided with increasing amenities and in its growing leisure has within its reach adequate facilities for sport and culture ; and the individual members of which are encouraged to migrate from one environment to another when qualities and surroundings prove incompatible ; is less likely to rebel against the economic system than to accept it with protests against its flaws. Unfortunately, it is not allowed to detect and remedy those flaws unaided. The politician and the economist insist upon advising, and even upon altering the details of the system. And both politician and economist suffer the grave disability of never being able to institute reforms in time.

The industrial revolution led to a new fluidity of labour and a new fluidity of goods. The railway age was born. The principle of private enterprise and unfettered competition applied to railways led to the creation of a network of lines and the misdirection of much capital and manual labour. Both statesmen and economists were quick to see the menace of this state of affairs, and almost as quick to see that in steam power there was a monopoly power growing in their midst. To restrict free enterprise was obviously a necessary act for the public good, but to restrict free enterprise was to leave the permitted entrepreneurs in the menacing position of monopolists. The monopoly must also be restricted. There had to be adequate services able at their inception to attract adequate capital and after their creation to attract adequate custom, but the controllers of those services could not be left with arbitrary power, because they might so burden the commodities they carried that trade with countries where no such monopoly existed would become impossible. After a generation of effort a complicated system of checks and balances was evolved and was functioning with moderate satisfaction to all concerned. But neither statesmen nor economists nor railwaymen had foreseen, or could have foreseen, that by the time the unpleasant mess into which the railways had got themselves and the country had been more or less cleared up, the internal combustion engine would have shattered the monopoly.

Labour was fluid, and because it was fluid new or expanding industries could attract to their areas more workers than were needed. The trade unions by their collective bargains prevented employers from using these surplus workers as a factor to obtain cheaper labour, so that employment did not ' go round ', as once it had gone round, the competing mass. Industries were displaying a tendency to localize themselves and their original rate of expansion was diminishing. The floating bodies of unemployed were both a nuisance and a menace. Somebody, surely, must need their labour. Obviously, State aid in job-finding was the need. Labour Exchanges to act as employment bureaus might match the two wants —the want of work and the want of workers.

Labour Exchanges were founded. How useful for their original purpose they have been need not detain us here. The real significance of their institution is that their mere existence changed the psychology of the people whom they were intended to serve. Labour had been fluid because the tradition of the race was that the onus of finding work by which to keep himself and his dependents is upon the man who needs work. If he cannot find work as a carpenter at Hogsnorton, he must perforce find work as a carpenter at Little Muddleboro'. If he cannot find work as a carpenter anywhere, he must perforce abandon carpentering and become a tinker, tailor, soldier, sailor or some other contributor to the community's services.

If the unions of the carpenters, tinkers, dockers, railwaymen, and all other crafts forbid a man entry to their body and are powerful enough to forbid employers from employing non-union workers, the workless craftsman is vitally handicapped. If he is told that his best chance of finding work at his own trade is to register himself in his own township and wait until a bureau has found work for him, his incentive to fluidity is gone. Both these factors operated when the labour exchanges were instituted. The man's working life which had once been his own responsibility was under the direction and supervision of his union and of a State department. The generations of workers born in the past thirty years have known no other system. Psychologically they are a different race from their fathers.

Even more decisive in destroying labour fluidity was the institution of unemployment insurance, and its concomitant, 'relief', granted through an office where the recipient registered for benefit. The total effect of these State interventions into the working life of the masses was to destroy fluidity just at that phase of national life when it was most needed, the phase of the post-war years when a world depression had slowed down the major industries, but changing habit and mechanical invention, with the later addition of Protection, had caused new industries to flourish.

Economists and statesmen have never been markedly astute in gauging the inevitable effects of war upon the economic lives of nations. They can hardly be blamed. He would have been an ideal reasoner indeed who in advance could have forecast accurately the resultant of so many balancing factors as those of the last great war. The stimulation to mechanical ingenuity; the two effects of a forcible uprooting from habit, one the desire to return home and to stay there, the other to refuse again the uneventful life of the past; the anger at the unjust distribution of material rewards during the period of national need and service; the entire dislocation of the labour market by a withdrawal of a large proportion of the man power and the intensity of the labour of the remainder, and later by the inflow of women labour; the complete disintegration of the normal balance of international trade and indebtedness; the clash of interest between replacement workers and trainees—these are but the surface problems of the deduction. If the ideal reasoner existed who could, from a knowledge that these forces must operate, deduce what legislation should be applied in advance to direct the totality of these forces in the best interest of the nation, he would still labour under the old disability, that however accurate the diagnosis, the mere administration of the prescription would set up what the physicians call an idiosyncratic reaction in the patient and confound the forecast of result.

If, for example, any economist advising a statesman had in 1917 forecast the industrial trend of 1921-28 and had urged legislation to secure the old fluidity for labour, his prescription would necessarily have included a vast housing scheme, for one of the most vital factors in reducing fluidity after the last war was the housing shortage. But if a housing programme had been projected on a national scale in 1917, it would not have been practicable, and if any other legislative means to restore fluidity had been successful, without such a scheme they would have been frustrated. Again, had an early housing scheme been possible, it would have needed more than economics as a basis for scientific judgement to prophesy in what localities new industries might flourish. In the early nineteen-twenties a Prime Minister could draw attention to the significance of the fact that industry was moving southwards, but in the early nineteen-thirties a President of the Board of Trade is able to say with some pride that his Government's fiscal policy has caused new industries to locate themselves in old and distressed areas, like Darwen in Lancashire.

It should be noted that human beings are not naturally fluid. The familiarity of scene and comradeship is one of the strongest ties known to psychology. It explains largely why colliers protest to violence that their trade is so dangerous and so filled with discomfort that it is all but intolerable, and yet send their sons down the pit generation after generation. It is inherent in the human and penetrating observations of Sir Austen Chamberlain on the slum clearance problem, that to uproot and transplant slum dwellers from their homes is to inflict upon them as great a psychological hardship as to uproot and transplant such a one as himself to Canada or Australia, there to begin life anew in strange and uncongenial conditions. The temptations to migrate have to be strong indeed before the normal family moves its habitat, or willingly sees its members move individually from the familiar—and *safe*—setting of habitude.

Even when the politico-economist is able sucessfully to diagnose in a given situation the seeds of coming discomfort and to make preparation for easing the incidence of the pending discontent, he is, thus, always faced with two allied possibilities—that his own addition of new factors to the economic complex may so alter that complex that his addition is itself changed, and that however desirable his preventive or his remedy, the people in whose interest it is applied may revolt from it from some non-economic motive, as when settlers in rural areas leave the promise of personal prosperity for the sake of gratifying their ingrained gregariousness in a township already overweighted with unemployed, as when men and women prefer to suffer malaise rather than subject themselves to the indignity of undergoing an inquisition by some lady almoner at a local hospital, or as when men prefer indigence to the rewards of menial service in the entourage of some arrogant rich person.

It is, perhaps, on the question of the growth and fluidity of population that the academic economist as forecaster and adviser is confronted with the most imponderables. He is also bedevilled by a host of social and religious conventions which make the application of his economic conclusions to the realm of sociology and politics always difficult and sometimes impossible. If, for example, a far-sighted technocrat in the first decade of this century had said, " Machinery and its organization by non-competitive, cartelized business has rendered the growth of population dangerous ; we must have an act authorizing infanticide and the driving of jaded old workers to State lethal chambers," he would, very properly, have been derided as a madman whose homicidal tendencies had permeated his economic thought. But, equally, had he in that decade published a work which contained the advice that all women should be instructed in some form of contraception and that facilities should be made available at public clinics and in works clinics, he would have been the immediate victim of the law, his work suppressed and his person attached. Had he merely said " The causes I have detailed make it essential that we should deliberately at some present cost evacuate this and that body of workers from those areas and remove them to these new areas," he would have escaped with the lesser charge of impracticability and heartlessness, and some Lancashire playwright would have seized on the proposal as a basis of a folk drama, as was done when Thirlmere was taken for Manchester's water supply.

But the problem of population has been the intimate concern of the economist since it was first realized that a shortage of commodities could be viewed in two ways—as too few commodities for the population or as too great a population for the commodities. The Mercantilists held that a rapid growth of population was a sign of prosperity, and that the denser the people in numbers the better the state of the State. A German economist named Süssmilch published in 1742 a work entitled *Die Göttliche Ordnung in den Veränderungen des menschlichen Geschlechts*. Süssmilch was that oddity, a God-fearing statistician. His text was " Be fruitful and multiply ", and his endeavour was to deduce laws from birth- and death-rates, the proportion of the population at various ages, and the like sets of figures. In his general tendency, Süssmilch was a Mercantilist, but his view of the desirability of a growing population was shared by some of the later Kameralists, notably Sonnenfels, who constructed a whole social system round the idea that the wealthiest and strongest nations were often the most populous. In Germany many public offices could be held only by married occupants, and similar regulations were canvassed as being desirable in England.

It is quite obvious to a generation which has become familiar with the term "cannon fodder" that a military State has a good incentive for encouraging child-birth. Napoleon, surveying the lighted bedroom windows of Paris on a frosty night, remarked " Ah, Marshall, a night like this is worth a thousand soldiers to France." It is also obvious that before labour is organized to maintain a wage level a dense population is a desideratum to employers wanting cheap labour. But one amiable Anglican clergyman, with a flair for economics, read Süssmilch, and remembering what he had read of certain native philosophers, including Wallace, Hulme, Smith and Price, saw a point of view very different from that of a militaristic State or a labour-seeking employer.

Spurred by the works of William Godwin—who taught that Government, though a necessary evil, is responsible for the unhappiness and misfortunes of man—the Reverend Thomas Robert Malthus published the first edition of an essay destined, like some high plain, to be a landmark and a battlefield. This was the famous *Essay on the Principles of Population ; or A View of its Past and Present Effects on Human Happiness ; with an Enquiry into our Prospects respecting the Future Removal or Mitigation of the Evils which it Occasions*. The first edition of this work was no more than a controversial pamphlet to rebut Godwin's notion of the perfectibility of man, and to show that an abolition of government could not restore the race to Eden, because the ground to unhappiness and misfortune is to be found, not in government, but in our weak and imperfect natures. In a century delighting in theological argument such a pamphlet was sure of attention. It went into six editions in its author's lifetime—the sixth being dated 1828—and each edition saw a widening of its author's material and thought.

The first stand which Malthus took was that human institutions, far from aggravating misery and the fear of misery, had tended markedly to mitigate them. His main premises were that " food is necessary to the existence of man " and that " the passion between the sexes is necessary, and will remain nearly in its present state ". From these postulates he argued that " the power of population is indefinitely greater than the power in the earth to produce subsistence for men. Population when unchecked, increases in geometrical ratio. Subsistence only increases in arithmetical ratio". Certain checks must restrain the superior growth of the population. There was the preventive check—foresight of the difficulties of rearing a family. There were the positive checks —poverty, disease, war and other human distresses. Marriage, Malthus recognized, might by foresight be postponed, but this, he thought, would mean vice, and vice to him was the parent of misery. By such foresight no happy state of society could be produced.

From this primary statement of his thought in the first edition of the Essay in 1798, Malthus moved far by 1828, but chiefly in the direction of discerning more and greater checks on human fecundity. What is known as " the Malthusian cycle " was unaffected. As Professor Haney in his *History of Economic Thought*, has succintly stated it, that cycle is thus :—

> In the generality of old states, Malthus held, there existed an oscillation or vibration in the relation between population and food. Assuming an equilibrium in which subsistence is just enough for the easy support of the existing population, the order of precedence, as he saw it, begins with an " effort " of population to increase. Then subsistence becomes more divided. As a result, the number of poor grows, and those already poor fall into deeper poverty. The price of labour falls, the number of labourers being out of proportion to the work in the market ; the price of provisions tends to rise. Then the difficulties of rearing a family discourage marriage, and population is brought nearly to a stand. But cultivators are meanwhile induced to employ more labour, and at last subsistence is brought up to a new equilibrium. Such was the normal and constantly

recurring cycle. Malthus, however, admits that it was liable to irregularities on account of bad crops, new manufactures, greater or less spirit of agricultural enterprise, and emigration.

It is not the purpose of our present enquiry to pursue the history of Malthusianism. It is our present purpose to note two points in the history of that notable doctrine, that it began a new quarrel between economists, and that the doctrine was formulated at the opening of an era when all the factors under the survey of Malthus were rapidly changing.

Malthus's reasoning was that, other things being equal it is easier for a population of four millions to add a million to its number and become five million than for a population of one million to add a million to its number and become two million—the tendency of population is to increase in geometrical progression. But land—the base of all subsistence—is under a strict law of diminishing returns. "It must be evident to those who have the slightest acquaintance with agricultural subjects, that in proportion as cultivation extended, the additions that could yearly be made to the former average produce must be gradually and regularly diminishing . . . When acre has been added to acre till all the fertile land is occupied, the yearly increase of food must depend upon the melioration of the land already in possession. This is a fund, which, from the nature of all soils, instead of increasing must be gradually diminishing."

Two pieces of knowledge Malthus lacked. One was the coming improvement in the technique and the growth of tolerance of birth control. The other was the pending improvement both in the means of increasing the fertility of land and in transporting food products from afar to dense populations, with means of preserving foods that in his own time were perishables. Long before statesmen and economists had finished squabbling as to the accuracy of the Malthus diagnosis and about its moral implications, and the lessons in practical statecraft which it inferred, the whole social complex had altered. Society had found, so to speak, a triple answer to the inevitability of the Malthusian cycle—accelerated long-distance transport, a technique of food preservation, and an aesthetically and socially tolerable means of birth restriction. Malthusian inevitability had been defeated by the can and the condom.

Malthus himself did not regard the cycle as a matter for despair, but rather as an incentive to activity. An increase in the population, after all, as Süssmilch had taught, was probably beneficial and necessary. The output of the nation would increase with the population. What the reverend gentleman thought must happen was that marriages would be postponed and that the number of children per marriage would decrease. Enterprising men of foresight and restraint would not create a situation wherein they would have to maintain four or five offspring when their means only allowed for the rearing of two. Foresight, prudence and virtuous abstinence would so adjust society that " all squalid poverty would be removed from society, or at least, be confined to a very few, who had fallen into misfortunes, against which no prudence or foresight could provide ". It was this faith in the individual citizen to which Malthus fixed his hopes. He disdained State action through emigration, industrial organization and regimentation. Unfortunately, however, the " ingenious teleology by which nature has made pleasant the process of reproducing the species " does not include at the climax of passion a prudent consideration whether the income of the potential parents can sustain another addition to the family. In an age when contraceptives were either unknown or decried as an offence against both morals and sexual aestheticism, the foresight and virtuous abstinence upon which Malthus relied failed to achieve the purpose for which he had designed them in his thought.

The doctrines of Malthus had two unlooked-for effects. They led Charles Darwin towards his doctrine of natural selection, which, perhaps more than any other factor, helped to change the whole outlook of organized society and to wrench apart the last links that bound the State (in practice) to the Church. They prevented John Stuart Mill from becoming a Socialist, for by his belief in the Malthusian doctrine of population Mill was prevented from advocating a thorough-going Governmental interference with wages.

It is obvious that to an industrialized nation, and particularly to a nation cooped within the boundaries of a set of small islands and dependent upon outside sources for its necessaries of food, the amount of population is the most vital of all questions. The history of civilization is the history of man's fight against the destroyers—battle, murder and premature death. Throughout the renaissance of science, which—for the moment—we can regard as stretching from the eighteenth century into our own time, man's effort to prolong the lives of men was not the least successful of his achievements.

The gradual attainment to a technique of public hygiene, the mastery of certain endemic and epidemic diseases, the abolition of recurring famines and the application of new forms of lethal weapons and of medical organization to warfare all helped to eliminate one of the checks upon population which Malthus had noted. (Modern weapons are less prone to deal wholesale death than those of an earlier generation. A clean-drilled bullet hole or a hit from a burst of shrapnel is a very minor matter compared with a hefty hacking from a two-handed sword or the impact of a trundling roundshot. The reduction of population by the world war of 1914 was preposterously small. Broken men were mended, and there was no devastation by plague.) The very science which preserved men from death stimulated the powers of production in mankind. Fewer and fewer men were needed to produce more and more sustenance as the nineteenth century wore on and the twentieth century began, but the State, still, like Mill, under the influence of Malthusianism, relied on the principle that had been deduced from a situation and a relationship of man to sustenance quite different from that which the machine age had created. There was no attempt to organize industry and migration, on the one hand, or to encourage a knowledge of some substitute for virtuous abstinence on the other. The private lives of citizens were their own affair; let them spawn at will and produce a menacing mass of potential labour welcomed for its effects on labour costs, even when those effects were thwarted by trade union organization and the conscience of the nation. Mr. Malthus had shown that there was a kind of natural check in these matters—and, in any event, there might be a world war at any moment, when a surplus population would be a very desirable asset. "Be ye fruitful and multiply" was still the economists' injunction, and when some crank ventured to suggest to the populace that small families could be arranged without any inhuman repression of the passions, a shocked State sent him to gaol.

So—despite anything that the thinkers might have urged or prophesied—the proletariat did not revolt, the population did not recede under the influence of shifting measures of subsistence, and labour fluidity was gradually lost. A new generation of economists was born, at Cambridge, which, apparently, conceived it its duty to begin and to end with a mastery of Marshall's new synthesis and remained a little in doubt whether, as the master taught, economics should be regarded as covering only those motives and desires of man which can be measured by money or whether, as he also taught, " even for the narrower uses of economic studies, it is important to know whether the desires which prevail are such as will help to build up a strong and righteous character ".

Organized Labour retained its pathetic faith in Parliament as a means of redressing all human ills, and the stock-jobbers and bankers continued to wax fat and powerful.

Chapter VIII

THE ILLUSION OF 1906

All historical divisions must be arbitrary. Having sketchily indicated a background whose perspective includes the Norman Manor in the far distance and the creation of such pleasaunces as Port Sunlight and Bournville in the foreground, I propose now to deal with the main purpose of this splenetic outburst and to discuss our present discontents. By " present " I mean those discontents which irk men and women of my own generation, many of which are inherited from the past, some of which have been newly caused within my own lifetime.

That such discontents may be properly displayed it becomes necessary to extend the word " present " from its narrower sense of the immediate now, and this I do, shamelessly, by taking a straight edge across the riband of social and political history at the year 1906, for the paradoxical reason that the great division occurs superficially at the year 1914. The justifications for the choice of the earlier year are many, and include these: to the generations now either in control or about to enter into control of the State—that is, the great body of men and women between thirty and fifty years of age—1906 is within continuous memory, and is notable for the " landslide election " which brought into power the Parliamentary majority of Liberals, under whose régime the great war was hatched. It is the year which opened the prologue of the new act in the national drama wherein the status of trade unions was to be changed, labour exchanges, old age pensions, insurance of the workers against ill-health and later against unemployment were to be instituted; the imposition and gathering of taxes was to be used as an instrument of social change; a nominal two-chamber form of government was to be made an actual single chamber form, with an attached debating society as a vestigial remembrance of the House of Peers; and wherein organized Labour was to control a separate Parliamentary party; wherein members of Parliament were to be paid from the tax-payers' money.

From the middle of the nineteenth century the House of Commons had tended to become more and more the representative body, in so far as its type of personnel was concerned, of the combined manufacturing and financial bodies. For a period the Conservative Party had—speaking very broadly indeed—been the party of the old land-owning interests. The Liberal Party had been the party of industrialists. A political question—Home Rule for Ireland—had effectually cut athwart the old distinctions. George Joachim Goschen when he became the Chancellor of the Exchequer in a Conservative Government was more than Liberal Unionist turning Tory in all but name. He was a portent. Goschen, who was in many respects the most remarkable public figure of his age, as a young man had produced a short classic on the theory of the Foreign Exchanges. He had been early made a Director of the Bank of England. He was of German descent, and his business life gave him an acute appreciation of the interlocking of the trade of nations. He was, in short, the descendant in type of Thomas Gresham. His deflection from the conglomeration of Whigs and Radicals symbolized a shifting of political allegiance far greater than that effected by the contemporary question of Irish independence, and it is highly significant that when the revival of the question of Protection in 1903 split the coalition party of Tories and

Unionists, the men of Goschen's type did not leave their new party to return to the old loyalty. They remained where they were, as dissentients.

What were loosely known as the propertied classes had been politically welded. That is not to say, of course, that the Liberal Party which came into power in 1906 was void of propertied interests. It had a very large share of such representative men as Harcourt the younger, the very personification of the Commoner-Aristocrat, Lord Elgin, Lord Aberdeen, Lord Ripon and Lord Fowler, in addition to representative industrialists like Sir William Lever, later to become Lord Leverhulme, and Mr. R. D. Holt, the shipowner. But the two political parties had fallen into new representative capacities. Liberalism stood for the new conception of a political party organized to further the ends of organized Labour. It included in its Cabinet a Minister who was definitely a Labour representative and who was included for that reason alone. Conservatism stood for the older tradition of a political party organized for purely political ends and observing as a principle the necessity within the community of social classes each depending upon the other for its existence and prosperity.

The Tory Party was, in a word, class-conscious ; the Liberal Party was class-antagonism-conscious. Contemporary Toryism honestly believed that to a normal mind the appeals of nationalistic patriotism, of the consolidation and extension of an Empire upon which the sun never set and where the bugles never ceased to blow, meant more than the appeals of a social or economic advantage over some other section of the community. If Britain waxed rich and remained great, all waxed rich and were great, and it was an unfortunate accident that a few thousand families who were patently neither rich nor great did not realize this. Liberalism appeared to be founded on the belief, inherited from Cobden, that if the workers were restless and discontented it was because the share-out of the nation's growing wealth was wrong, and could be adjusted by taxing the landlords. Trade must be free and industry unshackled, and the concentration upon landowners preserved this freedom, lowered industrial rents and permitted the disgruntled workers to see that Liberalism was their friend.

The new Labour Party, with fifty-one members, sat in the Commons less to forward a political philosophy and purpose of its own—" Socialism in our time " had not become a slogan—than to keep the Liberal Party in order.

But one purpose the Labour Party had. They were there to obtain a quick redress of an old grievance. In 1900 the principal railway companies had announced that following bad dividends they intended to raise the rates for goods traffic, including coal, and that the various directorates had come to an agreement in the matter. There was immediate public indignation at this frank disclosure of monopolistic powers, not untainted in their use by monopolistic arrogance. In the full tide of this indignation there was a strike of railway workers on the Taff Vale railway, a line much concerned with the carriage of coal for the navy. For once in a way, the owners had little public sympathy. An arbitrary raising of freight rates followed by a strike looked suspiciously as if the monopoly had another fault common in monopolies—bad management. The men had struck partly in anger with working conditions and partly over the case of a dismissed signalman, and with the folly of impatient men had weakened their own position by leaving work before the agreed notices had expired. The strike lasted ten days, and was settled on terms not unsatisfactory to the men. But the directors, having settled the strike, proceeded against the union for damages for unlawful picketing.

Mr. Justice Farwell found in their favour, believing that the law had never intended to set up bodies of men capable of holding property and acting as agents and yet not responsible in damages. The Court of Appeal reversed this judgement, but the House of Lords upheld it.

The workers realized that their trade union funds were at the mercy of legal actions agains the unions, just as if unions were not a specially sacrosanct creation, different in kind from all other organized bodies! It looked very much as if trade unions were to be stultified if they could be sued in damages for tortious acts perpetrated by their members, since picketing and peaceful persuasion were held to be tortious acts.

The new Government introduced, and eventually passed, a Trades Disputes Act, which laid down that " an action against a trade union, whether of workmen or masters, or against any members or officials thereof on behalf of themselves and all other members of the trade union in respect of any tortious act alleged to have been committed by or on behalf of the trade union shall not be entertained by any court ".

This looked surprisingly like victory for organized Labour and its policy of turning to Parliament as an instrument for making the world safe for a particular section of democracy. It had the immediate effect, however, of causing other sections of democracy to lose trust in that instrument. The trade unions had been put above the law. There might be one law for both rich and poor, but it was obvious that when torts were concerned there was one law for organized labour and another for organized non-labour. Why? Because the solid voting power of the unions in the constituencies and the fifty-one votes in the Division lobby of the Commons had intimidated the Liberal Party into an action which was morally unjustified. That—however exaggerated or unjustified—

was the conviction which swept those members of the petty bourgeoisie and the other classes who were not themselves trade unionists. In 1908 there was yet another Parliamentary triumph for the unions, which increased this conviction.

The same society as before, the Amalgamated Society of Railway Servants, was again the spearhead of attack. In 1908 a Mr. Osborne, a branch secretary of the A.S.R.S., sued the society to have it declared that one of its current rules which provided, *inter alia,* for Parliamentary Representation and the enforced levy of contributions from him and other members of the society towards the payment of salaries or maintenance allowances to members of Parliament pledged to observe and fulfil the conditions imposed by the Labour Party, was *ultra vires* and void.

In the first court the case went against Osborne, but the Court of Appeal reversed the judgement, and the House of Lords upheld that reversal.

The Labour Party in the House of Commons was thus threatened with the disappearance of the funds which kept it alive. The direct result of the judgement was the introduction of payment of members. If trade unionists as such refused to pay for their delegates in the Commons, then the populace at large must pay for them. The populace, not unnaturally, lost still more of its diminishing faith in Parliament, where the fear of *bloc* votes could so easily achieve so patent an injustice.

For a time the Labour Party had to honour the Osborne judgement, but only for a time. In 1913 it was able, through a Liberal Government still more dependent upon the Labour vote in the House, to reach a compromise in the Trade Unions Act of that year, whereby a political fund was permitted to unions from which those who objected could " contract out ".

The background politics of the Labour leaders was Socialism. The early enforcement of a political levy on members meant that Tory working men, of whom there were many, bred in the sentimental Disraelian tradition and emotionally fond of Church and State and the decorative aspects of aristocracy, and working men who happened to believe in private as opposed to State ownership, were compelled to pay money to support their political opponents in politics. The new Act of 1913 was not really of much practical help. It threw the onus of contracting out on the individual member, who might be either an indifferentist or a person easily intimidated by the opinion of those about him. After the general strike of 1926 yet another change was made. The political fund was allowed to remain, but the onus was for the member to " contract in ". Here, again, there was a wider difference in theory than in practice. Intimidation does not always mean the bludgeon and the knuckleduster, and it needs very often as much moral courage to refrain from contracting in as to exert the individuality needed for contracting out.

It may, indeed, be roughly, but truly, said that the whole decade before the war of 1914 was marked by a sudden extension of bureaucracy into the lives of private citizens. Where the State did not, on the plea of protective organization, intervene between the wage-earner and his modes of spending his pay, the trade union official or the employers' thrift departments did: very often, all three were concerned with the business of spending the workers' wages for them.

With this development of tyrannical paternalism in the State, the trade union and the employers' organizations there went, *pari passu*, a movement in industry which made for paternalism in other aspects of life. Popular literature, from the cheap periodicals written, in

Salisbury's phrase, by office boys for office boys, to cheap reprints of the classics, was produced at a cheapness not possible before the reign of the mass-producing machinery of the late nineteenth century, and not profitable to produce before the popular education introduced in the 'seventies had had time to create a large mob of semi-literate readers. The cinematograph passed through a short infancy into a lusty adolescence. These two channels poured into the receptive minds of the masses standardized thought, against which there contended a second strain of thought represented by the cheap pamphlets of the Fabian Society, the Rationalist Press Association and other bodies, and the novels and plays of Wells and Shaw, which found their publics because of their tremendous saleability. It was not the business of the commercial entrepreneurs who published popular literature to act as cultural censors, and one publishing house quite frequently produced mental pabulum which was compounded of the tradition and thought of the eighteen-sixties from the same machines which printed its antithesis in the form of a novel compounded of skilful propaganda for the spirit of discontent.

Unfortunately, the rebel literature, of which H. G. Wells's mid-period work is the type, was not directionally clear. Its major tendency was towards a reorganization of Society into a form where economic and social progress would be planned and administered by a *Samurai* of the State, but its minor tendency was towards a revolt from control. To a clear thinker it was obvious that young adolescent women who were heroines for rebelling against the convention of the old home and parental control would not be equally applauded for rebelling against the convention of the new Government Department and the bureaucratic control that would take the place of the natural parent. The charge against contemporary society was twofold, that it tied men and women to impossible duties and that it did not demand from men and women duties enough. It preached a new sexual freedom, but envisaged the day when society would be guided by a race of ascetics, voluntary renunciants of sex.

Both the literature of revolt and the political teaching of organized Labour were concerned, in effect, with the substitution of one discipline for another discipline. They were not concerned with the people's readiness either to change disciplinarians at a word of command or to develop life towards, rather than away from, increasing regimentation.

In an equal muddle was the contemporary trend of education. Generations of hard propaganda had by the early years of the present century inculcated into the mind of the majority the desirability of extending educational facilities not only in the sense of educating more and more citizens in the rudiments of culture but also in the sense of making available to as many as possible the benefits of higher education. New universities were chartered and established in the great industrial cities, but the incentives which took scholars there were very different from the incentives which had immemorially taken scholars to the older foundations. And—there was no collegiate life, or, to be strictly accurate, there was merely a grotesque parody of collegiate life through Students' Unions.

The hope of the pioneers of the new university movement, men like Haldane of Cloan, Walter Raleigh, Professor Macay and their like, was for a new race of enlightened workers. The hope of most of those who took advantage of the new universities was for a better job on the strength of some " degree " attained after lectures by hard cramming in the back parlour of the familiar bourgeois home. (In writing this sentence I intend no sneer and imply no judgement. I record merely what experience and research lead me to believe to be the facts of the matter.) There was no clear policy as between general cultural education and extended vocational education. In a very little time the modern universities had so organized themselves that men were walking an amazed earth as Doctors of Philosophy whose doctorate had been attained by a thesis for a degree in engineering or even in tanning or brewing. A man who had barely heard of Lotze might be a doctor of philosophy because he had caught the examiners on the hop.

The inevitable result of this rush for degrees was as Gilbert had insisted in an allied phase of life. When everyone was somebody nobody was anybody. M.Sc.'s were legion, and B.Sc.'s were three a penny. But before this result was reached, before anxious industrialists who had supported the new educational movement were driven to make work for the superfluous analytical chemists which the university of their area turned out through an examination mill, the fetish of advanced education had seized upon the superstitious reverence of the whole working-class movement. The able or lucky boy who advanced from an elementary school through some form of secondary establishment to a university and there met with a fair measure of academic success was hardly likely to take home his newly-found qualities and contentedly return to the trades of his forebears or his school contemporaries. The psychological urge in him was to find an opening in those professions and callings—schoolmastering or political agitation, journalism or commerce—where the ostensible marks of the educated product—the white collar and the black coat—need not be discarded.

The generality of the new type of " varsity man "—as they loved to call themselves—was not held by the old, almost unformulated ideal of the full man, the cultured scholar, but by a new ambitiousness to attain to an educational qualification as an open sesame to material and social advancement. The student " went in for " a particular subject and pursued it with an ardour directed to the ordeal of the examination-room rather than to the spending of a full life.

The same blight affected such movements as Adult Education and Workers' Education. Earnest tutors, both voluntary and fee-paid, laboured to inculcate economics and civics in potential trade union officials, Parliamentary candidates and agitators. Few indeed were the students who conceived their classes to be aids to a materially purposeless culture. Education had become a word of power, a shibboleth, by which doors could be opened without further effort.

The word of power proved increasingly impotent as more and more acquired its mastery ; the shibboleth failed ; the open sesame was of little avail if the opened door was jammed by a jostling mob of competing applicants for entrance.

Trade unionism seemed either to be placing trade unionists above the law or plunging them and their industries into strikes and stoppages, or mulcting trade unionists of their hard-earned cash to support ambitionists of their own class in the glamorous and comfortable circumstances of officialdom or Parliamentarism. Both the unions and the State seemed to be growing more and more dictatorial about the conduct of life as each year passed, and what the union did not order, some Government department did. Popular education extended beyond elementary tuition was proving incapable of the material benefits which it had seemed in prospect of offering. Toryism, the symbol of privilege, had been routed, and a conglomeration of anti-Tories, optimistically called the Liberal Party, had taken power, but the striking contrasts between rich and poor remained, and the occupants of the Treasury Bench were suspiciously like the gentlemen who had been evicted therefrom. There was the familiar complement of prosperous lawyers, commoner-aristocrats, wealthy industrialists with banking connections, and the usual sprinkling of amateur philosophers whose function, as the subaltern said of cavalry, was probably to give tone to what otherwise might have been a mere vulgar brawl. The Liberal ranks themselves contained in the Member for South Salford a notable satirist, Mr. Belloc, whose own estimate of the significance of 1906 was displayed in the familiar epigram :

> The accursed power which stands on Privilege
> (And goes with Women, and Champagne, and Bridge)
> Broke—and Democracy resumed her reign :
> (Which goes with Bridge, and Women, and Champagne.)

Against this background of disillusionment the younger generation was moving in an economic world of growing profusion. Lower costing, due to a variety of causes, and the discovery of substitute commodities, together tended to hasten the disappearance of the old class-distinctions in garb, amusements and—what was very important—idiom. Leisure was greater. As early as 1892 a Tory Government, already under the influence of that master-manufacturer, Joseph Chamberlain, had passed a Shop Hours Act which forbade the employment of young persons under eighteen years of age for more than seventy-four hours a week, including meal times, and by 1912 the Shops Act and the Employment and Closing Order Act were on the Statute Book. The forty-eight-hour week was a reality.

More leisure inevitably meant a change in the incidence of organized amusement in family and general social life.

Gladiatorial sport, the infant cinematographic industry, and spasmodic crazes like roller skating and " sixpenny hops ", became the normal essentials of young lives while they were still the abnormal extravagance of older lives. The monetary rewards of those who catered for the leisure of the masses—popular Scots comedians, film stars, the writers of " thrillers ", sporting celebrities, and their like—not only increased sensationally, but were regarded as a matter of public interest, the public being induced to revere its entertainers as much for their capacity to earn great sums as for their capacity to entertain.

A great Minister of State was convincing the nation that " the day of the cottage-bred man has dawned " ; drolls from the coal pits of Lancashire and Scotland were demonstrating that the ability to sing a comic song or perform a clog dance, or even to carry a twisted walking stick, was valued by the community at a far higher rate than the ability to dig coal, and certain strenuous livers were demonstrating that, by a judicious admixture of organizing ability and a knowledge of the technique of advertising, from soap or chemicals or cough cures or pills, the wealth of the Indies could be mined in townships like Widnes, Bolton or Leeds. The eighteen-nineties had taught that sudden wealth and power was possible to any playboy with sufficient rustic cunning to " best " gold-diggers of their claims or to corner diamonds in order to regulate supply.[1] The early nineteen hundreds taught that sudden wealth and power was possible to any pioneer who could effectually corner—in a very loose way—a domestic necessary, not by achieving control of all available supplies, necessarily, but by achieving some measure of agreement with his competitors as to spheres of sales and price regulations.

[1] *Cf.* Barnato's remark, " Rhodes must have been a genius, for he bested *me* ! "

These visible demonstrations of the arbitrariness of society in rewarding effort had, as usual, two effects upon the observing minds. With certain temperaments the reaction was, "It shall go hard if I do not better his example." With other temperaments the reaction was a mood of hot and bitter resentment at what seemed an economic system capable of creating, or at least not preventing, such illogical injustices. While one type bent its effort and will to snatching what prizes were possible in the merry game of "every man for himself and the devils of penury and frustration take the hindermost", another type bent its will and its effort to the task of limiting that game by new rules which would make the pace of the slowest the arbiter of advance. The consequence was a divided community between those who honestly felt that the race should be to the swift and the battle to the strong and those who felt that in the race and scramble for material rewards natural handicaps should be adjusted in order that none might fare better than his neighbour. Both schools of thought found their economic justifiers, and both found their emotional fuglemen.

It almost seemed in 1910 as if, under the stimulus of one of the most typical of individualists, Mr. Lloyd George, this division might lead to a clash of civil war, on the assumption—wholly fallacious—that a temperamental differentiation which ran through all sections of society was really a political question of "Peers or People?" As one might expect in Britain, the individualist was the spokesman of the anti-individualists.

The means by which the House of Lords became the symbol of oppression in two bitter electoral battles, and the means by which a growing generation was hopelessly confused as to the real significance of that body, were almost accidental. In 1894 Sir William Harcourt as Chancellor of the Exchequer was anxious to provide means of expansion for his Army and Navy estimates without making further additions to the income-tax. He lighted upon a device known as the death duties, whereby estates passing on death to new possessors yielded a certain sum to the State. To him and his contemporaries both income tax and death duties were fiscal expedients to fill the coffers of the State; to Mr. Lloyd George, the self-boasted cottage-bred man, they offered excellent means of re-adjusting social wealth between the various classes of society.

A wide-ranging programme of social reform, including such benefits as old age pensions and insurance against ill-health, demanded finance, and ostensibly there was no departure from precedent in raising that finance by the placing of new imposts upon the individually wealthy. To middle-aged Ministers under the influence of the standard economists of the later nineteenth century the symbol of wealth was still ownership of land. In Mr. Lloyd George's mind this belief was explicable. He had been bred in an area of Wales where the landlord was the local tyrant, and had built his early practice as an attorney chiefly by the skill and vigour he displayed in thwarting the will of that tyrant. Certain great noblemen were still the owners of vast estates which, by the discovery of minerals or by the growth of townships, had enormously increased in value. The Cecils and the Stanleys owned large tracts of Lancashire, the Duke of Northumberland owned wide mineral areas in the North-East, the Duke of Westminster was ground landlord of many rich sites in London. The Duchy of Cornwall and the Duchy of Lancaster were royal possessions yielding great incomes, each with its secretariat, and one actually having a Minister in the Cabinet.

An attempt to tax land in a new fashion caused the Lords as a Parliamentary Chamber to oppose the innovation. It was enough. The representative Chamber of noblemen who owned land was opposing the representative Chamber of cottage-bred men who did not own land, and on that plea the people was asked to consent to a change in the constitution, virtually making the Upper House legislatively impotent. By the erratic operation of the electoral system the appeal to the people resulted in sufficient power being given to the Liberal Government of the day to enable it to truncate the power of the Peers and set, as it were, the seal of democratic approval upon the technique of adjusting social class inequalities by the operation of Budget taxation.

Almost unobserved, a complete change in the functions of the House of Commons was thus completed. The representatives from the shires and the boroughs had in the far past gone to Westminster to decide to what extent they would tax themselves in response to the demands or requests of the king. By the immediate pre-war years the representatives of the various constituencies were sitting at Westminster no longer conscious that their function was to tax themselves, but believing that it was to tax somebody else. They were encouraged to feel that in them resided the honourable tradition of Robin Hood—they were to take from the rich and give to the poor, only the poor were not to be asked what form the gift should take.

Considerations of economic balance were little regarded, and weighed lightly against considerations of social impatience or resentment. A land-owning citizen or a citizen whose function in society included the control of enterprises employing large bodies of men and women was confronted by a situation in which the State was demanding more and more of his surplus wealth. Men who had gathered aggregations of wealth under an age-old stimulus, that of desiring to hand on to surviving dependents the fruits of labour or ingenuity, found that the imposts of the Exchequer no longer permitted the old gratification. The sense of continuity in possession was weakened where it was not destroyed. In its major aspects society was still economically based on the assumption that men were inspired to effort and industry by the hope of reward, and were moved to assume and fulfil certain duties by a combination of filial piety and paternal pride. In its minor aspects society was being changed on the assumption that the acquirement or retention of great personal wealth was worthy of reprobation. Those who inherited or acquired great wealth were subject to the especial attention of the tax-gatherers, and in being so subject were deprived of the old, inculcated sense of duty towards those by whose aids the possessions had been gathered. The incentive was no longer towards justifying stewardship by conduct. It was towards evading imposts that were felt to be prejudiced and irrational. If the State was determined to assume a paternal responsibility towards the community, the local patriarch was obviously relieved of his ancient duties. If the State was determined to screw out of wealth possessors as much as possible, the wealth possessors in this game of pull devil, pull baker, must obviously screw more wealth from the community, either by limiting expenditure or by extorting more from employed wealth creators. In a word, the change in fiscal policy which was apparent in 1909 was the end of *noblesse oblige* among the wealthy.

From the viewpoint of a cottage-bred man it might matter little, if at all, that additions to his nominal wages came to him not from the squire but from some local bureau. From the viewpoint of society at large the difference was vital. From the viewpoint of the Exchequer it might matter little that increasing taxation and death duties ejected one family from possession in favour of another—a great estate by a series of deaths within a short span of years might be rendered unsupportable by its original owners—but to the localities affected the difference was great. The old Hall, or the Manor, occupied by someone having long ties of inherited remembrances with the community about it, was a different factor in local life from the same dwelling occupied by some rich sugar refiner or some wealthy financier.

Whereas the late nineteenth century had still preserved an England which subdued the functional to the human relationships, the trend from 1906 onwards was towards an England wherein the functional relationship was dominant. To phrase it simply, just as in industry " the Old Guv'nor "—often called Owd Bob or by some familiar nickname—had become " the head office ", so in rural and communal life " the old squire " had become " the Londoner at the Grange ", and both had become fit objects for specially heavy taxation to finance social services directed from Whitehall in place of local humanities directed within the neighbourhood. Just as in industry, so in daily life, the State had fully and enthusiastically embarked upon a policy of incessant interference, but had evolved no fitting technique. It blundered in by trial and error, often as in the case of doctors under the State insurance scheme, having to use the tax-payers' money to bribe protestants against its policy into quiescence. It was working, in short, neither to a defined economic plan to which all social conveniences must be sacrificed (as in Russia at this day) nor to a defined social plan to which certain economic benefits must be sacrificed.

By 1914 society was in a mid-stage of transition, but a transition neither designed nor fully realized. Portents were very largely mistaken for accidents. The revolt of a large body of women against economic subservience was expressed as a political demand for a vote, just as the revolt of the organized workers had been so expressed, but the significance of that revolt was not really to be found in the speeches of feminist leaders like Mrs. Pankhurst; it was to be found in a representative work of the period, *Marriage as a Trade*, in which Cicely Hamilton expressed clearly what was really working in the new generation of educated working women.

There was no apparent attempt by the leaders of contemporary political parties to analyse and direct the economic-cum-psychological forces behind the suffrage movement. It was treated almost entirely as a political agitation which was a political nuisance. It was, in reality, the outward sign of a profound change in the national temper leading to a fundamental change in national economic organization. It meant that at the very phase of the national history when mechanical labour-saving devices were depriving both industry and domesticity of the need for hand-power, industry was being assaulted by a large new body of potential workers, many of whom were in temperamental revolt against the domestic life which was learning to dispense with them.

Hardy's ironic spirit must have seen something skilfully designed in the apparent accident that a world war was staged at this time, a war which drew masses of male labour from industry and opened the doors to more than equivalent masses of women. There are so many aspects to the question of how the World War affected the relationships of society that it is hard to say which of them transcends in importance all the others. Many of these aspects are highly technical in so far as they turn on economic and monetary changes and mismanagement. But there is one broad aspect to the question the importance of which is positively obtrusive however technically ignorant of economics the observer may be. The war caused the greatest change in history in the relations between labour in the mass and its employers and between individual workers as industrial and social units, but with the coming of peace the pre-war method of conducting industry was resumed and adjustments were not made to meet the changed relationships. The result has been that those who returned from war service to industry and the successive post-war generations entering working life have failed to find the few things necessary to human satisfaction and happiness.

The war, one may state flatly and dogmatically, was grossly mismanaged, both *qua* war and *qua* a violent transitional stage of national development. Before the causes and effects of that mismanagement are examined it may be useful to indulge in a digression in order that what in the writer's mind *are* those few things necessary to human happiness may be discussed and identified.

Chapter IX

THE HUMAN NEEDS

The test of good government is the contentment of the people. The contentment of the people does not imply a sottish acquiescence in a given standard of life or a given system of castes; it implies a confidence, probably unformulated and unenunciated, that the system of government and its administrators permit the society governed to advance in its standard of civilization as means allow, with neither injustice nor oppression employed as the means of advancement.

Liberty, equality and fraternity are by no means essential to contentment. Many citizens, many communities, temperamentally prefer discipline to liberty, the excitement of ambition to equality, and formal relationships in certain departments of life to fraternity. Even that mind, however, which shrinks from the responsibilities of liberty, in the broadest sense of the word, desires liberty to choose or reject the discipline under which it must live. Even that mind which prefers a graduated society through the grades of which the ambitious careerist may pass desires equality to be recognized in certain aspects of life—equality, for example, before the law. Even that mind which shrinks from the conception of fraternity in daily intercourse desires occasional expressions of fraternity in exceptional intercourse, as in moments of peril and crisis or great rejoicing.

Between the most cultivated and the least cultivated member of any community there is no difference in actual appetites. The differences lie in the manner of fulfilment of those appetites and the amount of restraint which is exercised in pursuing or enjoying their fulfilment. In the field of morbid psychology perversions are common to all grades of men and women, as are the normal appetites in the field of normal psychology. The elementary task of the statesman is to ensure that the necessary appetites are satisfied without the necessity for individual clashes of will and without the display of associated emotions which when unrestrained menace civilized communities with barbarism.

Self-preservation, say the copy books, is the first law of life. It is the primary duty of the leaders and organizers of the tribe to see that the fulfilment of that law is easy without recourse to murder and theft. The propagation of the species is the most powerful urge—however disguised. It is the primary duty of the leaders and organizers of the tribe to ensure that that urge may be satisfied without recourse to rape and riotous promiscuity, which might so disorganize the communal peace that collective survival would be threatened.

Food, shelter, covering, warmth, and the satisfaction of the sexual impulse are the common needs of all men and women, save those who are psychologically malformed. (In this regard—that is, from the viewpoint of the statesman—those abnormal persons who from some religious exercise or mystic discipline have achieved the sublimation of any or all of their appetites and become saints are to be called psychologically malformed, even though the malformation may seem admirable.) If any section of society finds it difficult to satisfy these needs while other sections find no such difficulty, if any section is compelled to satisfy such needs by efforts or in circumstances which contrast notably with the efforts and circumstances demanded from other sections, human happiness is thwarted and communal stability threatened, and this will be so whether the contrast is created by a flaw in the social organization or by the incidence of some taboo which falls unevenly. (It may be remarked in passing that such a contrast is presented forcibly to the minds of any modern proletariat by the common circumstance that the indulgence of the mildest latitude of conduct will bring down the censure and punishment of the law upon a pair of adolescents who may be stimulated to that latitude by watching upon a cinema screen the wildest latitude of conduct in adolescents held up to them as enviable specimens of society at its most spacious and gracious.) It is not enough that the State should prevent the economic organization of the community from endowing some with what it denies to others; the State must also ensure that taboos and rituals inherited from one phase of the communal development do not survive into another phase where their meaning has perished but their observance is still insisted upon. For example, there was a stage in society when, as Professor Frazer and others assure us, the exercise of the *droit de seigneur* was regarded as a boon by those whose brides and daughters were thus deflowered. Defloration was dangerous to any but a specially sanctified man, for it released evil spirits. But the exercise of that right long after the original superstition was forgotten helped to cause the French Revolution. In our own time the payment of tithes and the rendering of jury service have reached a stage wherein a privilege has in many minds come to be regarded as an imposition.

It should be admitted freely, of course, that if a man or woman be given the basic essentials for happiness, happiness may still elude their possessor. But happiness is not possible without those basic essentials. The normal citizen needs some certitude that food, clothing, shelter and warmth will not fail him, and that he will be enabled to mate with security. He does not ask this certitude as a gift, but as a return for his personal labours. If he finds himself in a society where, by ill-organized industries, he is prohibited from finding an outlet for his capacity to labour, he may then demand such certitude as what he considers a justified blackmail—as the price of his abstention from force in wresting his needs from the rest of the community. The final sanction of all government is force. As Trotsky has frankly implied in his *History of Russia*, the arbiter of success in revolt is not a quarrel just, but command of the machine guns. That State which must use or unduly display force confesses itself unsuccessful in organizing its wealth for the contentment of its components. Equally, that State which creates new discontents in some sections to allay the older discontents of other sections is confessedly unsuccessful in its task of organizing the whole community for common happiness.

The assurance to the normal citizen that the prime needs of mankind and womankind shall not go unsatisfied is not enough. As the mastery of man over nature increases, new wants are stimulated. It is not possible to confine the consciousness of those wants to selected sections of society. True, a coster girl in the East-End of London may not desire to have her face lifted merely because beauty specialists have discovered the technique of that operation, but if a certain cult of facial beauty is inculcated by the screen and the popular press she will feel the need for cheap cosmetics. A Lancashire pitman may not feel any burning desire for caviare as that commodity becomes more accessible, but if he is prompted by the hoardings and the newsprints he will feel a little aggrieved if his economic limitations prohibit Skipper Sardines for tea. A Yorkshire woollen operative will not fret for the joys of an ocean cruise to Tangier, but if he is induced by skilful advertisement to lust after travel, he will feel affronted if he is unable to participate in a cheap " chara " trip to Glorious Devon instead of taking his once satisfying vacation at Filey.

The State must, therefore, make itself responsible for an even spread of the satisfactions of those secondary needs which are created by the actions of its acquisitive traders if it acknowledges the soundness of acquisitiveness as a basis for society. It is, that is to say, not enough that when beach pyjamas become the rage in the wealthier section of society, they should quickly become procurable from Woolworth and from Marks and Spencer. Their procurability there will be but an added stimulus to discontent unless the economic organization enables those to whom they are offered to buy them without some corresponding deprivation. The State which permits the creation of artificial needs must, if it is to survive, contrive means for their satisfaction.

It is frequently held against the modern workers that in their cycles of prosperity they display the most amazing thriftlessness and expend in temporary satisfactions money which might well be garnered against what is tediously called " a rainy day ". If the charge is true—and it is true—the fault is not with the workers. It is not, perhaps, a fault at all.

When the whole of society conspires to raise the standards of taste in all its members, and to raise those standards in both senses, that of quantity and that of quality, it cannot condemn those sections which take the first opportunity of buying pianos or gramophones or wireless sets. When the whole of society conspires to applaud the sporting spirit and adulates those wealthy men who can afford to keep large racing stables, it cannot with any logic condemn the collier who takes the first opportunity to improve his whippets whether by providing them with better food or better treatment or a better strain.

If Lord Nob becomes a hero by the simple process of bankrupting himself with slow horses and fast women, plain Hob cannot be a moral criminal if he spends the rent money on the dogs. If a vast community of commercial entrepreneurs is encouraged to devote its enterprise to making and marketing new forms of commodities or new services for the enjoyment of its fellow men, those fellow men cannot be blamed for desiring to enjoy the new satisfactions to which they are attracted. They can hardly be blamed when they resent a system, or lack of system, which encourages the creation of those enjoyments and creates the temptation to their use only to thwart the tempted. A Tantalus justly condemned is an object of pity. A myriad tantalized men unjustly subject to his punishment should surely be the objects of understanding, if not of active sympathy. What appears to the statistician as an illuminating table illustrating supply and demand in a commodity appears to the impoverished citizen as an exasperating injunction to eat more fruit coupled with an inability to procure that fruit or a general condemnation for wasting on a banana fritter the pence that should have gone into the baby's money-box or a national savings card. It is necessary to human happiness that such a circumstance should not be condoned.

The first certitude that the natural appetites shall not be baulked must be followed by the second assurance that artificial appetites shall equally not be baulked if their creation has been the wilful work of society at large. The third need, as it seems to me, is that there should be some assurance, tacit, of course, and not necessarily expressed, that the conduct of life shall not be subject to arbitrary changes of whim in powerful persons or bodies of persons. If a worker is bred and educated to believe that his duty to his neighbour is to love her as himself, to join with her in the bonds of holy matrimony and therein to be fruitful and multiply, he must not be told in middle life, either flatly by some magistrate or County Court judge or obliquely by the community, that he and his mate are a pair of thriftless, feckless animals. He must certainly not be so told if he has been taught that any interference with the natural sequence of coition and conception is a spiritual and social sin, or if he has never been made aware that such interference is possible or even desirable. Similarly, a man and woman bred and trained to believe that their duty to their children is to provide them with " a better start than their parents had " must not—if they are to remain contented citizens—be encouraged to skimp their own lives of normal satisfactions for the sake of the children's careers only to be told, however inferentially, that they have made the fatal mistake of bringing up those children above their station with the result that, spoilt for labour such as their father and mother have known, they cannot be absorbed into circles for which their new standard of schooling has prepared them. If life is to be conducted on the assumption that in some mystic way a black-coated worker is a better and happier being than a worker in dungarees or shirt-sleeves, we must not be subjected to the shock of learning suddenly that the trainee for black-coated occupations is either a traitor to his or her class or an unwanted recruit to a section of society already too full.

(It must be emphasized that we are not at this moment discussing whether it is the duty of the organized State to prevent these things happening, or whether any form of government known to man could, if it would, prevent them. We are discussing, merely, what are the basic essentials for communal happiness, on the implied assumption that the nearer any form of Government comes to their provision the better form it will be.)

To the normal citizen bred in the traditions of the English race not only is it necessary to happiness that there should be some tacit assurance that the conduct of life shall not arbitrarily be changed at the whim of powerful persons, but it is necessary that the familiar unit of the family shall be as autonomous as is socially possible. The desire of the adolescent girl for " a home of her own " is no sentimentality ; it is a deeply ingrained biological sentiment. The sense of " cave-right " in the husband of a wife either with children or potentially the mother of children is strong because heredity implants and general environment nurtures it.

In theory every maker of a home devotes his labour to supporting that home, and every distraction of wage by the State or by an official body, such as a trade union, is felt either by wife or husband or by both as a weakening of the defences, so to speak, of the little family league which has been formed *contra mundum.* Communal efforts to take from the hands of the parents the direction of the children may be regarded by a bureaucracy as altruistic, but by the parents they are instinctively regarded as merely " interfering ". The attempt to subjugate the family unit to the communal unit arouses antagonisms which, however irrational they may seem, are profound.

The very approach to the sympathetic review of the problem of how a child is to be trained reveals a divergence of emotion which is pregnant with such antagonisms. The bureaucratic educator, for example, is dealing with a potential citizen whose culture must be shaped to an arbitrary mould ; the parent is dealing with " our Ethel " or " our Jim " whose immediate and future welfare is bound up with that of the family. This divergence is casually, but strikingly, exemplified in common idiom, where the phrase " putting ideas into the child's head " is not used as a tribute of praise but as an expression of disgust or alarm. It signifies a jealousy of the family autonomy even in " mind-shaping " which conflicts with all policies of communal, that is State, education.

It is quite obvious that with the development of complex communities the autonomy of the home must suffer. The need, as it was expressed above, is not to preserve intact that primitive autonomy which is the desire of the savage, but to preserve as much of it as may be possible. Where intrusions are necessary they should be demonstrably necessary. Where sweeping inroads upon that autonomy are to be made, they should be tactfully made. The interference of the State in private lives should, equally with the interference of the State in economic organization, be achieved by a reasoned technique, and not wilfully, fitfully, or as the result of some extrinsic expediency. It is conceivable, for example, that the State should assume and exercise the right to enter a private residence at all hours or any chosen hour, but for the State to assume and exercise that right merely because some monopoly service was suspicious that its facilities were being used without licence would be to invite resentment, and possibly revolt. (The modern State is quite capable of such action on such trumpery justification, as we have seen in the attitude of the authorities towards wireless sets.)

The conduct of the life of the citizen must not be arbitrarily changed and must not be subject to arbitrary interference, for so long as the citizen is trained to believe that he has a social and economic responsibility for the support and supervision of his family unit, if the community is to be preserved from emotions destructive of individual happiness. This is to say no more than that to each man and woman the " full life " cannot be designed and imposed upon the mind by some outside arbiter of conduct until and unless the inbred instincts of many generations and the open teachings of a generation yet alive are overthrown by a new teaching which can transform those instincts.

And any attempt to achieve that transformation and propagate such teaching must defeat its own object if it is so abruptly or peremptorily made as to arouse a " resistance complex " in the minds of the taught. The social temper of the Englishman has been embodied in a folk saying which, like all such, is a truism—" he will be led, but he won't be druv". The State which attempts to drive, actually invites a resistance which psychologically has nothing whatever to do with the virtues of the direction which is selected. That resistance may be passive, it may take time to show itself in any other form than that of a dumb resentment—it may remain, that is to say, a mental rather than a physical resistance—but it is a real thing, and a factor in the eventual arraignment by the protestants against the system of government or social organization which creates it.

The primal justification for toil is self-preservation ; the secondary justification is self-fulfilment. If neither incentive is present some artificial compulsion must be exercised. In a community where the life of the individual worker and those of his dependents are preserved, no matter what may be his circumstances in relation to the exercise of labour, the primary justification is weakened and possibly destroyed. If from men so circumstanced toil is to be extracted without the use of communal compulsion in some primitive and brutal form, the secondary justification, that of self-fulfilment, must be emphasized. A man who is drawing a subvention from his fellows of, say, 25s. a week, will probably refuse a job of unpleasant work at 30s. a week, not because he is a moral scoundrel, but because the margin does not represent to him a sufficiently tempting addition to his means of making life better worth living. If he were offered 60s. a week with the knowledge that such a scale brought him under some range of national or local imposts which would reduce the real value of that reward by half, he would not be deceived. He would in all probability remain content with his idleness and his subvention. Similarly a man engaged upon some business or occupation not in itself attractive to him, but necessary as his means of livelihood, might well, with an easy conscience, restrain his efforts at a given point because his earnings after that point would be so reduced by the tax-gatherer that the net extra reward was unattractive.

The avocations which are more desirable than leisure are few, and to those engaged in them extra effort must be weighed in the mind as the assessment of the means of making leisure more pleasant against a diminution of the leisure which can be so improved. A man working a five-day week at a pound a day would, in refusing to work a five-and-a-half day week, be merely purchasing a half-day's leisure for 10s., which might seem to him a cheap purchase. A worker having done a seven-hour night shift might consider that the eighth hour at time-and-a-half was not preferable to that eighth hour taken at his ease. In so deciding, neither would be guilty of any moral obliquity, nor would either show himself as anything but a sound thinker on the lines laid down by generations of " business men ". The mental justification of the choice would be the old adage that money can be bought too dear.

The type of communal organization which breeds discontent is that in which certain classes of the community have to work too obviously harder for their self-preservation than do their fellows ; where the secondary justification of self-fulfilment is ill-adjusted, so that the worker is not tempted to the extra effort because the reward is less valuable than the satisfactions of leisure ; and where rewards are either so illogically or so unevenly apportioned that large masses of workers cannot by putting forth their maximum effort and sacrificing the maximum amount of leisure attain to even a bare parody of the self-fulfilments enjoyed and obtruded in enjoyment by some smaller sections of society. When into such a mal-organization is intruded, from whatever desperate need, an assurance by the community that the prime need to labour for self-preservation has been removed, the complications multiply. The psychological effect is not gratitude for subsistence without labour, it is resentment that society should consider bare subsistence enough for some while permitting others to enjoy adornments and fulfilments which all have been trained to desire. To strain an analogy, it may be said that the beggar at the gates of Dives is less resentful of the circumstances in which he finds himself than is some idle scullion sitting at the feast below the salt and forbidden to taste the dishes which he sees and savours as they pass from hand to hand.

Unevenness of reward in a society can be prevented from causing discontent only in one of two ways ; by the acceptance of a series of taboos or the acceptance of a series of fetishes. When the king was generally regarded as a divinely anointed and sacramental man, he and his appointed deputies appeared to those whom they commanded to be beings of a superior kind. The respect paid to them was a form of fetish worship which prevented the mind of the worshipper from challenging the human " fairness " of the difference in the material lots of the worshipped and the worshipper. When knowledge was the close preserve of a select caste, the realization that the educated person had powers not possessed by the uneducated person created a similar fetish worship. But this control of the emotions by the adulation and fear which a fetish arouses cannot be maintained when the king and his officers are no longer regarded as men possessing specially delegated supernatural powers and when knowledge has become the free possession of all grades of society.

In a community where the masses form an uneducated mob the acceptance of authority can be achieved by the mere possession of power in the hands of authority, but when the masses have been trained and encouraged to acquire knowledge, and to exert mental powers in challenge of existing appearances, authority must not only show its power but show also its reasons for possessing power. To this extent the old Tories were right who maintained that popular education was bound to be subversive to the maintenance of society as they had known it before that alleged blessing was dowered upon the masses. To this extent the modern Left Wing is right in applauding as incentives to discontent the weekly presentation in the illustrated Press of photographs and descriptions of the wealthier sections of society at play.

A population of illiterates and the suppression of the more flippant illustrated weekly periodicals would doubtless permit the existence of a community fundamentally happier than that which now inhabits these lands. But since it is no longer " practical politics " to achieve a population of illiterates—or, indeed, to outrage the freedom of the press by suppressing such organs as are provocative of revolt against the prevailing economic and social systems—the position is created in the realm of ideas which reproduces that in the realm of material satisfactions. A nation cannot be happy and politically contented when cultural appetites are deliberately created and their complete fulfilment baulked. It cannot be happy if those appetites are created and fulfilled, but their application to life rendered supremely difficult. The mob can only be bribed into acquiescence by bread and circuses when bread and circuses represent the limit of its desire for sustenance and amusement.

Humorous critics of our existing organization have remarked on the fact that collective feasting has disappeared from our working lives. There used to be a joyous ceremony of harvest-home, but it has not been replaced by a similar joyous ceremony on striking the trial balance. May Day was once a kind of innocent saturnalia when all rejoiced together. It has become a day of some anxiety to the authorities responsible for the maintenance of law and order. Once the workers gathered to make merry. Now they gather to make gloomy and menacing speeches. Jack-in-the-Green has been supplanted by Jack-on-the-rostrum, and the Lord of Misrule construes his title in no jocular way. Men once sang about their work, in both senses of the phrase, singing its pleasures and singing as they performed it. Despite the efforts of contemporary satirists, such as the admirable "Beachcomber", to supply new chanties for our new occupations, men do not now sing about their work.

These things are jests, but they are jests with a core of sinister truth. That truth is not merely, as some have insisted, that the form of modern labour is more artificial than the form of primitive labour. It is that the simplicities of labour and refreshment no longer satisfy the mind of working man, for his mental—and, if one may use the word without danger of misconstruction in this context, his spiritual—appetites have expanded. They have expanded under the direct stimulus of the communal will, but the communal will has not yet been powerful enough to adjust the terms and conditions of labour and leisure to the expanded need.

The lack of such adjustment would not in itself be a social canker. What irks men to the point of active discontent is the lack of assurance that the prevailing form of social organization permits such an adjustment and the fear that it actively prevents it. The shoe pinches because it cramps the growing foot. Individual aspirations, not only condoned but actively encouraged by society, are left unsatisfied, and the dissatisfaction is not appeased by the ancient annealings of accepted fetish or taboo worship as it might once have been.

At its simplest, the gap in satisfactions may be expressed thus—the failure of a small enterprise, a farm or a little business, to supply all the material comforts or mental refreshments which a citizen desired might be compensated for by an impalpable reward in the shape of a glow of self-conscious virtue in having assisted in the maintenance or progress of a joint venture in alliance with a congenial or respected or merely familiar master; the failure of a large enterprise, divorced from human contacts as between worker and eventual consumer, and worker and eventual controller, does not supply that impalpable. A small and simple enterprise with a tradition of continuity pays its workers in more than coin; a large and complex enterprise with a tradition of abrupt changes of personnel cannot add to its ostensible rewards of wages and organized "welfare". That a local harvest is good is a matter for general rejoicing in which all have reason to share; that an annual balance-sheet is good gives the rank and file of the workers cause rather for new resentment than for rejoicing.

It is true that such resentment may be illogical and "short-sighted", since a prosperous business, in theory, means some security of tenure for those who staff it.

But it is also true that the individual worker cannot connect his personal security of tenure with the state of that prosperity. He may be dispossessed of his claim on the business by the sudden obsolescence of a process or by a change in proprietorship wrought over his head. A lifetime's devotion to the joint enterprise leaves him with no greater claim upon it than did his first week's work. He feels, indeed, that the longer he spends with the business, the more menacing the threat of dismissal. (It may be remarked in passing that it is not without significance that in great modern enterprises the attainment of long service by employees is made the occasion for celebration and, often, the giving of medals, and talks on " loyalty ". In the smaller businesses of an earlier day, and in agricultural life, long service was the expectation of the entrant.) Neither happiness nor contentment is possible in a society where sections that have a separate entity of effort have no such entity of reward, where, that is to say, the betterment of the whole does not show itself in some way as the betterment of each.

It may be argued that at no stage of society has the betterment of the whole of a section meant the betterment of each unit within it, and economically such argument could be well sustained. But some stages of society have provided, and future stages may provide, " betterments " which the economist cannot assess but which are of recognizable value to the psychologist. Man does not live by bread alone ; he lives also, at the most sordid, by circuses. The task of the statesman, surely, includes the delicate business of realizing what particular kind of circus is fitted to each phase of a changing age, and of knowing when each type of circus has become outmoded in the advancing minds of the spectators. More important still, that task surely includes the business of realizing whether organized super-circuses are less or more satisfying than impromptu entertainments locally arranged. To cling to a somewhat troublesome metaphor, human happiness may depend less on the occasional anodyne of an efficient fête on the village green than upon the constant resources of individual back-gardens.

In primitive states of society, when food, shelter and adequate clothing failed, it was possible for the lack to be blamed either upon the unfathomable whims of an angry deity, or upon the malignity of some demon, or upon the machinations of a known and personified tyrant. The identification of the cause of disaster was itself to some extent an anodyne. A wrathful god might be placated, a malignant demon might be exorcised, a tyrant might be fought. In complex states of society such identification is not usually easy, though men attempt it. The ills of the masses are blamed upon some abstract but undefined thing—the capitalist system, the custom of primogeniture, or what not. Actually the thing which irks men is the knowledge that their ills are almost haphazard, and befall them despite visible efforts to organize the community on a basis of fairness and efficient distribution of material goods. It is when some abstract cause is elevated as the reason for men's discontents that distress is most likely to become despair, and despair most likely to breed physical revolt. Men can work or fight against a callous or inept tyrant, and can pray against the visitations of an Old Testament God, but what can men do when confronted by such objects of inhuman power as the Economic Laws ?

In practice, of course, they can do either of two things. They can deny the Laws, or they can deny that their economic and social governors have rightly construed and applied them. The usual and easier course is the second course, and it gains force when their governors are seen to be actively tampering with what was once demonstrated to be an unalterable fiat of nature. For example, a generation of consumer-producers which has been taught that the price of goods is governed by some mysterious operation known as the law of supply and demand cannot but feel sceptical either of the truth of that law or the honesty of its interpreters when it finds that by cartels and restriction schemes supply is being " rigged " to the detriment of those who constitute demand. It cannot but feel sceptical when it finds in some phases of its economic life there are more kinds than one of supply and demand.

For example, the value of a share in an enterprise is obviously fixed by the earning power of that enterprise; it turns upon the operation of supply and demand in so far as that affects the products of that enterprise. But he would be simple indeed who thought that this alone governed the value of his share, for it is also, and far too obtrusively, affected by the operation of supply and demand for the share itself, quite apart from the products of the enterprise. The share that I buy to-day for 20s. may to-morrow be worth 22s., not because the enterprise has suffered any change, but because the market in the shares themselves has been caught short in the face of a sudden demand. Similarly, it needs no great measure of experience or imagination to teach the simple fact that supply and demand are themselves terms governed by circumstances of time and place. The lesson, indeed, is explicit in a once popular music-hall song concerned with the man who was asked sixpence for a quantity of sulphur and grumbled that he could get it for fourpence at Boots', only to be told that he could get it for nothing in Hell.

The tendency of mankind when told that economic and social relations are governed by abstract laws is, thus, not to deny the validity of the laws but to deny the competence of governing persons to apply those laws or to organize society in such ways that the incidence of the laws is changed. If a community feels that it is being left by its governors to the mercy of abstract laws when human ingenuity could change their incidence, it will grow discontented. It will grow more discontented when it feels, whether justifiably or not, that those laws are indeed being evaded or deflected, but only for the benefit of a favoured few.

This aspect of discontent has itself more than one phase. An excess in supply means that for a time supply must wane until demand again overtakes it. The complete closing down of an enterprise will ruin the happiness of those dependent upon it for their livelihoods. The partial closing down will create differences in treatment between work-people. The attempt to continue production on the old scale and to overcome the lack of outlet by some system of storage will eventually imperil the whole enterprise. Those affected will then turn their resentment against a world system which has made possible such cycles of temporary over-production or against a local system which, knowing that such a cycle is operative, has failed to organize itself in such a way that the periods of unwanted labour can be endured without suffering.

In a capitalist State the criticism is apt to take a detailed form once the workers who are personally hit by the cycle have been educated into an understanding of the financial and economic history of the undertaking they serve. The existence of dividend equalization reserves and the non-existence of wages equalization reserves becomes a matter for bitter comment. The possibility of a company paying high dividends for a period of years, only to pay no dividends and to turn workers away at a time of unexpected trade slackness, is reviewed with an understandable impatience by those bereft of work or income. It does not soothe the consequent discontent to explain that, in the case of this or that company, or this or that industry, no prudence could have obviated the situation. Even if it be successfully shown that in the heavy industries the deflection of all the earnings paid in dividends to the wages fund would hardly benefit the individual worker to an appreciable extent, the feeling will remain that in a world capable of being organized not only for " plenty " but for evenly spaced " plenty " someone is either blundering or plundering.

Of two things one—either the world is capable of such organization, or it is not. Either selected pockets of humanity in the world, say the British or the American people, are capable of being so organized that spaced plenty is possible or they are not. Either the advance from the uncertainty of primitive society, confined to hand labour and slow transportation, to the relative certainty of our own day of generous production and swift transportation has been a miracle of luck and cunning, or it has been a tragedy of unused chances and misused appliances.

The masses—that is, the volume of people who do the work of the world with little or no direct share in its government—might be reasonably contented to know on reliable intellectual authority that their present discontents are not only inevitable but are commendably few compared with the anxieties and deprivations which would have been theirs but for that miracle of luck and cunning. They might even be reasonably contented to know that, despite the misused and unused opportunities of the recent past, economic experts are now at one in devising the means of repairing the folly of their predecessors. They cannot be other than discontented when intellectual authority speaks with two voices, and when the method of advance recommended by one school of thought enjoying temporary power as the adviser of Government is immediately criticized as an approach to chaos by some other school of thought claiming equal right to confidence, and with the potentiality of being itself the adviser of Government on the occurrence of some casual political change.

The divided voice of economic and political authority might with an illiterate audience cause merely a splitting of the auditors into two opposed camps. With a literate audience it can only cause authority as such to fall into contempt. The average man, unschooled in and impatient with those subtleties of economic thought which, when enunciated, sound to him the veriest sophistries, tends to reason thus—" The essentials of personal happiness are few and simple, the means of supply are adequate ; are, indeed, we are told, more than adequate ; but the essentials of personal happiness are not supplied. Why ? Because something has been mishandled, and that something is almost certainly those means of supply. The State is no longer obsessed with the need to protect its citizens from famine, plague and assault. It is no longer obsessed with the need to seek new fields of wealth. The reward of human labour measured by the material return from a given effort has increased enormously by the invention of machines and the growing perfection of means of exchange. That reward is badly distributed, not always in the old sense that one section of society gets more and others less than a ' fair ' share, but sometimes in the new sense that to any individual citizen the reward is erratic and its incidence outside any personal control. Since the growing perfection of means of exchange has itself arisen from the advance of mechanical aids to, and replacements of, labour, it is probably the mechanical aids which have been mismanaged. Again, why ? A machine which does the work of ten men causes nine men to idle on inadequate means of filling their leisure, and one to work as hard as ever he worked. Why ? Should not that aid to labour have eased all equally, and, if not, should its productivity not in some indirect way have eased the lot of all concerned with the original operation which it now performs? If the invention of machinery was hailed as the dawn of a day when the curse of Adam—labour—was to be eased, why to-day is a growing list of unemployed regarded as a menace and not as a fulfilment of that promise?"

Such reasoning may be jejune and ingenuous, it may omit many considerations—the application of mechanical means to quality, for example, and the creation by mechanical means of new fields of demand—but it is reasoning accepted by growing masses of men and women. It leads to two conclusions—either the old machine-wreckers were right, or the society which has so mishandled machines must be radically altered.

Phrased differently, the clash of possibilities lies in the communal choice between a return to modes of life less ornate and less varied than those which the machines have made possible, and an advance to a mode of life infinitely more complex than we have yet known in which centralized authority must increase in power and the individual citizen must sacrifice liberty for luxury.

CHAPTER X

1914 AND 1926

THE industrial revolution, by the deceptive appearance of permanence which it gave to each advance in mechanical mastery, caused re-arrangements of population which themselves had the appearance of permanence. If steam-driven locomotives with a trail of carriages running on metal lines seemed to be the culmination of man's transporting ingenuity, the crowded factory towns of the north of England seemed to be the permanent result of power-worked factories. Few, if any, saw how rapidly the internal combustion engine was to disturb the permanence of the one or how soon the technique of British trading was to shake the permanence of the other.

The congestion of the North led to the inevitable clash between those who saw in the new conditions an immeasurable advance from the old and those who saw in them a pitiable failure to attain without unnecessary delay to possible better conditions. The town labourer of the mid-nineteenth century was far better housed and fed than the country labourer of the mid-eighteenth century, but his housing and feeding were obviously on a standard far below what was possible to the communal means. Back-to-back houses in serried streets arose under the compulsion of economic convenience not as the best shelters that could be provided but merely as shelters that could be provided quickly and cheaply in such a way that the labour force was encamped near to its field of operations—the pit or the factory. The early industrialists were only too palpably sincere in regarding the working conditions of factory life as more comfortable for the workers than the conditions of rural and home-workers' lives. So sincere a reformer as Theodore Roosevelt on the verge of the present century worked desperately hard to save the tobacco workers from home labour on the very grounds which the early industrialists adopted in defence of the young factory system.

The change from the moral shambles which was depicted with such terrible force by Disraeli in *Sybil* to the relatively ordered and spacious life of an industrial township in the early nineteen-hundreds was accomplished with remarkable quickness, but that change never overtook—could not, by the nature of things, overtake—the aspirations of the workers housed in such townships, particularly after the flood of a new culture, though it was but the culture of Board Schools and W. T. Stead's penny classics, had borne in upon the minds of the masses. The growing tightness upon the individual citizen of the organization of his working life by employers converting individualism into cartellism and by unions striving for a complete control of the totality of workers in any given trade, and the growing insistence of the State upon a larger and larger share of control in the ordering of private lives warred with the still vivid and theoretically desirable tradition of personal liberty, of freedom, of individual responsibility. There was still a general belief in what one can only call the superstition that representative government in national and local affairs somehow gave this liberty, freedom and responsibility, though it was visibly being used to destroy them. Ruskin could tell an earnest working man, seeking advice on how he and his fellows could make their voices heard to better effect, that his voice was not worth the bray of a donkey, and Huxley, as early as 1887, writing for a popular audience,[1] could warn his readers that

[1] *Hume*, by Professor Huxley, "English Men of Letters Series," 1887. (Paper cover 1s., limp cloth 1s. 6d.)

> . . . the members of the House of Commons are not yet delegates ; but with the widening of the suffrage and the rapidly increasing tendency to drill and organize the electorate, and to exact definite pledges from candidates, they are rapidly becoming, if not delegates, at least attorneys for committees of electors. The same causes are constantly tending to exclude men, who combine a keen sense of self-respect with large intellectual capacity, from a position in which the one is as constantly offended as the other is neutralized . . .

but upon representational government the faith and hope of the masses remained fixed. The woman's suffrage movement seemed almost to elevate the vote to the sanctity of a mystical symbol of all emancipation.

But—as we have seen in an early chapter—despite this attachment to the form of representational government, there was a general awareness that it was not functioning to the satisfaction of the normal citizen, just as there was a general awareness that the system of industrial relations was not satisfying the new mental and material demands which it had helped in its haphazard century of growth to create.

The record of industrial disputes between 1906 and 1914 is significant of the uneasy temper of the times. In 1911, the Coronation Year of King George V, an epidemic of small stoppages culminated in a general railway strike at a moment when only the death of King Edward had called a halt to a political contention that was threatening to split the unity of the nation in a way not known in living memory. The combination of political, industrial and social unrest, including recurrent demonstrations of "unemployed", which in some cases in the provincial cities involved the use of force by the police, but in London chiefly took the form of bedraggled processions with collecting boxes, continued to fret the nation until 1914, when labour troubles in England, a virtual mutiny of army officers in Ireland, and the spectacular contempt shown by the suffragists towards law and order, very naturally misled foreign observers into the conclusion that the disintegration of British social life was all but complete. That conclusion in a foreign mind is the more understandable when it is remembered that the British Isles were under the government of a Liberal administration, which surely implied absence of repression, and thus also implied either a complete decadence in the moral fabric of the race or a complete breakdown in the whole system of administration.

The historic hope of all statesmen menaced by revolt at home is an external menace sufficiently strong to re-knit the ties of domestic unity. William H. Seward actually contemplated the creation of such a menace as a means of avoiding the War of Secession. In 1914 the Statesmen of Europe had little need to create such a circumstance; the ineptitude of themselves and their predecessors had relieved them of that necessity. Calling upon God to defend the right and to strafe the Godless enemy, the Allies and the Central Powers took arms not only against each other but against the sea of troubles that had till that moment menaced the fabric of the various States. The old black magic worked well. The Socialists who in the name of universal brotherhood were by striking to have made a modern war impossible, forgot to strike, such was their enthusiasm for the national cause.

If any to-day think that the nations entered the war in any mood of chastened pride, he deceives himself. The mood of 1914 was expressed by young Asquith's sonnet which opened with the fervent line, " Now God be thanked, who has matched us with His hour," or the popular marching song, " When we've wound up the watch on the Rhine." The glut of sombre war novels which took the public taste some ten years after the war was over, acclaimed as realism, falsify the spirit of the opening years. That is more faithfully conveyed by Ian Hay's *The First Hundred Thousand*, which was a piece of day to day psychological reporting. By 1918 war had become a vulture, but in 1914 most people thought it was a lark.

The reasons for that mood are plain. Whatever else about war was unrealized, one thing was everywhere appreciated. After such a cataclysm, the world could never be the same again. Even those bounding optimists who declared that the whole thing would be over by Christmas knew that when it was over all relationships would have suffered a change. To those who flocked to the recruiting offices in 1914, from whatever personal motive, whether to prove that Britain's word was Britain's bond, or to escape the nagging of a termagant wife, or to put to the proof Mr. Kipling's assertion that soldiering was the lordliest life on earth, or to escape the odium of not enlisting, or to remain one of a band of friends, to these, I say, the war offered two gifts. One was an immediate escape from a mode of life which had become irksome into a mode of life that was compounded of a discipline that gave unexpected freedoms and a continuous excitement. The other was the promise that at the end of the war "things would be different".

How soon that initial mood was shattered those who suffered C. E. Montague's *Disenchantment* well know, but while it lasted it was real. There was a conviction that all had subjugated all class and personal needs and motives to the common call. I can speak only for the English as I, an Englishman, moved amongst them, but it must have been so with most other nations. Because the end was common to all, and because the end transcended any spur to action that living men had known, the English had become a band of brothers, each in his temporary degree prepared to work with his fellows selflessly and devotedly.

If on 4 or 5 August 1914, the Prime Minister had conscripted the nation, as a nation, for the duration of the war, the nation would doubtless have accepted that fiat with acclamation. For reasons many and various, and mostly preposterous and contemptible, that was not done or even attempted. Britain entered upon the serious business of the war as a serious business—wherein services were rendered for profit, and supplies were obtained by bargains with private enterprises which, though very often unwillingly, prospered by the nation's loss. The recruitment of the new army was achieved on a voluntary basis by the employment of publicity agencies to exploit the emotionalism of the masses, and the derided men who stayed at home comforted their hurt pride by finding fat jobs. Those who had no stomach for that fight had no need to depart, they stayed where they were and (in our vivid modern idiom) let the other poor mutts depart. The consequences of the failure to take advantage of the nation's mood of high resolve—for that *was* the nation's mood—were many and sinister. Among them were two of special significance; a new national unity, possible then, became less and less possible as each week passed, for reasons shortly to be examined, and the wrong men were allowed to enlist for combatant service. By the wrong men being allowed to enlist is meant that for a while the recruiting phrase " Your King and country need you " was applied only to the fighting army. There was no realization that in a conflict of the kind upon which the world was embarked the service of fighting might be less useful than the act of performing some other service which permitted others to fight efficiently. That, indeed, came later, and was applied; but it did not come in time to prevent the loss of valuable skilled men nor the bitterness which was engendered by the difference in reward to various classes of servitors.

The lack of economic foresight in the organization of the nation for war was the prime cause of most of the social discontent which followed the armistice. It filled all sections of the community with resentment, the first sign of which was the bitterness of the uniformed men for the stay-at-homes. This bitterness arose primarily from the knowledge that the men at home had stayed there by choice and not because a dictated duty had kept them from the rigours of the line. It showed itself in many obvious ways, only one of which need be remembered here. One of the popular music-hall songs which had caught the fancy of the troops in 1915 had as the opening of its refrain, the lines "*I wore a tulip, a bright yellow tulip, and you wore a red, red rose.*" After the slaughter of the brickfields by La Bassée this ceased to be sung in the original form and was sung in a parody, so loosely constructed as to bear on its face the hallmark of its origin as a genuine folk-song of the trenches. That parody ran, roughly, thus:

I wore a tunic,
A dirty khaki tunic,
And you wore your civvy clothes.
We fought and bled at Loos
While you were on the booze,
The booze that no one here knows.
Oh, you were kissing wenches
While we were in the trenches
Wearing a full-pack load,
For you were a-slacking
While we were attacking
Down on the Menin Road.

There was a period when the very resentment of the serving soldier for the non-serving citizen was used to encourage recruiting under the voluntary system. The poster " What did you do in the Great War, Daddy ? " and its fellow poster showing a gap in the ranks over the legend " There's room here for you ! " were reflections of the knowledge that non-serving civilians might expect the scorn of their uniformed fellows which would pass on to posterity.

As all know, that scorn did not pass to posterity, for several reasons. The voluntary system failed, and fighting men had to be conscripted. The war revealed itself in quite a new light as the years passed, and the first fine careless rapture of the 1914 recruiting offices looked in retrospect less like divinely inspired courage and more like foolish hysteria. But the conviction remained that the community as a whole had not had a square deal in the first organization for war. Glory and a shilling a day might together constitute adequate payment for all the sacrifice which early enlistment involved, but a shilling a day and no glory was rather a different matter. Not only did the laggards secure " cushy " jobs as civilians, but when they eventually did enlist they secured the best jobs, very often, as soldiers. The Territorial Army units and the early Kitchener battalions kept in the ranks for too long men fitted by education and training for command, and many of these found themselves by 1915 and 1916 officered by men who had squeezed through the " lubbers' hole " of an O.T.C. into commissioned rank with neither comparative length of service nor experience. Of the bribery and corruption of most units, and all cadet schools, others than Montague have told. There seemed to be muddle within and without, and the mood of high resolve changed to a mood very different.

Even when conscription was adopted it was prefaced by a period of muddled organization and broken pledges, and it was confined to the combatant forces. The egregious Derby scheme, with its broken promises to the married men, was regarded as a measure of the ineptitude of the contemporary rulers. Conscription, when it came, came too late to soothe the feelings of injustice. The permission to " key " men and " indispensable " men to remain outside the economic deprivations of service and wax economically fat in civilian jobs and enterprises remained a rankling grievance to half the nation. It was, very often, a grievance to those forced by circumstances to benefit from it. (It was this sense of grievance in Mr. Baldwin which led to the secret gift of a tenth of his fortune to the nation as an example to his fellows of how the injustice wrought might be voluntarily repaired. Never, perhaps, had so splendid an example so disheartening an effect.) Not all the beneficiaries of mal-organization felt that their gain was in any way wrong. Some felt that it was inadequate. The Welsh miners struck for more. The national unity which had been possible in August 1914, which could have been achieved by the bold but simple measure of conscripting all service, by 1915 had given place to a disunity more apparent than any which had shown itself in the troubled years between 1906 and 1914.

The army itself had other causes for discontent. The war was only too obviously being bungled. Not only were the politicians at home immersed in intrigue and the perpetual fight for personal power, but the soldiers in command were inadequate to their work. Offensives were ordered over ground which had not been properly surveyed. Colonel Hutchison has well written, " History must write of Passchendaele that it remains a military crime, a complete misunderstanding of ground, a misinterpretation of the quality of troops, and a misreading of the intentions of the enemy. No possible excuse, no extenuating circumstance, political, strategic, tactical, exists for the futilities of Passchendaele. . . . And it is recorded that an officer from G.H.Q., who persistently had urged Haig's offensive, in November, for the first time since its opening, visited the front, and wept, crying: ' To think that we asked men to fight in that ! ' "

In the services men were struggling for a variety of personal ends—cushy jobs, decorations, promotion and the like. In politics at home the motives for changes that themselves seemed good, and even inevitable, were doubted and dubious. In the *Encyclopædia Britannica* Captain Liddell Hart notes the events on " the Home Front " in 1915 in a short passage teeming with significances.

> Perhaps one of the most significant landmarks of the transition of the struggle from a " military " to a " national " war was the formation of a National Ministry in Britain which occurred in May 1915. For the prototype of Parliaments to abandon the deep-rooted party system and pool the direction of the war was proof of the psychological upheaval of traditions. The Liberal Prime Minister, Asquith, remained, but the real lead began to pass insensibly into other hands, notably those of Lloyd George. Churchill, whose vision had saved the menace to the Channel Ports and made possible the future key to the deadlock, was shelved, as already had been Haldane, the creator of the expeditionary force.

Since the end of the war the pitiable shifts and expedients of the National Ministry and the Second Coalition which succeeded it have been displayed frankly enough by many of those who were party to them. The memories of that time in such works as Mr. Churchill's *The World Crisis*, Lord Beaverbrook's entertaining volumes, and the official biography of Lord Oxford and Asquith, display (as it seems to me) adequate proof that the distrust of the fighting forces about the motives and capacity of the politicians was justified, just as the memories of the men who fought and the men who commanded them justify the distrust which was felt of the capacities of the higher command.

What, it may be asked, has this momentary return to old emotions to do with our present discontents, with which this book purports to deal ? It has much to do with those discontents, for it was surely during the war years that there was created and brought to a point of passion in many minds that " mistrust of all men governing " and that contempt which now frets us for a system which had till then retained its status of a fetish.

The blunders and misjudgements of the war as cues to bitterness and contempt might have been assauged, and perhaps forgotten, had they not been supplemented by the blunders and mismanagement of the demobilizing period. The whole aspect of industry and social life had been changed. The attitude of men employed to men employing had also been changed. The treatment of employees by employers had greatly differed as between group and group. In some cases business enterprises had added a man's normal salary or pay to his army pay. In other enterprises the difference between the two amounts had been made up to the serving man by his employers. In most cases the enterprise sent the man away with patriotic fervour and human good will—and struck him off the pay-roll. In many cases foolish promises had been given to " keep the job open ". In applying the word foolish, one makes no reflection on motive, but only on foresight. Between the making of such a promise in 1914 and 1915 and its redemption in the late months of 1918 or the early months of 1919 all jobs had changed, and the needs of the returning man had changed. No census was or is possible, but the number of cases where the promise was faithfully kept must have been high, and the number where the keeping of the promise led only to new resentment must have been almost as high. Youths who left their civilian employment returned men, often married men with family responsibilities. They were expected to return gratefully to a job and a wage that were no longer adequate. Temporary replacement men and circumstances had together changed the value of the man to the enterprise and the use of the enterprise to the man.[1] Into this changed world of business and industry a mass of men had to be returned, and the admitted task of the statesman was to return them with the minimum of dislocation and of personal injustice either to them or to those employed in their stead. My own testimony to the chaos of that time is prejudiced by emotions of anger still warmly recollected in tranquillity, which is the right mood for a Wordsworthian poem but the wrong mood for the writing of this book. R. H. Gretton's *Modern History of the English People* will supply the lack of detachment in me. He writes of the effects of the election of 1918 :

> But in the very process of consolidating its position the Ministry took solidity out of everything else. They had let loose a vociferous haste, and in the rush of it the whole nation, civilian and military alike, slipped rapidly out of hand. All the careful plans for gradual and systematic demobilization of war industry and the armies began to go wrong, and fell

[1] A certain man, once my colleague, having served with distinction from 1914 to the end of the war, and having been twice wounded, returned to the job which had been kept open for him, and received the boy's wage which had been his when he enlisted with the good will of his superiors. On his suggestion that it was now inadequate he was told by his immediate superior—now, I am happy to say, dead, " Well, you see, so and so, from our point of view, you've wasted four years . . ." In this case there was no economic justification for the attitude, but had there been any, the bitterness created by this remark would hardly have been less.

> within a few weeks into the angry confusion of wholesale methods, which were the very thing the authorities had most wanted to avoid. Soldiers clamoured to go home, their people at home clamoured to have them back. Pre-war labour clamoured for a clean sweep of all dilution labour, and especially of the women who had taken men's jobs. Dilution labour and the women hotly resented this brushing aside of all they had done ; and now that women had votes, politicians did not find this phase of the difficulties easy to deal with. Ugliest of all, a great part of the labour world which had stayed comfortably at home all the time actually wanted to prevent the men who had gone from coming back ; they were jealous and frightened about the flooding into the labour market of those millions of men.

For those whose war years were spent at home there had been evolved a special kind of discipline, of which food rationing was an example, and from this discipline there was a natural anxiety to get free. The time under restraint had not been long enough to permit the new circumstances to change character. There had also been imposed on great masses of the people the worry and hardship of wages that lagged behind rising prices. The unorganized blackcoats were particularly the victims of this anxiety. These, with the returned soldiers, were stirred by resentment against what were known as " war profiteers ". When the impatience of the men waiting for demobilization led to actual mutiny and riots—there were deaths and woundings in the quelling of these disorders—resentments were intensified. Whatever other virtues the contemporary statesmen and their economist advisers had, they lacked the great virtue of preserving, or even of recovering, for the community the national camaraderie which had marked the opening of the War

With the year 1919 there opened a decade of discontent and suspicion, of restlessness and resentment, of which the succeeding labour and social troubles were the symptoms rather than the cause.

In 1919 itself there was such an epidemic of strike threats that the Defence of the Realm Act, a wartime measure providing for special disciplines and repressions, had to be invoked against the menace of direct action by organized Labour. In 1918, with the war at its most critical phase, there had been strikes of transport workers, miners, police, shipwrights and other workers, and the need to keep the nation at war had resulted in ready concessions to their demands. From 1919 to 1926 there was not the same urgent political reason for ready concessions. Those that were wrung reluctantly from various sections of industry neither satisfied the strikers nor pleased the consuming sections of the community. The General Strike loomed very close in 1921—there was a second abortive police strike which caused a unit of the Tank Corps to park itself in the centre of Liverpool—there was further trouble with the transport workers and the miners—and in 1926 the General Strike became an actuality.

While this ferment of labour unrest and social dissatisfaction agitated the community at home, a faulty Treaty abroad followed by a series of unintelligible attempts to achieve what was supposed to have been achieved by the first twenty-six articles of the Treaty of Versailles (forming the Covenant of the League of Nations) and an era of grim civil war in Ireland caused the common man more and more to distrust the capacity of his elected governors and the system which permitted them to perpetrate their follies and ineptitudes. The unexpected merit of the General Strike was that it revealed the fact—at once a disillusionment and a warning—that the much vaunted alternative to the existing system and its users, government by a Socialist-cum-trade-union *bloc*, was even more pregnant with ineptitude than the system and men which it opposed. Having seen the Trade Union Congress in action, the people at large were not likely to depose their leaders to make that body of uncertain and un-nerved mediocrities king.

It has been frequently said that the commonsense of the English people killed the General Strike. It would be nearer the truth to say that the very disunity which caused that strike caused its collapse. Between well-intentioned but inept leadership and attempted sectional dictatorship there was for the ordinary person no choice. The ordinary person preferred the good intentions. It was the sectionalism of the attempt to coerce the community which was resented. Before the strike itself was launched, and that by a blundering accident in a newspaper office where a section of a section got out of control of the trade union leaders, the public sympathy was broadly with the miners and against the mineowners. Once the strike was launched, sympathy swung round. But in swinging round it did not swing away from the coal miners, who had been the primary cause of the trouble, but only against the trade union junta who were trying to help the miners in the wrong way. Much of the exasperation against the general strike leaders was aroused by what seemed to the normal citizen their suicidal folly. For a section to apply pressure against the Government of the day might be legitimate, but to apply a kind of pressure that threatened everybody—including the section itself—with starvation and ruin, however legitimate, seemed stupid. It was the technique of cutting off the nose to spite the face.

The general strike was prefaced by the grant of a large subsidy to the coal industry to prevent the general strike.

This subsidy was admittedly uneconomic. It was Danegeld. But

> We've proved it again and again,
> That if once you have paid him the Danegeld,
> You never get rid of the Dane.

The Prime Minister publicly in the House of Commons prayed for peace in his time and handed over £20,000,000 of Danegeld to buy off a general strike—and the general strike came. It was an impressive lesson in the ineptitude of modern statecraft. It was almost as impressive a lesson in the value of economic advisers.

The collapse of the general strike found both sides a little ashamed of themselves. There was to be no vindictiveness. Broadly speaking, there was no vindictiveness. A new Act reached the Statute Book which curbed a little the powers of the trade unions in politics—the "contracting in" clause previously discussed was part of this measure—but there was wisely no manufacture of martyrs. Unfortunately the grievances which had caused the strike were not eradicated, and the lesson had been learnt that there was, in Great Britain at any rate, no possible sudden remedy for them in direct action by organized labour.

Even while this industrial turmoil was boiling, there was preparing in the witches' cauldron a much more infernal brew which was to present itself to the palate in the sweet form of the stock market boom of 1928.

Between 1918 and 1928 that fateful decade of waste, muddle and confusion, there had been fashioned by statesmen—or despite them—a post-war world the characteristics of which were pretty grim to the wise eye. The peace treaty of the war-to-end-war had left Europe seething with potential strife. The Communist coup in Russia and the Fascist coup in Italy had demonstrated that Parliamentary democracy had ceased to command the confidence of restless peoples irked by the irrationalities of reward and power under the haphazard organization which was dignified by the name of the Capitalist System, but which was in reality a sustained transition from free enterprise and competition to monopoly control. In certain countries, England for example, demobilization had been bungled; the provision of houses had been bungled; the adaptation of such things as roads and townships to conditions formed by the advance in mechanization which had been made during the war years had been bungled; the creation of labour fluidity to meet a world in which the topographical centring of industry had changed and was changing had not so much been bungled as thwarted, where it was not ignored as a need. The irritation of organized labour with its working and social conditions had been aggravated rather than smoothed away. Politicians were ironically congratulated upon having created, in the words of Mr. Lloyd George, "a world fit for heroes to live in" since they had produced a world in which none but heroes could live.

Politically, in England, economic questions of great complexity had usurped in Parliament the place once occupied by political questions of relative simplicity of principle and no great complexity of detail. The electorate had been increased by a flood of politically illiterate voters whose very numbers made intelligent political education a matter of great difficulty. These had reached the register at a time when the concentration upon non-political interests of the popular press, the cheapness and availability of amusements ranging from public tennis courts to cinematograph theatres, and the availability to persons of moderate incomes of motor-cars, had distracted the public mind from politics as a continuous interest and a constant study.

The electorate was thus wayward in its allegiances and had to be wooed by catchwords, since it had not the faculty of earlier electorates for wading through columns of close print to absorb the arguments which its political leaders provided for it on platforms and in Parliament. Even had it possessed that faculty, the columns of close print were no longer provided by those sections of the Press which reached the masses. The masses had, in a word, lost all sense of continuity, of cause and effect, in politics and in those phases of economic development and organization which presented themselves as phases of politics.

The English electoral systems, wherein constituencies vote as constituencies for one of a list of two or three candidates on the principle that the candidate with more votes than any other candidate is elected, makes the election of a Parliament erratic. The number of votes cast over the whole nation for a particular party does not affect the result. The quickest way to demonstrate this is by an absurd simplicity. If there were 600 constituencies each of 40,000 voters and in each of these a Tory defeated a Socialist, the new House of Commons would contain 600 Tories. If in each constituency the victory had been by a majority of 2,000 (Tory 21,000, Socialist 19,000) the Tory vote over the whole country would be 12,600,000 votes worth 600 seats, and the Socialist vote would be 11,400,000 votes worth no seats. If at the next election three candidates contested each seat and (again using a grotesque simplicity) the result in each case was Tory 14,000, Liberal 13,000, Socialist 13,000, we should still have 600 Tories in the new House. The Tory vote would be 8,400,000 votes worth 600 seats, the Liberal vote 7,800,000 votes worth no seats, and the Socialist vote 7,800,000 votes worth no seats. The Tory vote of 8,400,000 would be worth 600 seats—the anti-Tory vote of 15,600,000 would be worth no seats. If at the following election one thousand and one voters in each constituency changed their allegiance and voted Socialist, the result then would be that 600 Socialists were returned although the total turnover of votes was but 600,600. We get the result in each constituency: Socialist 14,001, Liberal 13,000, Tory 12,999. Over the whole country we have 8,400,600 Socialist votes worth 600 seats; 7,799,400 Tory votes and 7,800,000 Liberal votes worth no seats. In effect the turnover votes (600,600) have been worth 600 seats to the Socialists.

In practical life this sort of thing does not happen. True. Something a little more unfortunate happens. In one constituency a Socialist (shall we say ?) is returned by a majority of 100, in a neighbouring constituency a Socialist is returned by a majority of 10,000. In the first case the seat represents 20,050 votes and in the second case 25,000 votes. But in the first case, an "unsafe" seat, any trivial cause—a wet day, for example, or the unpopularity in one suburb of the candidate—will change the representation at the next election. In the second case, a change-over of 6,000 votes is needed to effect such a change. And in both cases a third party candidate may poll a large vote with no chance at all of winning the seat.

The effect of these and similar vagaries in the system is to make voters, and particularly young voters, acutely aware that the voting strength in the House of Commons bears no relationship to the voting strength of parties at the polling booths, and to make party managers aware that an electoral freak wrought by these vagaries may defeat all party hopes.

The presence in Parliament itself of three parties also leads to the presence on the Government benches of a minority party—the two Labour Governments were in this position. We thus get the possibility that the majority party in the House of Commons may be the minority party in the country, judged by total votes cast, and that the major party (that is the party with more members than any other single party) in the House, whether it be the majority or minority party in the country, may not be the governing party. The result of this alternative of irrationalities is called " government of the people, by the people, for the people ", or, alternatively " fooling all of the people all of the time ", according to the taste of the describer. Whatever it be called, it was this confusion which confronted the vast new electorate created by the post-war extensions of the suffrages.

Not only was the world prospect grim and the domestic prospect murky towards the end of the first decade after the Armistice, but the new and largely untutored electorate was being asked to judge on two questions of extreme complexity—the virtue or viciousness of tariffs and the virtue or viciousness of the gold standard. On neither of these questions was there any hope of unanimity among professed economists and statesmen. On both of them there had been historic quarrels in the past. On each the only hope of the unlearned mind was to find some trustworthy authority and prepare to follow it.

The history of tariffs as a controversy I have written in some detail in another place. The question had been abruptly obtruded into the consciousness of the English masses in 1923 when the Prime Minister, Mr. Baldwin, master of a great Parliamentary majority, announced with characteristic honesty that he could not " steer the country " through the winter of 1924-25, with its menace of increasing unemployment, unless he were given a mandate for Protection. The mandate was refused and a Labour Government was returned to office, but not to power. It survived but a few embarrassed months, and

Mr. Baldwin returned to office still lacking his mandate for tariffs, but able to use the expedient of Safeguarding, Protection's natural son.

In the composition of his new Administration Mr. Baldwin gave the Chancellorship of the Exchequer to Mr. Winston Churchill. It was a gracious act. Mr. Churchill, for all his brilliant versatility, had shown no signs of possessing any unusual command of finance, but his father had resigned from that office without introducing a Budget, and the son, from understandable motives, must have aspired to it. In his maiden speech he had rhetorically " lifted again the tattered flag " which his father had left " lying upon a stricken field ".

Mr. Churchill has the misfortune to enjoy, unjustly as I think, a reputation for instability and erratic action. The strongest psychological incentive upon him as Chancellor of the Exchequer was to prove himself a sound and conservative financier. In 1924 the hallmark of a sound and conservative financier was a belief in the gold standard. On 28 April 1925, it was announced that Great Britain would immediately return to that standard.

Before examining the causes and effects of this return it is interesting to note in passing how divided were the professing economists as to the wisdom of the step. Not only were they split into two camps—the pro and the anti—but it was possible for an economic thinker of the quality of Professor T. E. Gregory to write in 1926 :

> There are some acts of State which close historical controversies. The decision of the Baldwin Government to return immediately to the gold standard was one of these.[1]

By the end of 1931 Britain was again off the standard, and in the interim the controversy over the wisdom of the

[1] *The First Year of the Gold Standard*, by T. E. Gregory, D.Sc. (Econ.). (Ernest Benn, Ltd., 1926.)

return was more hotly debated after the act than before. Far from closing an historical controversy, the act of State added virulence to it.

Professor Gregory's own first comment upon the situation then created implied doubts, hesitations and pain in certain bosoms.

> Those who agree with the School of Mr. Keynes, that the gold standard is *intrinsically* undesirable, will find in the experience of the last year and a half—(i.e. from April 1925 to September 1926)—additional reasons for regret. And even of those who approve, on general grounds, of the gold standard, some may believe that it would have been better to wait for a more propitious moment, or, whilst thinking that the moment had come for a return to gold, would have preferred to have seen a new parity point fixed between the paper pound and the re-created gold pound. Others, again, deny that the immediate sacrifices incurred outweigh the immediate and future benefits to be derived from the return to gold on the basis actually chosen. And, lastly, it is affirmed by some and denied by others, whether supporters of the gold standard or not, that the period of transition is over and that the difficulties of adjustment have been successfully surmounted.[1]

Whatever the difference of opinion among economists, the deed was done. Britain returned to gold and stabilized her £ at pre-war parity. Upon that deed much that followed—including the general strike of the following year—was blamed. But whatever else was wrought by the restoration of the gold standard, one thing was achieved, for good or ill. The whole community became " currency conscious " as never before in its history, and in attaining to that mental state achieved a still deeper

[1] *The First Year of the Gold Standard*, by T. E. Gregory, D.Sc. (Econ.). (Ernest Benn, Ltd., 1926.)

distrust of the wisdom of its statesmen and their academic advisers.

The currency controversy had, indeed, one peculiar effect. Theretofore it had been possible for certain distrusters of the politicians to aver that the political parties spoke with a divided voice because that sham fight suited a small body of hidden and secret financial controllers who spoke with a single voice to the political puppets whom they manipulated. The party system in politics, said these doubters, was a skilful camouflage to hide from the people the fact that their destinies were really controlled by " the financiers " who were at one. But when the currency question assumed the form of a prolonged and running public debate between deflationists and inflationists, between the advocates of a stable currency based on gold and a managed currency based on some other and less tangible standard, it became apparent that even " the financiers " were divided.

The cynic on the soap-box might advise his hearers to ascertain what was the real desire of the financiers and then to vote for the opposite, but the advice became a little confusing when the apparent real desire of the financiers showed itself as two contrary desires. The old conception of an international financier as a sombre Machiavelli gifted with superhuman cunning and sub-human ethics faded and gave place to the new conception of an estimable gentleman baffled and bewildered by the complexities of his own function. As with the industrial capitalist, so with the financier—the hurts and discontents of the community were not caused by his malign machinations but by his professional ineptitude. The cause of industrial and financial maladjustment began to be seen not as selfish callousness, but as what Dr. Johnson might have called " ignorance, pure ignorance, ma'am ". Anger and resentment in the discontented classes gave place to impatience and pity. It was even noticeable that the popular caricatures changed with the popular mood. The presentments of bloated capitalists and bankers were no longer men of fat paunch and complacent mien ; they were men with the vacuous faces of idiots and with straws in their hair.[1]

While these two complex questions—tariffs and currency—formed the staple of public discussion and controversy, and while the industrial population settled back into its mood of discontent after the failure of the general strike and the botching together of a peace in the coalfields, while the European situation passed from phase to phase of its menacing development, like a child in convulsions, the glorious potentialities of the machine age suddenly presented themselves anew.

The £ was stable again ; the greatest menace of living memory, the general strike, had been met and defeated ; the shattered regions of the Central Empires had been succoured ; America, the traditional land of prosperity, seemed more prosperous than ever, and machines and scientific research applied to such primary activities as agriculture were able to pour out wealth with a minimum of effort and to manufacture commodities at low cost. A new era was opening—with the promise of unlimited personal profit for those who participated in the enterprises which would serve it. The English nation had become currency minded, it had come to grips with the mysterious subject of finance, it had been taught by the War Loan propaganda that savings were as safe in pieces of paper as in a savings bank or a building society or an old tea-pot. It became stockmarket-minded. The boom of 1928 was born. It deserves a chapter to itself, for it intensified some and created others of our present discontents.

[1] See especially the caricatures of Low, where this attitude is most marked between the years 1926 and 1933.

CHAPTER XI

FROM BOOM TO CRISIS

THE stock market boom of 1928, which was the feverish prologue to the catastrophic world slump of 1929, was at once a symptom of a deeply-rooted social and economic malaise and the cause of a new ague from which the body politic still suffers. We have spoken in Chapter VII of the steady growth through the nineteenth and early twentieth centuries of the stock-jobbing community and of the increasing power of the banks. Both these developments were essentials to, as well as the results of, the expansion of man's power to produce more and better goods at less human effort and to transport and exchange those goods with a constantly decreasing use of time and energy. Once the world was made smaller by mechanical aids to communication, transport and exchange, primitive methods of finding capital for enterprise could not suffice. More and more complex methods were needed, and in the devisal of such methods the banking system and the Stock Exchange played vital parts.

In 1802 the Stock Exchange in London opened with a list of 500 subscribers. In 1933 there were nearly 4,000 members. In 1802 there were under a score of stocks dealt in. In 1933 the official list quoted nearly 6,000, to a total value of £18,371,459,742, plus 43,717,752 shares of no par value. In 1932, a year of stock market depression, the Committee of the Stock Exchange gave permission to deal in securities to the total value of

£782,589,141 and 1,724,666 shares of no par value.[1] In 1825 there was a noticeable prosperity abroad in the land. At the beginning of that year there were 276 joint-stock companies in existence in Great Britain. In 1933 the Stock Exchange official list contained under the general head of commercial and industrial securities no fewer than 1,468.

The tendency of any piece of scrip representing a share in an enterprise is to acquire a double life. As a literal share in that enterprise it has a value ; as a " thing in demand " it has another value. A share worth one pound in a company may, by reason of the good profit-earning prospects of the enterprise, become worth, on a sage and conservative estimate, thirty shillings. If those prospects are generally apparent there will be a demand for such shares. In vacuo, one could assume that the shares would find a new level round the higher sum. But other factors influence the situation. There may be a bigger demand for the shares than the number of shares available can supply. This will force the value upwards. Or, the shares having touched the new level, many holders who paid a pound each for the securities will see an opportunity of making ten shillings profit by selling. They will offer their shares on the market. The supply will thus exceed the demand, and the price will fall. But in the meantime the profit-earning capacity of the business has not changed. On a sage and conservative estimate the shares are still worth around thirty shillings.

Again, knowledgeable men may have reason to suppose that a company is facing an unprofitable time, or even

[1] For the benefit of the uninitiated it may be well to explain that a share of no par value is not a worthless share. It is a share representing the equity of the business, issued for cash or assets. These shares differ from other shares in having their dividend expressed as an amount per share, since there is no nominal par value on which to base a percentage. These shares were created by astute minds in America as a means of escaping liability to Stamp Duty.

some kind of disaster. When that knowledge becomes public property, holders of the shares will want to be rid of them. The market price will fall. These knowledgeable men, therefore, sell the shares before that fall takes place, and if they have no shares will sell shares that they do not possess, knowing that by the time delivery is demanded the shares will be freely on offer at a lower price. But the profitless time which was foreseen or the disaster which was counted upon may not eventuate—it may not eventuate because the knowledgeable men have been wilfully misled by others more astute than they. To meet their commitments they must have shares, and will make offers for them freely and at a high figure. The market price of the shares will rise rapidly, even dramatically. But the position of the enterprise behind those shares has not changed. Real value has been stable, and only market value has fluctuated.

So different may be the market value of shares from the earning-power value which they represent that in the case of a gigantic combine, like the Unilever group or Imperial Chemical Industries, a startling article in a financial journal of standing has been known to wipe out many millions of market value between the close of the market one evening and its opening the following morning. Similarly a tactless speech by a Minister has been known to depress gilt-edged securities for just as long as it takes to have a second speech made by another Minister to repair the damage done by his colleague.

The true purpose of a stock exchange is to facilitate the flow of capital into productive industry. Savers will not lend their savings if a loan means that the money is not to be readily available in time of personal need. Those whose work is the supervision of other people's money are loth to "freeze" funds in long-term use. A bourse which maintains an open market in securities means that enterprises are sure of their capital, but that the suppliers of that capital are equally assured that they can recover their own contribution with a minimum of delay. If an enterprise is launched with a capital of £100,000 and I buy the right to a one-hundredth share in its prosperity by providing £1,000 and suddenly desire my money again, I procure it by persuading another to buy my share from me, and not, as in more primitive communities, by persuading the enterprise to "buy me out". But when a bourse is so conducted that the value of the shares in which it deals is liable to erratic fluctuations apart and in addition to the fluctuations in the fortunes, or the prospects, of the enterprises as such, the true purpose of the organization is hindered if it is not overlaid by a second purpose—the provision of a casino in which gamblers may grow rich by taking advantage of the ignorance of others. It was as a joint casino that the London Stock Exchange and the American Stock Exchange presented themselves in 1928.

After the destruction of the war years there came inevitably a period of reconstruction which brought goods and services into strong demand. The general public had seen to its amazement that war itself means personal prosperity for individual workers, and had not realized that the national wealth had been dissipated or pledged in five years of destructive effort. Still less did that general public realize that the post-war boom consequent upon the immediate reconstructive need was in effect merely an adding to the great debt incurred between the outbreak of war and the armistice. When the immediate post-war boom in certain industries subsided the feeling was abroad that this diminution in demand was but a temporary lull in a process which could not for long be stayed. To take shares in enterprises which existed to provide those things needed by a world that was intent upon rebuilding its shattered fabric was obviously a method of hitching the personal wagon to a financial star that must soon again be in the ascendant.

When it was realized how readily citizens of human avariciousness and great technical ignorance were prepared to hand money to entrepreneurs who could promise a share in the brave new world which was to be built, such entrepreneurs were not lacking. The stock gambling mania on two continents swelled into a frenzy as devastating to common prudence as, and far wider spread than, the South Sea Bubble, whose characteristics were reproduced even to the impudence of a request for funds to be used for a purpose yet to be revealed.[1] For a time it seemed only necessary to make an offer of capital to the public for the issue to be oversubscribed, and for dealings to open at a premium—that is, for a company to offer its shares at, say, par—£1 for a £1 share—and for those shares to change hands at the first available moment at something over that figure. In consequence money was subscribed by hordes of persons who had no intention of retaining the shares allotted to them for more than the few days necessary to show them a profit.

Among the technicians of the stock market there have always been operators known as " stags ". These enterprising gentlemen apply for an allotment of a new share and send in the small amount of money demanded with the application. Before the second remittance is demanded they dispose of their allotment at whatever profit it shows. When an unprecedented mass of new shares was being offered with most of its components going to an immediate premium on the market, the small body of

[1] If any reader doubt the exactitude of this statement, let him turn back the newspaper files to the prospectus of Anglo-Foreign Newspapers, and read there the expert criticism upon it, particularly in those newspapers which refused to publish its terms in their advertisement columns.

professional " stags " was greatly augmented. " Stagging syndicates " were formed among office boys and junior clerks in city offices, and such was the volume of applications for allotments in newly offered shares that no matter how patently futile an enterprise might seem to the calm and even moderately sophisticated mind, its proffer of shares would meet with such a response that the initial demand would force the security to a premium.

The very minds which detected the impudent imposture or puerile optimism behind a proposed venture would thus be tempted to apply for shares, in the firm hope that a sharp profit would be made and all responsibility in the new enterprise abandoned within a very few days. Nay—to make certain of a share in this easy money, the very persons whose training and native astuteness warned them of the eventual hopelessness of a sustained profit being made by a new venture felt compelled to apply for far more shares than they were disposed to take, even for this gamble, to prevent their being kept out of the haul by the allotment of only a small proportion of his desire to each applicant.

Even the most timid of private investors seeing such profits being made, and being instructed that a new era of prosperity was opening for all enterprises, was tempted from his or her natural caution. These unfortunates were those upon whom the new shares were eventually " planted ". A sharp-witted and unscrupulous man with a useless idea could vend it to a new company for shares ; that company under his direction would float a public issue ; this issue by genuine applicants and " stags " would open on the market at a premium—and the instigator would then unload his shares. The technique was susceptible to many variations. By making the original company the " parent " of a group of subsidiary and associated companies the promoter could exploit his original useless idea many times over at the expense of the ignorant investing public,[1] and could postpone the inevitable day of reckoning when the shareholders would learn that their money had not fructified in some wealth-creating enterprise but had disappeared into unknown pockets, leaving them with no dividends on their investment and probably no capital to recover from its wreckage.

Until these days of reckoning began to occur and to obtrude themselves on the public notice, the stock markets maintained the aspect of a legal casino, a place of automatic profits and little risk. The Stock Exchange became " news ". Nothing is, indeed, more enlightening as to the mood of that mad time than a comparison of the place occupied in the daily perspective of a popular newspaper by stock market movements in, say, 1925 and in 1928.

The responsible members of the Stock Exchange were, let it be said, not happy about the mania of the public and the way in which it was being exploited by rogues. The legislature was equally unhappy. It was realized that the existing Company Law left too many loopholes through which men of fraudulent intent could creep to entrap the public. A new Companies Act was drafted and was expected to reach the Statute Book during the boom year itself, but in the event it failed to do so, and became the Companies Act of 1929. As so often before, the statesmen and their expert advisers had diagnosed a malady and devised a partial remedy, but by the time it was prepared and ready for application, the state of the patient had undergone a complete change.

A stock market boom so artificial and so swollen could not by its nature persist long. The public, after all, contained a large number of persons who bought shares,

[1] This technique is examined in detail in the author's *How the Stock Market Really Works.*

in the old-fashioned way, to keep. A variety of salesmen, known as " share-pushers ", contrived to sell worthless shares at high prices to such persons, but there was an approximate saturation point in one generation and there was also a growing fear of purchase which arose from personal or vicarious experiences of purchases that had proved worthless within a very short time after acquirement. Knowledgeable men, to whom the devices of the crooked promotors and operators were obvious, shared with the first flock of victims the mood of Sam Weller when he cried, " Ain't nothin' to be done in consequence . . . . ain't nobody to be whopped for taking this 'ere liberty ? " A number of persons, ranging from an illiterate little joiner to a peer of the realm, were eventually to be whopped, and the process of whopping them precipitated the crash and reaction from boom to slump.

Whatever the economic forces which wrought the change from the buoyancy of 1928 to the despair of 1929, the psychological factors included three criminal trials. In January 1929 a new chairman took office with a group of companies that had enjoyed a vogue with gambling investors—the Ner-Sag companies—and in May the original chairman, a Mr. Brandreth, was sentenced to four years' penal servitude for publishing a false balance sheet and making false entries in an invoice book. The circumstances of his arrest and trial caused a considerable sensation at the time, and did much to increase the uneasiness of the community at the state of affairs in that mysterious region " the City". It checked perceptibly the public confidence in the easy belief that the area between the Old Bailey and Old Broad Street was a Tom Tiddler's ground where all might gather easy money. But the machinations of Mr. Brandreth had not affected a very wide circle ; his was not the type of enterprise with which solid and substantial financial institutions concerned themselves. He was duly sentenced, and the City had one petty malefactor the less. If any wondered that such manipulations with grouped companies could be possible without earlier retribution befalling the manipulator—not to say that they should be possible at all—the reassuring answer was that it was an unscrupulous rogue who was to blame and not the system which had given him his opportunity.

Group finance was the finance of the new age. It had the cachet of such towering figures as Lord Melchett, Lord Kylsant, Lord Leverhulme and other members of the Upper Chamber of the legislature. It was a necessity to the new process of rationalization. Rationalization was a word of power, popularized from public platforms by an eminent capitalist as the true retort to the wild demand for nationalization. Nationalization meant a State monopoly under the inept direction of bureaucrats: Rationalization meant a private monopoly under the apt direction of trained business executives. Nationalization meant the serfdom of the community; Rationalization meant the glorious freedom of being able to work for—or not to work for, to buy from—or not to buy from—the great monopolistic corporations. Nationalization meant stagnation; Rationalization meant progress and enterprise and the right to take risks with other people's money that no bureaucrat would dare to take. Unless companies were merged and grouped, and their finances grouped and merged, rationalization would not be possible. The way to complete rationalization was through bigger and bigger aggregations of capital inspiring bigger and bigger groups of associated enterprises and exploiting wider and wider markets.

Looking for something to rationalize, some industry in a palpably bad way, a Mr. Clarence Hatry, a young financier of great charm, undeniable ability and more than usual courage, found that which he desired in Steel. By a complicated procedure, too intricate to be expounded here, but well within the law, he began the public-spirited enterprise of rationalizing that great industry. His end was to be attained by a skilful shuffling of shares. His purpose was honest ; his original methods were not dishonest. But, during the process of share shuffling, the market began to go against him. He was threatened by failure and loss. Personal vanity and a desire not to involve those who had trusted him with their money in such loss led him to take a step which so many misguided young men have taken. He committed an arrant piece of fraud in the hope, and possibly the belief, that conditions would change in his favour and permit him to make adjustments which would save his enterprise and prevent any knowledge that a fraud had been committed from ever reaching any but his own immediate associates. Like any miserable clerk, he would falsify the books, and when the horse won he would make all right again. The very simile was applied to him by the judge who eventually sentenced him to a long term of imprisonment.

Clarence Hatry had not, like the pettifogging Mr. Brandreth, busied himself with companies of relatively little importance and small capitalization. He had dealt magnificently in millions. His frauds affected certain of the great joint-stock banks and practically every stockbroker in the industrial market. His fall from grace to open disgrace shook the stock markets of the world. So interlocked is company finance in our time that the failure of the Hatry ventures brought down the market values of the best of stocks, because men faced with the need to meet Hatry company commitments had perforce to offer their good stocks as a means of attaining liquidity. Those who had from London plunged heavily into the Wall

Street market had to realize their American securities at whatever figure they might fetch to secure funds for the meeting of obligations at home. The professional operators were hard hit, and the ordinary investor, even he who had escaped direct personal loss, was frightened. Those who held Hatry stocks saw their possessions rendered worthless ; those who held other than Hatry stocks saw their possessions devalued to a startlingly low figure. And—worst of all—confidence in all investment was shaken. So this was what was meant by modern rationalization and group finance ! Not an honest man's means to prosperity, but a veritable rogues' paradise.

And the banks were hit. Everybody knew it. The bankers had forgotten the old English principle of banking, that money and credit should be lent to a man on his known character and standing, with certain security which he could provide. They had not lent money *to* Clarence Hatry ; they had lent money *on* certain securities that Hatry had pawned with them—and the securities had turned out to be forgeries.

In that difference was all the distinction between banking and mere money-lending. The banker lent *to* a customer : the money-lender and the pawnbroker lent money *on* a security. What had caused this change in banking technique ? The answer was only too obvious. Rationalization and grouped finance. The banks themselves were structures as large and as complicated as Hatry would have made the steel industry. The average citizen began to wonder if it were not inevitable that every large aggregation of capital and effort must sooner or later pass a line were not only the old human relationship between employer and employed was no longer potent, or even possible, but where, too, the human relationship between provider and customer was eliminated.

And, oddly enough, though all knew that some banks had been badly hit by the frauds, the balance sheets did not show much sign of damage. Again, why? The answer that passed readily from lip to lip on mouths that had but recently learnt the formation of the words, was "hidden reserves". Were hidden reserves, then, something which enabled an enterprise to conceal its true position from the world at large, including its own proprietors?

The answer to this question came from an unexpected quarter. At the end of 1929 Hatry was sentenced for fraud; by the middle of 1931 the Chairman of the Royal Mail group of companies was in the dock charged with an offence which amounted to the handling of hidden reserves in such a way that the public had been misled as to the trading position of the Royal Mail Steam Packet Company, that old established, honourable and famous concern. His conviction shook again what returning investment confidence had been visible after the shock of the Hatry debacle. Hatry might have been the inevitable rogue or fool against which any system can hardly hope always to protect itself; but here was a great public figure, a man far above any suspicion of roguery for personal gain, a man protesting that he was unaware of having perpetrated any wrong against the established code of company law. The auditor of the company had been charged with the Chairman in respect to certain of the balance sheets of the company. It could not be denied that these sheets were misleading to the ordinary person, but a galaxy of famous accountants testified that the auditor in passing them had done nothing that any leader of the profession would not have done. The auditor was acquitted on those charges, as was the chairman, but the public still felt that after such a revelation no balance sheet could be trusted as a guide to the exact state of a company's prosperity, that no buyer or seller of a share could be sure of even placing an approximate value on his purchase or sale.

A stock market which for a space had the appearance of a philanthropic casino and then presented itself as a kind of thieves' kitchen—which prided itself upon its high standard of professional honour but which permitted, or at best tolerated, manœuvres suspiciously like chicanery and roguery—but which remained the only free market for the exchange of shares, began to trouble the public mind as a symptom of faulty organization in the industrial relationships of the community. Surely the honest and technically ignorant worker, anxious to contribute his savings to some useful and fruitful enterprise in which personal gain and communal betterment would be allied, could be protected from such deprivations as were now likely to befall him. Surely the mass of the people, particularly the younger generations, could be protected from the unsettling influence which had played upon the wage-earner during the boom of 1928. The function of industry was not to provide gambling counters ; it was to provide necessaries, in the widest use of the word, and those gracious adornments to life the provision of which was one of the characteristics that distinguished civilization from barbarism. Surely the perversion of this true function could be prevented.

But, while the great mass of men appeared to be thinking thus, the entrepreneurs of business and enterprise were as urgently vocal that honest and fruitful enterprise was being stifled or aborted by too much control. The assurances which the State already needed that a projected enterprise was competent to satisfy the demands of the law were so crippling that many a potentially fruitful undertaking never passed from conception to execution. In the brave days of laissez-faire a young man with an idea and the command of but little capital might launch his venture and by ploughing back its first profits might bring it to the stage of its development when public money might be solicited and the infant enterprise grow into a great service. To-day such a one, having to file this and that return, having to pay this and that minimum to his first employees, having to find insurance contributions, having to satisfy inspectors that his workshops or factory conformed to certain rigid requirements, could not hope successfully to launch his venture. Even the need to keep his books in a specified way and to have them audited by a qualified accountant in order that returns might be made at certain periods to Government departments might impose an extra cost upon the venture that would mean all the difference between its being " worth while " and not " worth while ". Far from the ordinary investor and worker being left unprotected, the protections which the State sought to give him were so burdening to the enterprising creator of new industries and businesses that a premium was placed upon lethargy instead of upon initiative.[1]

Although the ears of the detached observer might be smitten by the contending cries of " too much control " and " too little control " he could at least discern that those who blamed a too rigid system of restraints and restrictions, of prohibitions and insistencies, for the decay in trade were themselves perturbed by the effect which the boom of 1928 and its attendant, if delayed, scandals must have had upon industry. A burnt child dreads the fire, said the copy-books. A " stung " investor dreads the bourse. The just must suffer for the unjust. Daring enterprise is not possible if people are too fearful of fraud or loss to provide capital. But the Companies Act, which

[1] Sir Ernest J. P. Benn, in *The Confessions of a Capitalist* and *The Return to Laissez Faire* has expounded this complaint forcibly, lucidly and in all necessary detail.

had been postponed from 1928, reached the Statute Book in 1929. All would now be well, and confidence would return.

Unfortunately, in 1932, M. Ivar Kreuger—who had been displayed to a wondering world as the new saviour of society, the financier achieving a saving internationalism where statesmen had failed, the apothesis of the strong, silent man whose foible was service and whose ideal was rationalization—blew out his brains in Paris. For nearly a decade his progress from humble, and obscure, not to say shady, beginnings to a dominance over many millions of pounds of savings and investments and over the fate of many millions of workers, had been watched with complacent applause by those who were regarded as the most astute business and financial brains in the world. His suicide was hailed as an international tragedy. It was the death of a genius for whom a temporary world set-back had been momentarily too unsettling. Organs of opinion of the standing of *The Times*, the *Economist* and the *Financial News* devoted to him editorial threnodies that would have been slightly exaggerated in their exuberant grief had he been a composite reincarnation of George Washington, Abraham Lincoln, William Ewart Gladstone and the Apostle Paul. The chairman of one of his English companies—an ex-Minister of State and a leading Parliamentarian, and, incidentally, the chairman of a group of financial journals—was advertised to broadcast an appreciation of the dead genius who was understood literally to have killed himself under the Herculean task of rehabilitating the finances and trade of a shattered world.

The broadcast appreciation was not delivered, and the tone of the Press changed, for the truth about Kreuger was suddenly known.

Ivar Kreuger was a proved fraud, and is suspected now to have been in the last years of his life a syphilitic in the first stages of General Paralysis of the Insane. The strong, silent man, the selfless ascetic, was revealed as a commonplace lecher with an itch for power and wealth, whose genius consisted in a mastery of forgery and fraud which made the unfortunate Clarence Hatry seem a mere bungling amateur. But—and here was the rub—the admitted masters of finance and international banking (with a few honourable exceptions)[1] had accepted him at his own valuation. Economists like Sir Arthur Salter had paid tribute to his value as a saviour of society. Against his machinations the safeguards of experience, shrewdness and commonsense—those virtues of the financially great—had been as valueless as the safeguards of the stock exchanges. His death not only exposed the criminality of Ivar Kreuger; it exposed more immediately and relentlessly the gullibility of those who had surrounded, supported and applauded him.

Those trained watchdogs, the financial journals, found themselves in an awkward dilemma. Kreuger flotations had been approved and Kreuger securities freely recommended. Either the recommenders had been singularly inept in their task of distinguishing the true from the false and the good from the bad, or they had been influenced by a consideration of tenderness to sources from which advertising revenue flowed into their coffers. The inference to be drawn from the horrid incident was plain—either they were incompetent for their function or they were venal. The non-technical Press, like the befooled statesmen, might, perhaps, be excused on the ground of invincible ignorance; but the technical Press, like the financiers and bankers, could hardly claim that excuse and hope to retain the confidence of those whom it had misled.

[1] It is on record that once, when denied access to Mr. Montagu Norman, Kreuger said with a laugh, "Does he think I am a Hatry?"

The affair of the harassed and wretched Mr. Brandreth had been a cloud no bigger than a man's hand ; the Hatry collapse had been a veritable typhoon ; the Kylsant case had been a heavy reminder that the storm was not yet over ; and the Kreuger debâcle had shown that neither in intensity nor scope was the cloud-burst limited. This then, was rationalization and this was group finance, despite the protections and annealings of the brave new Act which Britain had passed to the Statute Book in 1929.

The blessed word Rationalization, which had had so much to do with creating the stock-market boom,[1] began to be suspect from another cause. The rationalizers were displaying a suspicious inability to perform what they had promised. One great combine, for example, had embarked upon a great new works at Gillingham, and the head of the enterprise had glowingly explained to the shareholders that with rationalized methods the steady volume of orders must be such that these works as an overhead charge would be subject to a steady and full use that would bring low the cost of production and that the orders would flow because this great works could turn out products at so low a unit cost that the world would consistently buy them. When the works were complete and the orders did not flow in sufficient volume to keep them fully occupied, they were justified in quite another way. It then seemed that the justification of rationalization was that it could meet any demand that might occur, no matter how large, and part of a rationalized policy was to have the means available to meet a sudden demand of great size. Either explanation, of course, was tenable but both could not be right.

The popular revulsion from rationalization was shared in some industrial and financial circles. One of the

[1] See pages 19 and 20 of Mr. G. D. H. Cole's *Intelligent Man's Guide Through World Chaos.*

earliest achievements of those who were left with the task of restoring the Royal Mail Steam Packet group to prosperity was that of disintegrating the aggregation. In April 1933 Tweedales and Smalley, textile manufacturers, took steps to prevent the company's being drawn into a combine by the quiet acquisition of its shares in the market.

But was rationalization or the failures of inept rationalizers or the discovered frauds of rationalizers like Hatry and Kreuger the cause, or even a main contributory cause, in the creation of that slough of despond into which Britain and the world entered pell-mell in 1929, and in which the statesmen and financial leaders still flounder like so many mud-larks groping for the scattered pennies of a past prosperity? Some authorities thought not. Dr. Paul Einzig in his *The World Economic Crisis* (first and second editions, 1931 and 1932) was under no doubt of the relative importance of such incidents as the Hatry crash and its effect on investment confidence.

> The monetary causes of the crisis played a prominent part in Great Britain. As London was practically the only free gold market in Europe, she had to stand the full burden of French gold purchases. At the same time the high money rates in New York during the Wall Street boom diverted a considerable portion of foreign balances from London to New York. As a result the Bank of England had to raise its bank balance to 6½ per cent in September 1929, and it was by no means certain whether even this rate would be sufficient to safeguard the Bank's gold reserve. This rising tendency of the Bank Rate was largely responsible for the liquidation on the Stock Exchange popularly attributed to the Hatry Crisis.

There is room for argument as to what was the first cause of the breaking boom, because any selected cause must needs have an antecedent. Mr. Cole has written: " . . . it was first of all in America that the wave of prosperity which had seemed to be sweeping over the world from 1924 to 1929 broke in a cloud of spray on Wall Street", but the American collapse followed the effect on the Wall Street market of the Hatry crash and its consequent liquidation in Great Britain. Professor Irving Fisher in the introduction to *The Stock Market Crash—and After* (1930) examines no fewer than fourteen of the " many causes that have been assigned for the stock market crash of 1929 ". They range from blaming President Hoover for unduly optimistic statements about business conditions which were alleged to have worked the country into a fever of speculation to blaming the bankers for getting everybody into debt, and from blaming Mr. Babson for saying that a crash must come sooner or later to blaming Professor Irving Fisher himself for " always insisting that all was well and talking of prosperity, a new era, and increased efficiency of production ". Professor Fisher does not underrate the effect of the Hatry collapse.

> Few realize to-day (he writes) that the greatest fall of stocks in British history, comparable only with the Baring Panic of 1890, preceded and was an actuating cause of the American panic, and that a coincident fall in Paris and Berlin accompanied the British liquidation. It began with the failure of the banking house of Clarence Hatry in August, followed by his arrest in September and subsequent conviction for a gigantic forgery of stock certificates. This started the British liquidation in London and in New York.

It may be that Professor Irving Fisher overrates and Dr. Einzig underrates the significance of the Hatry crash, but it is more likely that Professor Fisher is sound and that Dr. Einzig a little misleads us by his method of statement —that the monetary factor was not a hidden cause for the effects " popularly attributed " to the Hatry factor but was the cause of Hatry's collapse—a cause precedent, as well as a cause coincident.

Be these things as they may, there is, at any rate, general agreement that the world slump was precipitated by the stock market boom. Either the monetary system stimulated that boom, or the boom perverted for a time the sound working of the monetary system. In either event the monetary system is faced by a grave indictment.

The banks were either the villains or the victims of the initial tragedy. In either case the banks are faced by a grave indictment.

Either the political and financial leaders of the community encouraged that boom to dangerous proportions or they were powerless to check it despite their awareness of its potential dangers. In either case the leaders are faced by a grave indictment.

On whichever prong of the fork they choose by their apologias to be impaled, they must expect either contempt or execration. " These be your gods, O Israel ! "—either men chastised by the nemesis of their own avarice or men scourged by the Frankenstein monsters of their own folly.

Chapter XII

MR. NORMAN AND M. KREUGER

The statesmen, with their economic advisers, and the banking houses, with their intelligence departments staffed by trained economists, either led the community into the morass where it now flounders or failed to prevent a communal landslide into that morass. The catastrophe having happened, they devote their energies in part to discovering explanations for the disaster and in part to devising and debating plans for the return to firm ground of the hosts they nominally lead. Neither in apportioning blame nor recommending restorative action do these experts agree.

The return to gold in 1925 was an error. The refusal again to return to gold is an error. Rigid State economy is an error. Generous State expenditure would be an error. The cause and remedy for our discontents is to be found in the monetary system. The monetary system cannot be either the cause or remedy. Wages must be forced down to decrease costs. Wages must be kept up to increase purchasing power. Prices must be raised and stabilized by restricting either the production or distribution of commodities. The restriction of commodities is the wrong way to raise and stabilize prices. To buy in the cheapest and sell in the dearest market is still the secret of prosperity. There can be no prosperity until such anomalies as "cheap" and "dear" markets have been eliminated by fiscal and trade arrangements and agreements. A currency unlinked to gold is a benefit. A currency unlinked to gold must be artificially "pegged" from day to day because it is not a benefit. The community must save. The community must spend. There must be a rigidly planned economy, for, otherwise, cycles of under- and over-production will continue to imperil civilization. There must be no rigidly planned economy, for that means a static civilization without the necessary stimuli to individual enterprise and an end to aesthetic progress. There must be State control of banking and investment, because uncontrolled banking and investment has led to a riot of over-speculation which has caused the present slump. There must be no State control of banking, because that would lead to stagnation and the proved inability of bureaucratic control to display adaptability in the allocation of credit and capital. There must be an abandonment of the primitive fear which leads men to strive for national self-sufficiency. The state of the world is such that only national self-sufficiency can save the State from eventual disruption by external aggression. The world as an international economic unit, governed by friendly agreements, is an imminent possibility. The variations in standards of living are such that the world as a single international economic unit is an idle dream of a far-flung future. The world as a single economic unit is within sight as a practicable ideal, but the British Empire as a single economic unit can never hope for actuality because of the intense national selfishness of its components. The Empire as a single economic unit is the only hope of the survival of the race, but beyond the confines of the Empire economic unity is impossible because of the intense national selfishness of other races.

For each of these, and many other contradictory assertions, authority can be found. Occasionally the same authority is found preaching a new economic gospel in seeming antithesis to that which he originally enunciated, as when Mr. J. M. Keynes, having taught his disciples that gold as a currency standard is an outworn fetish, begins to teach them that in a return to gold lies salvation.[1] But Mr. Keynes has never been other than frank as to the flux of his own thought. The preface to his *magnum opus* contains the honest, almost naïve, warning:

> As I read through the page proofs of this book I am acutely conscious of its defects. It has occupied me for several years, not free from other occupations, during which my ideas have been developing and changing, with the result that its parts are not all entirely harmonious with one another. The ideas with which I have finished are widely different from those with which I began.

If for a moment one removes that confession from the forefront of *A Treatise on Money* and places it in the forefront of some *Treatise on Surgery*, it becomes obvious that its writer may hope to command respect for his intellectual honesty, but should hardly hope for confidence as an adviser and consultant. One does not from choice submit one's body to a practitioner whose ideas at the end of a régimen or an operation may be widely different from those with which he began. One would naturally be a little chary in accepting the ministrations of the pupils of such a teacher. They might have retained, and insist upon applying, the wrong early ideas. An artist is permitted an early bad manner, but a curative practitioner cannot expect such tolerance.

Influenced by the grave warnings of certain leading economists, the electorate of Great Britain in 1931 approved the fall of the Labour Government because it would not balance the Budget and threatened to allow Britain to be driven from gold. In 1933 the same electorate was invited by leading economists to rebuke the National Government for a pedantic insistence upon

[1] Compare *A Tract on Monetary Reform* (1923) and *The Means to Prosperity* (1933).

balancing the Budget. Such a turn-round in opinion in so short a time would no doubt have caused more amazement had it not been for the precedent of 1931, when a Government was disintegrated in order that its successor might keep the nation to gold, and that successor sought "a doctor's mandate" partly on its achievement in giving to the nation the benefits of a departure from gold.

The phrase "a doctor's mandate" was happily chosen, for the Government which received it acted in the way made famous by Thomas Hood, whose lively verses celebrated a doctor, it will be remembered,

> Whose dose was so pat
> However it acted
> One speech it extracted,
> "Yes, yes," said the Doctor,
> "I meant it for that!"

The antics of such a Government would almost certainly have caused a greater revulsion among the electorate had it not been for the almost universal conviction that, had its predecessor been permitted to continue in existence, not bewildered discomfort but the agonies of final dissolution would have been the fate of the body politic.

One lesson, indeed, the populace learnt well during the years between the slump of 1929 and the present moment—that whether the Budget was balanced at great sacrifice to the individual tax-payer or left unbalanced, as an incident in the political year the Budget was more important than many had thought it when they had looked upon it as a kind of arbiter for another year of the amount of income with which they were to be left and the price which they would have to pay for certain commodities. It was a great advance in the general political education, but it was, unfortunately, not accompanied by a thorough exposition of what balancing a national budget might mean to national wealth and welfare. That exposition was not forthcoming, one suspects, because the pundits themselves were quite in the dark as to all the implications of a given fiscal action.

The frenzy of over-speculation which culminated in the boom of 1928 was followed by the slump of 1929, which produced in Great Britain the crisis of August 1931 and in America the crisis of March 1933. The instinct of the English is to blame the Government of the day for whatever disasters may befall the people. In the middle of 1929 a Conservative Government under Mr. Baldwin had given way to a Labour Government under Mr. Ramsay MacDonald. But the outgoing Conservative administration, with Mr. Churchill at the Exchequer, was generally believed to have conformed in its financial policy to the views held by Mr. Montagu Norman, the Governor of the Bank of England. To him, rather than to the Chancellor of the Exchequer, the praise and blame for a return to the gold standard, at the old parity of the £, in 1925 was, rightly or wrongly, allotted.

For many generations it was an accepted convention that two departments of statecraft were beyond the intelligence of the average man with his average education, whoever and whatever this man and this education were. One was foreign affairs, the other was currency. The convention in the case of foreign affairs weakened but did not disappear during the framing of the Treaty of Versailles. The convention in the case of currency disappeared abruptly in 1931, for only on the assumption that the average man was a master of currency theory could he be awakened to a realization of the plight into which events had led him. The value of the £ became a theme of absorbing interest and the future of gold a public obsession—with, of course, the reservation that these things were thought upon only in the scanty intervals between the pursuit of the usual avocations of securing a livelihood, wooing or keeping a mate, educating children, managing a domicile, searching for health, amusement and happiness.

In order that no doubt might remain as to the competence of the ordinary citizen to grasp the involutions of money a myriad tutors thrust their services upon him. The classic theory of the foreign exchanges as enunciated in the eighteen-eighties by Goschen was re-expounded and upheld or re-expounded and pulverized. The value of a currency fluctuated in relation to other currencies as the indebtedness of one nation to the other changed in balance. If a currency rose too high it became advisable to ship gold in payment of the balance. If gold began to flow out, the rate of interest on discounts was raised, and gold began to flow back from centres where it could not earn so high a return. A high bank rate attracted gold and a low bank rate did not. ("Eight per cent", said the proverb mongers, "brings gold from the moon.") On the amount of gold in the possession of the Central Bank depended the amount of currency available to a community whereby to effect exchanges of goods and services. A safe financial and monetary centre paying a good rate of interest attracted the surplus funds of all other centres. Those funds would be lent at an even better rate of interest, and all would be well.

It was beautifully simple. Unfortunately its simplicity could not be protected from the complications created and introduced by abnormal external circumstances. Funds flowed in and were re-lent. The great danger, so remote in normal times as to be utterly negligible, was that those who had sent in the funds might want to withdraw them at the precise moment that those to whom they had been re-lent could not repay. The original providers of the funds might want to withdraw them hurriedly for one of two reasons or a combination of both—a loss of faith in the centre where the funds had been deposited and an urgent need for their repatriation caused by trouble at home. That combination of both reasons occurred in the mid months of 1931—and the funds had been largely lent to certain foreign centres which could not repay them. When funds are urgently wanted at home to meet a desperate contingency no rate of interest abroad, no matter how attractive, will keep them. In July 1931 gold poured from London, and nothing could stop the flow.

What had caused the urgent need to repatriate the outflowing funds ? What had caused the loss of confidence in London as a centre ? The answers to these two key questions are the explanation of the crisis. Could either circumstance have been foreseen and guarded against ? If so, who failed, and why, to exercise that foresight and to provide the preventive measures ? In the answers to those questions lies the identity of responsibility, the discernment of who should have been " whopped ".

When the frenzy of speculation in Wall Street gave place to the stock market slump in the October of 1929 there were not wanting competent economists to welcome the change. This withdrawal of funds from speculative purposes, it was explained, would benefit trade, for the released capital would go to stimulate genuine trade. The Wall Street slump had been preceded by a fall in commodity prices, which became accentuated after the crash, but, even so, the economic wiseacres were not unduly perturbed.

It was, indeed, what the ancients would have hailed as the grace of God which drove home the realization that the world was seeing no ordinary cycle of alternating boom and slump. Europe had a record crop in 1929, and the blessing which had descended upon the husbandmen inaugurated an era of ruination.

There was no need to buy outside the continental boundaries, and the growers an dhandlers of wheat on the American side found themselves with accumulating and unsaleable stocks. Wheat had joined coffee, rubber and sugar in a crazy world wherein prices were so low that the producer, even if he could sell at all, must sell at a loss. In an earlier day the remedy for this state of affairs would have been cruel and simple. There would have been many bankruptcies; many producers would have gone out of existence; the supply would have narrowed, and, after a sufficient time-lag, prices would again have risen. In a still earlier day the accumulating stocks might have been commandeered and distributed to the needy.

As things were, skilful economic organization prevented bankruptcies and the passing out of production of certain producers. Artificial methods of restriction were applied. The firms remained alive, but their capacity to employ workers and thus distribute consuming power to absorb stocks was weakened. The decline in the purchasing power of the primary producers reacted on all industry, which in turn reacted again on primary production.

By easily discernible stages the slump grew in intensity until the May of 1931, a fateful month. Behind all modern trade stands the system of modern banking, differing in its mode of application in various countries, but based always and everywhere on the ancient principle of the goldsmiths, that as all depositors of wealth will not demand a return of their assets at the same moment, more may be lent in the form of credit than has been borrowed in the form of tangible assets. There was in Austria an institution, the *Creditanstalt*, regarded as one of the world's leading banks and above all suspicion of unsoundness. In May 1931 it suspended payment, and caused such a wave of distrust in the soundness of Central European banking that foreign credits were hastily withdrawn. In

Germany the withdrawal of foreign funds and the exit of capital from so unsound a resting place caused in June the suspension of payments by the Darmstädter-und National Bank. The German Government, with its own currency affected, seeking to prevent the spread of panic runs on German banks, imposed restrictions on bank payments. When the nerves of the community permitted, these restrictions were removed from internal transactions, but foreign creditors had perforce to agree to a long postponement of the repayment of their short-term liabilities.

The situation in Central Europe caused banks to fail in many countries. The menace of runs, which all banks faced, caused an urgent need for all funds lying abroad to be brought home. London suffered heavy withdrawals from this cause. But London was the great lending centre, and her loans to central Europe were known to be frozen. The virtual interruption of all normal exchange business made the future of the English £ doubtful. There was in political office a Labour Government which was thought to be spending wildly above the nation's means, chiefly on social services. London, in short, was embarked upon a financial Rake's Progress. Those who felt no need at home to recall their funds were not disposed to leave them in a centre so shaken from its old stolid trustworthiness.

While the industrial and financial structure of world society was thus shaken, and trade between nations was already threatening within ascertainable time to come to a virtual standstill, the statesmen and economists were still agitating themselves about the capacity of Germany to continue her payments on reparation account, and of the other nations to pay (and in America's case, successfully to collect) their war debts. There was in the mid-June of 1931 no clear-cut, general appreciation of how acute the world crisis had become.

(For some years it has been part of the professional duty of the writer of this book to convey by each outgoing mailboat to New York a survey of conditions and tendencies in Great Britain. Such reports, while necessarily superficial, have, to ensure their continuance, to be honest and conscientious. A passage from a report posted on 14 June 1931 is illuminating as to the then state of mind of many persons in Great Britain. It reads :

> . . . Not even the grave necessity which compelled a change in the German bank rate on Saturday has convinced many British observers that the situation which presents itself is genuine—there is a wide tendency to regard the whole position as having been wilfully manœuvred. By the British public at large, Germany is still not trusted. Informed opinion, however, realizes that apart from the political uncertainties there is an urgent reality about the economic crisis, which affects not only Germany but the whole of central Europe and affects the credit and financial stability of countries the world over. In this crisis the dramatic fall of prices is seen to affect more than the burden which Germany carries in the shape of reparation annuities. This price fall has been such as to bring many nations other than Germany within sight of repudiation ; if not downright and avowed, certainly partial ; to be achieved through special imposts, as has been suggested in Australia. In view of the plight in which such countries as Australia find themselves, the reality of the German difficulty cannot, except by ill-informed and prejudiced minds, be seriously doubted, and if there is no price recovery the re-opening of the whole question of the Young Plan will prove inevitable. The task of the Statesmen becomes, therefore, not merely to deal with the political situation in

> Berlin, but with the economic world-ill of which the political malaise in Germany is but one symptom.
>
> The visit of Dr. Brüning and Herr Curtius to Chequers (the residence of the British Premier) has already had the effect of concentrating British attention upon the German problem, and the intention of Premier MacDonald and Minister Henderson to visit Berlin has convinced the ordinary elector that the question of Germany's capacity to pay is not only urgent but is being treated in such a way that its seriousness cannot be doubted.

Reading that passage two years afterwards I stand, like Clive, " astonished at my own moderation ", but even more astonished at the ingenuousness of my rulers in their concentration upon the German symptom.

For the distrust of Germany which still lingered in so many minds there is some excuse, for the populace had not forgotten the once applauded warning, " They will cheat you yet, those Junkers," and many who were dimly aware that the ship of civilization was in a desperate plight saw in Germany's attitude a reflex of the attitude of the excellent mariner in the popular, and much broadcast, song :

> The mate said : That's O.K. with me ;
> The shipwreck suits me to a T.
> I owe ten bob to Captain Brown,
> And I'll have enough to pay him
> As the ship goes down.

It was, indeed, war debts and reparations which filled the mind of the ordinary reader of popular newspapers, rather than the gravity of the real crisis, and there was a tendency among politicians and expounders of the mysteries of high finance and international trade to imply, if not flatly to state, that once war debts and reparations were abandoned, the god of prosperity would be again in his heaven and all would be right with the world.)

The whole tangled history of German reparations had been eloquent of the inability of economic specialists to justify their alleged importance. The breach in the original unity of the Conference of Paris, when Mr. Keynes abandoned his official status to utter a trumpet warning of folly in powerful places, had a little shaken most men's faith in those negotiating his new world for him, but the sequence of events after that Conference even more forcibly shook his childish faith in experts.

The Reparations Commission of 1921 had fixed the payments due from Germany at £6,600,000,000, equal to thirty annual payments of £220,000,000. In 1924 the Dawes Plan was evolved, which changed the average annual payments to £125,000,000. In 1929 the Young Plan made the annual average payments £100,000,000. From 1921 to 1929 the payments were shared in 92 parts thus: France 52, Britain 22, Italy 10 and Belgium 8. From 1929-32 a further allocation was made in 230 parts, France 130, Britain 55, Italy 25, and Belgium 20. From 1932-36 the allocation was to have been in 276 parts, France 156, Britain 66, Italy 30 and Belgium 24.

On 8 July 1932 these various changes of demand culminated in the cancellation of reparations at Lausanne, leaving Germany with an obligation to make an eventual payment of £150,000,000 by means of bonds as from the year 1935. The bonds were deposited with the Bank for International Settlements—created in 1929 by the Committee of Experts on Reparations and under the inspiration and force of Mr. Montagu Norman—and may be marketed from 1935-47, under certain safeguards for German credit, at a price not below 90. They carry interest at 5 per cent, with 1 per cent amortization, which will extinguish them in thirty-seven years. This agreement so to end reparations in their old form became known, by a magnificent stroke of irony, as the Gentlemen's Agreement.

But the agreement of Lausanne would not have been possible had not the rising apprehension of 1931, the growing realization that the world crisis was a world crisis indeed, caused President Hoover to offer to his country's debtors a twelve months' moratorium on debt payments. Oddly enough, to English eyes, this offer was almost rendered abortive by the refusal of France to accept it immediately and gracefully. If the burden of war debts and reparations was the main obstacle to world recovery, such a moratorium—with, perhaps, an implied promise that it would be endlessly renewed—was surely a relief at which to snatch gratefully, and the peasant-like fear of France that she might loose on the deal a short-sighted piece of avariciousness. Why—Britain herself was quite cheerfully prepared to lose £11,000,000 on the deal, and had never since the Balfour Note striven to make any personal profit on the difference between the debts paid to her and the amount she paid to her creditor !

President Hoover, it was true, insisted still that war debts and reparations had in American eyes no relationship to each other, but to the knowing European this only meant that President Hoover was dressing his economic wisdom in a camouflage domino for the benefit of his awkward and economically unsophisticated Middle West. The one year moratorium presaged an eventual review of the whole creditor-debtor position. The major powers of Europe would forgive Germany a large part of her trespasses and in due course have their own trespasses forgiven—not from any magnanimity on either side, but because it had become obvious that a policy of Shylockry was a particularly painful policy of self-destruction.

This happy English viewpoint was more than a little myopic. Although by 1932 the agreement of Lausanne had been concluded and Reparations eliminated, America was not prepared to renew the moratorium. In the December of that year a war debt payment was called for. England, protesting that it would be world suicide to pay, paid—and protesting that the payment was a capital repayment only, which should not fall into the Budget of the year, contrived to admit it to that Budget. Experts had said that the departure from the gold standard in 1931 would be the ruin of England. Experts also said that the war debt payment could not without crushing effect be found from the annual Budget. Experts then hastily pointed out that the departure from gold was a rich blessing and that the accounting in the Budget of the debt payment was a master-stroke of financial management.

> However it acted
> One speech it extracted,
> " Yes, yes," said the Doctor,
> " I meant it for that ! "

One of the simplest methods of explaining why Britain was driven from gold is to revert to the classic theory of the exchanges and to say that she was spending more than she made. Her bill for imports was more than her account for exports. Now, a war debt payment is in reality a gigantic invisible import—an import of " nothing " costing the amount of the payment. Such an invisible import by all theory should leave the country, and its currency, weaker than before. Actually the payment of December 1932 left the £ sterling stronger. After the departure from gold in 1931 the Legislature created the Exchange Equalization Fund with total resources of £175,000,000 (borrowing powers of £150,000,000 and the remnant of the old Dollar Fund of £25,000,000) to support the £. The debt payment of 1932 was followed by a period when this facility had to be used not to keep the £ from falling away to lower and lower values, but to prevent it from rising. In 1931 the bogey had been a falling currency; in 1933 the embarrassment was a rising currency.

In 1931 the Fund had been envisaged as a prop, in 1933 it was being used as a ground anchor. Its devisors had, of course, meant it for that.

The economic effects of war debts differ not at all in kind from those of reparations. If a customer is paying old debts he obviously has not the same means wherewith to buy new goods. If a creditor community is receiving large payments—that is, calls on goods and services—from some helot debtor it does not call to the same extent upon the goods and services of its own nationals. In the case of payments in kind this is easily grasped, but between payments in kind and any other form of payment there is in eventual effect no difference at all.

Again, if a creditor expects a debtor to fulfil old obligations from current earnings, it is obvious folly to take all steps to prevent that debtor from having any current earnings. To insist upon payments from the debtor and then by tariffs and other devices to limit the debtor's trading capacity is to embark at once upon two self-contradictory policies.

From one angle it may be said that to the creditor nation, debts fully paid had exactly the same effect on the internal economic life as machines—they meant more wealth for less effort. Either the effect of that wealth had to be distributed evenly in the shape of greater leisure for the same standard of living or in a higher standard for the same amount of effort, or it would mean total leisure for some and none extra for others. That in its turn would mean a changing incidence of purchasing power with all the deducible effects upon the relations of community to State and of individual citizen to individual citizen. If Fritz and John and Jonathan consume a given number of units of production, and Jonathan insists that Fritz shall go short and that John shall not increase his consumption, the result is an accumulation in Jonathan's storehouses. Either Jonathan must arrange for the consumption of that accumulation or his own productive faculty will itself become an embarrassment. There will be a state of glut, even while there is a shortage of consumption among those who would gladly consume.

Consumption will never be effected while the old superstition remains that before a man or a woman is allowed to consume he or she must earn the right to consume by a personal production gauged by a standard which new rates of production have rendered obsolete. Consumption can never be effected while national economic organization is based upon, or chiefly affected by, local vested interests in profit-making and job-filling which prohibit distribution based on available wealth.

What most of the supporters of capitalism[1] have never realized, though it has been insisted upon by not a few commentators, is that the system, in so far as it is a system, has survived by means of periodical fits of generosity, when its products have been virtually given away. Company Law, that is to say, does not insist upon shareholders having presented to them a Profit Account, but a Profit and Loss Account. Unless the imminent possibility of loss is envisaged, the tolerance of fluctuating profit becomes irrational as a system of rewards for enterprise. The cycle of boom and slump in industry, which until our own day was taken more or less for granted as a necessity to trade, really meant the occurrence of periods when high rewards for some forms of trading service were

[1] Of which, strangely as it may read, the present writer is one.

balanced by low rewards for other forms of the same service, or even by " drawbacks " by the community in the shape of losses to the entrepreneur, which always meant, broadly speaking, that the community was consuming goods which had " cost " it less than they had " cost " the makers and distributors to provide.

What has always irked labour under that system has been the fact that whereas workers are penalized during these periods of forced generosity, they are not admitted to the rising benefits of the preceding and succeeding times of boom. What has caused many employers to oppose systems of profit-sharing has been the fact that organized labour, while willing to share in rising profits, cannot bring itself to share in falling profits, by abandoning a trade union minimum rate of wage when " times are bad ", to which Labour has replied that even in times of boom its share of the gain, judged by human needs, has been too small to permit of further diminution.

By a paradox, times of slump occur when the community is sated with products. If between them a nation's producers and its debtors have produced more than the community is prepared to consume, production must slow down if consumption cannot be further stimulated. In a simple and primitive community the very local glut which caused the diminution of production could be used to tide over the producers in temporary idleness until their faculties were again demanded. (That, in effect, was the secret of Joseph's statecraft.) The same application of the temporary surplus could be made in a complex community if there were sufficient discipline to overcome the sectional selfishnesses and fears.

Such a discipline is hard to attain even in the confines of a nation ; it is impossible in a world of nations. The consequence is that when those who foresee the economic effects of the collection of reparations and war debts in a world of national trade barriers enunciate their foresight, means cannot be found to prevent the foreseen chain of cause and effect. Owners of capital resent and resist taxation devised to adjust wealth as between class and class, they resent and resist diminution of personal gains from dividends and interest. Workers resent and resist the disappearance of their jobs, and those who are left without work ask for a standard of maintenance equal to their abandoned standard of living, which is refused because its provision would mean a further changing of the incidence of wealth as between citizen and citizen, class and class, and because such a method of pooling and re-distributing national income during a period of diminished production would result in some other pocket of humanity (called a competing nation) ousting the pioneer nation from all markets and thus depriving it of its means of re-entry to the expected era of returning production. All must continue to produce and to produce at a low cost for as long as possible, because none without the simultaneous action of the others dares to distribute present surplus by any new test of the "right to demand".

What is—and what was—that "right to demand" in the eyes of the older economists? The debate has filled generations of time and acres of printed paper, for it is the interminable argument about the theory of value, and it has never been wholly freed from a confusion of ethics with economics. "Discussion of the ethics of value", says Professor Cannan in his *Review of Economic Theory*, "is much older than discussion of the economics of value. . . . The beginnings, at any rate, of the transition from ethical to economic discussion are perceptible in the seventeenth century." It is a transition which has not yet resolved itself, for to the economist's explanation of the cause of values, that is of the differing rights to demand among the community, the exerciser of such a right instinctively opposes a set of ethical values. It may be economically clear why a stock-jobber in five minutes can acquire more rights to demand goods and services from the community than the producer, who gives value to the shares in which the jobber deals, acquires in five hours—it may, perhaps, be economically justified that this difference in reward should be as it is—but economic lucidity does not prevent the producer from feeling that such a system of rewards is ethically wrong. It may be economically clear why a creditor nation having lent a measure of goods and services at one period can reclaim goods and services to a far greater measure at a later period, but again economic clarity does not prevent the debtors from denouncing as ethically wrong a system which not only permits but causes such a discrepancy between loan and repayment measured in terms of actualities as apart from the fluctuating token whose nominal value as written in the original bond has not changed.

If a nation borrows goods and services worth, let us say, £1,000,000,000 when the £ is worth 4·86 dollars' worth of gold, and has to repay goods and services equal to the same amount of gold when gold is costing more in £'s, the nominal repayment will be a far larger amount of £'s—gold being the measure of goods and services. The transaction can be viewed as one in which more goods and services have been repaid than were borrowed, for the debtor is being compelled to give back more than he borrowed. But when he protests, he is told that goods and services are not the denominator of the debt, and that in the token measure the amount is unchanged. Ten thousand tomes may explain why this apparent injustice comes about without easing the sense of injustice.

If the multiplex bargains of humanity are seen as a ragged and unorganized pooling of products and services, the existing method, whether applied to immediate return for work contributed or to delayed payment for work or services contributed in the past, consists in a man withdrawing from that pool a personal share assessed on the arbitrary value placed on his contribution at the time he made it. But that arbitrary share is assessed in terms of tokens, which may themselves fluctuate in value between the creation of a right to withdraw from the pool and the moment of its being exercised. The effect is that no matter what surplus of products and services may be in the pool, none may withdraw from it until he has established a right based on the value of a contribution (or, in the case of a dole or of local relief, based on the value of somebody's contribution made over to him for his use) and no withdrawal is guaranteed to be of equal value in goods and services to the right when established.

Irrational as such a system may seem, there is a defence for it. The pool is no simple aggregation of means to life upon which the world community amicably draws. It is a pool created by innumerable contributions produced under innumerable variations of conditions. If men drew upon a world stock of goods and services without first being compelled to establish a right through some contribution of their own, all would tend to draw more freely and to contribute less regularly. The alternative to some such system as now exists is a dictatorship able to say, " To each according to his needs, from each according to his ability,"—but who is to select the dictator ? Even if a world of warring national traditions and different standards of civilization were to compose itself sufficiently to select such a dictator, by what means could he ensure that from each would come contributions according to ability, or that withdrawals would not exceed actual need ?

If, as is freely charged, the existing system of trade into and out of the ragged pool of world possessions is " rigged " by greedy men, what guarantee can there be that under the alternative system the same greedy men would not " rig " the dictatorial system of " indentation according to need " and " requisition according to ability ", since both need and ability are vague matters subject to human assessment ?

Irrational as the existing system may seem, there is, I say, a defence for it. Even were there not, the system was in being from the moment that the Treaty of Versailles began its domination of European economic relations. Its vagaries were implicit, and were deducible. A debt contracted at one date for settlement at another date in a given currency was liable to represent a different volume of calls upon humanity when paid from that which it represented when contracted. The real charge against the managing men, the statesmen, bankers and economists, is not that between 1920 and 1933 they tolerated and even clung to a faulty system—any system in operation would be faulty—but that they failed to provide adequate protection against the operation of known faults, and even by a particular policy aggravated those faults.

In a Europe baffled and depressed by the changed value in realities of its reparations and war debts stood London as the leading financial centre, with calls upon it for the repatriation of funds lent to it but unable to bring home the funds which it had lent to Central Europe. By what ineptitude had such a situation been allowed to arise ?

Banking experience, it must be reiterated, teaches that all depositors will not make a sudden and simultaneous demand for the return of their deposits and that all debtors will not make a sudden and simultaneous default. Still more remote in recorded experience is a situation wherein both these improbables occur together. But such —speaking with allowable exaggeration—was the situation in 1931. Why had the frozen funds been lent to doubtful debtors like Austria, Hungary and Germany ?

Was it not true that the very countries from which it was proving impossible to call home to London the lent credits were those which were calling home their short-term deposits from London ?

The answers to both questions lie in what for convenience we may call " Normanism ", that is, the central banking policy inaugurated and conducted by Mr. Montagu Norman.

" Mr. Norman ", says his biographer, Mr. Einzig, " has often been criticized as a man who placed international considerations above domestic considerations, and who paid too much attention to helping foreign countries to recover their stability, and too little to helping British industries to attain prosperity." Such a criticism is the product of ignorance, so phrased, and Mr. Einzig is guilty of no perversion in his phrasing of it. To a man bred in the traditions of international banking, it is not possible for British industries to attain prosperity unless and until foreign countries recover their stability. Mr. Norman's policy of helping foreign countries was merely the common-sense policy of any business house in " carrying " a customer over a period of hard times in order that his custom may not be irrevocably lost by his premature and unnecessary failure.

" Another criticism against Mr. Norman's policy ", says his biographer, " was that it was inspired by political rather than by economic motives." Here, again, the criticism so phrased is redolent of ignorance, ignorance of the very meaning of the word politics. Politics is the science and art of government. No central banker can be expected to ignore the problems which we roughly group under the term " world politics ", for upon the sound conduct of world politics his work depends for its success. If funds are lent to an ex-enemy State to help her to restore her economic fabric, the motive is obviously that of a desire to see her re-established as a sound economic entity. To men charged with the profitable use of funds left in their care—profitable, that is, to the whole community, including necessarily the owners of those funds and the bankers directing their use—the economic factor must dictate the political aspect of the world which such men view.

The primary need of the banker is simple. It is to find for funds customers who will use them fruitfully. Capital is most fruitfully used when all nations prosper. The instinct of a trained banking mind is to assist distressed customers back to prosperity, for their recovery will augment the prosperity of those customers already free from distress. No more subtle motive than this is needed to explain satisfactorily Mr. Norman's policy in lending generously to Germany, Austria, Hungary, Bulgaria, and Danzig, and (later) to Belgium, Italy, Poland, Greece, and Rumania.

> One of the main justifications of Mr. Norman's policy is its success during the period between 1923 and 1929. It resulted in stabilization in Austria, Belgium, Hungary, Italy and a number of other countries. In 1923, when he first embarked upon his gigantic task, conditions in Europe were desperate . . . indeed it appeared as if Europe were heading towards financial, economic, political and social disaster. It was the constructive policy pursued by Mr. Norman that has checked the process of decay, and that has set Europe on her legs again. . . . Within a few years he had created stability all over the continent. He removed the danger of collapse in many countries, and those whose currencies actually collapsed he assisted in establishing new monetary systems. He granted credits providing a breathing-space that enabled Governments to balance their

> budgets, and to restore their credit at home and abroad. He paved the way for an international flow of funds, thus enabling countries which had suffered through inflation to reconstruct their working capital and their savings.

The last few lines of that panegyric by Mr. Einzig might almost have been written of Ivar Kreuger, and the truth is that the Swedish fraud and the English banker were both between 1923 and 1931 endeavouring to achieve the same object—the restoration of the fallen fortunes of smitten countries by the loan of other people's money, at a profit, but with a view to the future benefit rather than the immediate return. Both were thwarted by the onslaught of depression in 1929.

Mr. Norman's international policy, it may be said, failed, but it failed for reasons and causes beyond human control. It did not wholly fail, for the restoration which was achieved by the stricken countries between 1923 and 1929 gave to Europe a resiliency which enabled it to withstand the shock of the great depression as it could not have been withstood lacking that restoration. In Russia after the revolution there was a return to barbarism which in some areas reached the pitch of cannibalism : there has been no such return in Europe during the present depression. There might well have been had not the stricken areas been bolstered up by the support of international funds directed through London in the six years when " Normanism " was applied to the post-war world.

But the policy failed. Why did it fail ? Very largely because the technique of internationalism in finance was incomplete. In textbooks and financial newspapers and the serious Reviews it is the habit to talk of nations as if they were single entities. " The trade of Germany ", " the indebtedness of Austria ", " the adverse balance of France ", " Europe's trade with America ", are all familiar phrases. Actually no such entities exist. The trade of Germany comprises innumerable bargains by innumerable men with innumerable other men in various countries. The indebtedness of Austria is a single debt only so far as it is a State debt ; the commercial indebtedness is again comprised in innumerable debtor relations with individual creditors. When Austrian funds are suddenly called home from London they are called by frightened men acting as frightened men, not by a State acting as a political entity. When British funds cannot be called home from Austria it is not because a State refuses to return them, but because a myriad men who have had the use of parts of those funds cannot find the wherewithal to repay.

Trade is conducted, as life is lived, man by man—but the collection of funds to lend and the gathering of those funds to re-lend introduces two " bottle-necks ". A central bank is fashioned to collect and divert credits hither and thither. The banks which lend and the banks which borrow are responsible one to the other in the creditor-debtor relation. But behind each, in the final analysis, is the mob of lenders and borrowers whose claims to goods and services are being temporarily transferred from one set of hands to another. Because Smith in Manchester does not chose to exercise his claims, Schmidt in Hamburg may exercise them, and because Schmidt in Hamburg exercises them Straus in Berlin may have claims to lend to Jones in Bootle, and Straus may call home his claims before Schmidt is ready to repay the claims borrowed from Smith. In the resultant unpleasantness Jones of Bootle may well wonder why he was not lent the temporarily unwanted claims of Smith of Manchester, instead of their being diverted through Hamburg and Berlin. The short answer to Jones is that the claims upon goods and services must go with the minimum of delay to where they are *immediately* wanted, and that he has no cause for personal complaint since he is repaid, in default of Schmidt's remittance, by somebody else's temporarily unwanted claims. The world, in short, is larger than the islands which contain Smith of Manchester and Jones of Bootle.

There enters another " but ". In the islands which contain Smith and Jones, Jones and Smith have some measure of control over the social and economic rule under which they live and trade. The idle claims that are temporarily passed elsewhere pass under control of those over whom Smith and Jones have no influence. The idle claims of Smith may be lent to a Herr Schmidt who uses them, either directly or indirectly, to Smith's hurt. Smith may be a maker of matches and Schmidt a maker of match-making machinery. The use of Smith's idle claims may enable Schmidt to make machinery for Russia which will pour cheap matches into Smith's own markets, to his embarrassment. Or the lent claims of Straus may eventually help a British maker of match machinery whose renewed activity will so injure Schmidt that he will not be able to repay his debt. Or Schmidt and his fellow-borrowers, from some psychological urge not suspected in them, may turn wilful defaulters, and the bank which " bottle-necked " the loans at first distribution may not be strong enough to meet the claim of the creditor bank, and its myriad of claim-lenders, on behalf of these defaulters. Or Schmidt and his friends may be honest, but the State under which they live may have to prohibit the export of foreign exchange.

It is, one sees, an extension of the position surveyed in an earlier chapter with regard to usury. Once the relation of borrower to lender passes from the personal contact and becomes a matter of interveners trading with other interveners, the old securities as to good use, in either an ethical or a financial sense, are ended. The psychological factors and the economic factors and the political factors become too many and too subtly interwoven for the human mind to grasp the resultant complex for use as data for safe deduction as to the trend of the future. The imponderables outweigh the ponderables.

The end of the matter is that the central banker, as such, must confess himself unable to see more than a step of his way. He must, if he be honest, say, as Mr. Norman said at the Bankers' dinner in 1932:

> For most of us, "One step enough for me." That is as far as, on the whole, I can say. The difficulties are vast, the forces so unlimited, so novel, the precedents are so lacking, that I approach this whole subject not only in ignorance but in humility. It is too great for me. I am willing to do my best.

In other words, the pose of the witch-doctor with the infallible remedy and the right to smell out the heretics of his tribe must be abandoned. Humility and a pledge to do his best must replace the austere haughtiness of the master craftsman who has hitherto stood above and beyond suspicion of bewilderment in his craft.

But—and here, for many in all camps of thought, is the rub—the "best" that is proffered may not satisfy, and yet the profferer remains irremovable. The humility may be genuine, but the convention of the tribe may still demand that the humble confessor of bewilderment must be treated as sacrosanct.

By common consent the head of a great Central Bank has more real power over the daily lives of a community than almost any other occupier of office. A General whose plan of campaign fails—whether from ineptitude in conception or misfortune in execution—is removed. He is "Stellenbosched"—"dégommed". The Admiral who fails may not, like Byng, be shot *pour encourager les autres*, but he is at least susceptible to the decisions of a Court of Enquiry. The Central Banker, however, is re-elected by a small body of persons after nomination by a caucus of his fellow directors, and he neither offers nor is called upon to offer any explanation or defence of his policy. At no point of his working year is he subject to examination, as is a Minister of State. His smile or frown is so potent that those working in close association with him, even though outside his own organization, are not tempted to sacrifice the one or invite the other. Particularly in the face of a political agitation for a complete change of system to something which they conceive to be worse are they tempted to remember when they look upon the Governor and directors of the Central Bank that all within the existing system must hang together lest all hang separately.

What, it may be asked, is the grievance? Is it suggested that because a man or body of men trained in the delicate work of banking has failed to prevent a world crisis beyond the prevention of any single group of experts he or they must be replaced by others of the same kind? Is it suggested that they should be replaced by men ignorant of banking? Is it suggested that the system which they operate, and which has evolved itself from the needs of the expanding community, should be jettisoned and replaced by some "paper" system devised by theorists completely ignorant of the complications arising from the diversified human relations which constitute the world of trade and banking? Is it even suggested that the "best" which is proffered with such winning humility could be bettered by another chosen because he represents an opposite school of banking thought?

All these things have been suggested from various quarters, but all that is suggested here is that the existing situation and the comment upon it by Mr. Norman is yet another proof of the failure of the expert, and that, in the light of such failure, the imposition upon the community which suffers from it of the need to impose unquestioning confidence in the experts who have failed is irrational. It is also suggested that the trend which has led to failure may rightly be suspected of being wrong, and that progression in the same direction may be expected to worsen rather than to repair the ills which have been created.

That tendency has been away from the small unit and the personal responsibility of the individual citizen to his own affairs towards " rationalization " into large units and the delegation of responsibility to men who have already reached a position where the mastery of the large-scale operations committed to their charge eludes the scope of the human mind.

In finance, as in politics, the admitted benefits of large-scale operations and internationalism have had to be bought by the sacrifice of satisfactions and fulfilments only possible under less complicated systems demanding fewer delegations by the individual citizen to " experts " and elected or nominated persons.

If the aim of government is to secure to the individual the highest potentiality of happiness and " the full life ", opinion must obviously divide upon the question of what constitutes the full life. The suggestion here made is that whatever it is, one thing it certainly is not—it is not a life in which the material circumstances of the individual pass almost entirely from his own control, in which the security of his livelihood rests not upon the exercise of his ability but upon that of monopoly controllers remote from him, in which the conduct of his home is dictated largely by bureaucrats equally remote from him, and in which his very amusements are dictated by the social theories of one group of remote persons and the ability to maintain a communal material standard of another group of remote persons.

Chapter XIII

THE NEW TYRANTS

There have been many glib definitions of man. " Man is a tool-making animal." " Man is a political animal." " Glory to man in the highest, for man is the master of things." It is possible—I do not know, for I have not looked—that a volume like Benham's *Book of Quotations* would give many additions to these three aphorisms selected from the rag-bag of memory. One aspect of man may be displayed in a similar aphorism—man is a managing animal, a contriver who delights to control his contrivances.

If any deny that premise, whatever point or direction this book has is for him fallacious, for the direction of this book is towards the conclusion that the freedom to contrive and manage has been withdrawn from the mass of men and monopolized by the few. With the beginnings of centralized government over wide areas the tendency began; with the dawn of the machine age it was quickened; to-day it has become almost intolerable.

The more a man has by circumstances to delegate the primary functions and selections of life, the further is he removed from happiness. The more remote his delegates are from him in the exercise of their functions, the more removed is he from contentment. The exercise of functions by experts may make for material betterment and that vague state of being known as efficiency, but does not necessarily make for general happiness.

Allied to the right to manage one's own life is the right to possess property, and to control it. A personal possession has a quality of satisfaction-rendering which is not inherent in a communally possessed equivalent. Even the mystics who strive to attain to a state beyond the lust to possess admit that the pleasure-giving quality of possessions is a temptation to be conquered by stern and persistent discipline. In possession is the tradition of the human race. The human objection to the man with great possessions is not that he possesses but either that he possesses beyond his rightful share, and so prevents others from having the satisfactions of ownership, or that he uses the power which his possessions bestow upon him to the detriment of his fellows.

If any deny that personal possession is a source of happiness this book is, again, a mere fandangle, for the direction of this book is towards the conviction that the ownership of property in the real sense of the term has been made progressively more difficult to the citizen and that, despite admitted advantages from collective ownership, happiness and content have declined with the progress from individual to collective ownership. The effect upon the citizen of a centralized government undertaking an ever-widening range of functions and that of limited liability in the proprietorship of enterprises is the same—it gives him a nominal share in ownership without the actual responsibility and sense of possession of real ownership. It tends to make him the puppet of his own delegates, in the selection of whom he has only a nominal choice, since large electorates, whether of political voters or company shareholders, must in practice confine their selection of representatives to a choice between candidates nominated by a caucus.

In finance the use of a citizen's money has tended through the past century to pass further and further from his cognizance and is quite beyond his own sense of responsibility. It is directed by the agents of his agent's agents to uses which the owner can neither trace nor comprehend. This means that the ownership of money—representing calls upon the goods and services of mankind—is utterly divorced from personal responsibility. It is lent for what it will fetch, and not for what it will do. To such a state of divorcement has ownership from control and responsibility come that—to use our earlier example—the embittered head of a Purity League may by her personal savings be helping to subsidize a camouflaged brothel. (When quite recently it was discovered that the Bank of England was interested in the ground site of a certain celebrated café much patronized by gaiety-seekers, the jest went freely round the City of London that here was a pleasing example of the oldest bank subsidizing the oldest profession. The Bank was obviously able to hold its hand from inconvenient foreclosure by virtue of means whose eventual control may well have been the possession of persons to whom the café and its clientele would seem abhorrent.) Similarly a man of strong political convictions may be putting out his money for eventual use for purposes in direct opposition to those convictions. A firm believer in the policy of squeezing post-war Germany "until the pips squeak"—oh, pleasant, Christian phrase of yesteryear!—may actually have contributed to the Norman policy of rehabilitating the object of his vindictiveness. A trade union adulator of Leninism may, through union funds left with bankers, have contributed to anti-Soviet adventures of the most vigorous kind. Protesters against low wage rates for one body of workers may have been responsible for the imposition of low wage rates upon another body of workers.

If any hold that this divorce of responsibility from ownership is but a light price to pay for the enormous material benefits which come from centralized control and direction of investment funds, he is entitled to his opinion.

On a balance of disadvantages argument is too often futile. But it is one of the many murky purposes of this book to imply that such a price is not so light as it may superficially seem, and that from such a divorcement many evils spring which are not of very obvious parentage.

But it cannot be denied that communal possession and control of certain assets and powers and the delegation of function and responsibility to the chosen specialist is the very beginning of civilized life ; it is the step which leads from barbarism to culture. In social and political governance, as in economics, such a trend marks the development of man from savagery to civilization. Even were it not so, in a world of trading men and nations now so many centuries old, linked by so many relations from the past, unit to unit and part to part, attuned to habits of interdependence by the cultivation of appetites which only continued interdependence can satisfy, and divorced from any central authority whose dictated discipline is freely and generally accepted—as was the mystical authority of the old religions—it is not possible to contemplate a return to simplicity, if for no other reason, at least because the transition would be more terrible to endure than a continuance in the present trend away from simplicity.

By the failure to understand and control certain economic forces at the time of their creation and release—the power potentialities of steam, electricity and the internal combustion engine, for example—mankind was whirled into a new mode of life willy-nilly. Those observers who discerned the effect upon human happiness of that mode and its subsequent developments, as Ruskin did in *Fors Clavigera* and Butler in *Erewhon* as Wells did in his early romances, as Cobbett did with unusually clear vision, were derided as cranks or simpletons. They were, indeed, simpletons, but only in the sense of men who espoused the simple as against the complex, who looking at happiness saw the truth of the ancient rune that " it is not given for goods or gear, but for The Thing "—whatever " The Thing " may be. They were not simpletons in the other sense. They did not imagine, as their deriders appear to have imagined, that an increase in man's material possessions contrived at a time when avarice had become the test of a man's right to social applause and honour somehow changes the temperament and alters the inherited traditions of the mass of men, leaving the powerful few to retain both unaltered. They did not imagine that a sense of injustice as to the sharing of benefits disappears if the smaller, and supposedly unjust share, is increased in quantity and not in proportion. They did not imagine that an abrupt change of environment can in a generation or two generations induce contentment by shaping the psychology formed in other circumstances to the new surroundings. They did not imagine that men who had resented tyranny under a known tyrant would cease to resent it under remote tyrants, and would serve complacently in an unnatural mode of life merely because that mode had substituted new discontents for old, had removed the fear of famine and the presence of chronic ill nourishment and under-clothing only to replace these things by the fear of the degradation of pauperism at recurring intervals and the presence of created appetites with satisfactions perpetually within sight but generally out of reach.

The economic simpletons were disregarded. A larger body of economic simpletons than that represented by such " intellectuals " as Ruskin, Mathew Arnold[1] and Samuel Butler earned even more violent derision. The early machine wreckers, the Luddites, were patently

[1] It was Arnold who first derided enthusiasm for a quickened transport which merely took its users more speedily from a dull and illiberal life in one place to a dull and illiberal life in another.

stupid men whose economic ignorance was but little less resented than their violence. But Luddism in the early days of the twentieth century took another form—a refusal to expend full effort in working the machines in order to keep work in hand either for the employed workers or their fellows. "Ca' canny" was but a negative form of Luddism. The case against workers who preached and practised ca' canny was sound. The lower the cost of an article, the lower the selling price, and the lower the price the greater the demand. To refuse to work machines to their fullest advantage was wilfully to limit demand, and so to limit work.

A wonderful example of the misjudgement of the economic simpletons among the workers was found in the history of such additions to human betterment as type-setters. The linotype machine, for example, which did the work of the hand setter at far greater speed, was feared by compositors as a threat to their employment. In practice its capacity to set type cheaply and quickly caused so great an expansion of demand for printed matter that it—and inventions of its kind—created work in vast quantities. It is true that by the time the linotype was introduced organized labour was more than a little wary of the use of machines to benefit their owners without consequent betterment of their workers. Trade union rates of pay for piece-work prevented the cheapness of printing from benefiting only the owners of the machines and the readers of print, and kept some of the benefit for the workers—but here again was a wonderful argument against any negative form of Luddism. Because of rigid trade union rates, costs for many projected ventures were too high to permit the enterprises from coming to birth—other ventures because of heavy costs had to confine their activities to a narrow field. If printing were cheaper through the readiness of men to set type at a low reward at machines of great setting speed, many more periodicals would be launched and work created for typesetters; unemployed typesetters would not be a charge on trade union funds; the real wages of all would thus be higher.

This type of argument still persists. It is a sound argument in certain circumstances. It is not, however, valid in all its applications. What the economic simpletons foresaw when they invented and pursued the policy of ca' canny was exactly what any student of new power forms must see—that if a labour-saving device is invented it saves labour, and the saving in labour must have one of certain effects. Either it enables the same volume of goods at the same cost to be produced by the use of fewer hands, or more goods at lower cost are produced by the same number of hands. If the demand for the product is elastic, it is better that more goods at lower cost should be produced, but as this means more profit (under a profit system) for the enterprise, that profit is susceptible to a labour bargain. Men may rightly demand—though they may not get—a share of the increase in return for their toil even if their toil has not increased. If the demand for a product is inelastic and the machine merely displaces human labour, either the machine must "carry" the dispossessed workers or there must be a transition period for them until they find other labour during which they will be a charge on somebody else's labour, whether as machine pensioners or as looters of other's earnings. In any event, the advent of the machines changes the whole economic situation, and the presence of the workers affected is still a factor in costing, whether direct or indirect.

The treatment accorded to the original Luddites, the early "aesthetic" protesters against machinery, such as Ruskin and Wordsworth (who is said to have sought a good railway investment while he protested against the desecration of the landscape by locomotives and their trains) and the ca' canny trade unionists was that of contemptuous impatience with ignorant and greedy men. Either they were blind to their own eventual interests or they wished to preserve certain local amenities or a certain familiar culture at the expense of the world's material betterment. Industrialists tutored by economists and statesmen tutored by economists held that " production, production and ever increased production " was the secret of man's advance from lower to higher standards of life.

Not until the post-war years did the attitude change and not really until the whole effects of this blind concentration upon production had helped to create the recurring crises of 1929-33 did what one may call official opinion condone and even advocate ca' canny as an acceptable doctrine of economic salvation. The short day and the short working week were either reluctant concessions to pressure from organized labour or the amusing experiments of progressive employers with a whim for displaying philanthropy in that form rather than in the form of free libraries or playing fields. It was never even explained to a bewildered proletariat that cartellization with its voluntary restriction of output in certain markets and such experiments as the Stevenson rubber restriction scheme were but manifestations of the philosophy, unformulated but held, of Luddism, ca' canny, and Erewhonism.

In 1933 there came the complete reversal of " official opinion "—that is, the opinion of men in high political office held and uttered either after instruction by professed economists or without immediate and violent contradiction by the whole body of such—in the shape of admissions in the English House of Commons that technological unemployment must be regarded as a permanent or very long term factor and in America by the drafting of the Thirty Hour Week Bill. An observer must be forgiven if in this progress he sees a sign that the opinion of the expert is apt to lag behind the conclusion of the non-expert, and that a truth dimly discerned and wrongly applied by the masses of the workers comes to be clearly discerned and applied by his academic betters only after a very long time-lag.

Delivering his Presidential Address to Section F of the British Association in 1931 Professor Edwin Cannan, Emeritus Professor of Political Economy in the University of London, gave it as his opinion that politicians " for the most part follow the economists with a sixty or seventy years' lag ". This is a pregnant dictum. If it is true, the applications of economic thought which are so tardy cannot be helpful. The economist is primarily under the disability that his conclusions must be derived from observed data, and by the time the conclusion is reached and enunciated the data from which it was drawn may have passed from the realm of current actuality to that of recorded history. A proposed remedy might thus—indeed must almost always—be too late for the malady it proposes to cure. If there is a further time-lag, on Professor Cannan's evidence, of sixty to seventy years before the remedy when advised is applied, its futility, and even its danger, is apparent.

But Professor Cannan's dictum contains a naïve belief that the economists are one and speak always with an undivided voice. Assuming for a moment that his estimate of the time-lag is accurate, which are we to suppose—that in the year 1993 or 2000 the politicians will be implementing the conclusions of the Cambridge School, or those of the London School ?

When, as we saw in the earliest chapters of this book, there was an acceptable and accepted central authority whose discipline all obeyed, when the ethical code of the

Church directed the economic activity of the worker, when good craftsmanship and fair dealings were the touchstones of public appreciation and tolerance, there was a directing voice by which the acts of the contemporary politicians could be inspired or judged. It was a single voice. The substitution of the economist as witch-doctor for such an authority has not produced a single voice, but a veritable Tower of Babel. If the politicians lag sixty or seventy years behind the economists, which particular group of jarring economists do they lag behind? If they are to shorten that lag, with which group of warring economists are they to fall into step?

Sir Josiah Stamp (in his foreword to *The Riddle of Rationalization*) has written:

> The majority of those who give thought to the present amazing sickness of the world, and the inability of modern industrial society to take proper advantage of its own development and power, are coming to see that extreme and unco-ordinated individualism may not only fail to do justice to our possibilities, but even bring us to the verge of poverty. Nearly everyone is prepared to introduce some degree of conscious co-operation and control in industry—such as prevents municipal and civic affairs from falling into chaos—in order to prevent waste, overlapping and complete misjudgment of economic wants by a large aggregate of uncorrelated decisions. Everywhere there is a feeling that "planning" of some kind must be introduced at different key points in the economic machine to make it function, either at all, or to a better advantage than now. Schemes and suggestions fill the air, and the main questions that emerge are: "Who is to do the planning?" "Do you admit the democratic principle?" "Do you control ultimately by politics and the vote?"

> " At what stage do you stop, if you *can* stop ? " " Is there any place for ' profitability ' as a test of survival ? " " Is there any scope for individual initiative, and especially for the *new* individual ? " . . . We are all assuming, without much examination, that the fundamentals of human liberty will remain intact, or that what is left is more precious than our present rag-bag of doubtful rights.

There is no unanimity among professed economists in the answers to those questions. If the politicians are content to take their direction from economists, from which answerers must they receive instruction ?

The duty of the statesmen, I premise, is so to direct the State that its subjects are content, but with no ignoble contentments. The test of the " nobility " or " ignobility " of the satisfactions which create content opens a new field of argument. One must be arbitrary in defining such a test, with a readiness implied to argue upon this theme elsewhere until the eyelids will no longer wag. Those satisfactions are ignoble which dull the faculties of those who receive them. Deprivations of responsibility make for an ignoble contentment in those skilfully taught to abhor responsibility. The acceptance of inferior handicraft as a means of avoiding the mental or physical exertion of procuring better handicraft makes for ignoble contentment. The acceptance of " soft comforts " in exchange for the right to exercise the personal faculties in the arrangement of a life makes for ignoble contentment.

Admitting that it is impossible to define such a term as " the good life ", one may yet say that " the good life " is a term generally understandable, whether it be in the sense of Pater or in that of St. Francis, the sense of Nietzsche or the sense of Christ. That organization of the State which renders the good life difficult either by the excess of material temptations to its antithesis or by the lack of means whereby primitive barbarism can be escaped is a bad organization. The duty of the statesmen, then, is to season the instruction of the economist with that of the ethical teacher, if he can.

But the choice of an ethical code by the State is a danger to the moral liberty of the subject, which is itself to many the gravest of evils. The duty of the statesmen must in this direction of activity be negative rather than positive—the instruction of the economist must be seasoned with a perpetual apprehension of the danger of allowing a code of law to increase national wealth at the expense of justice or of freedom, since in freedom alone can be retained the one comprehensive source of noble contentment, the potentiality—if not the actuality—of living that undefinable but recognizable " good life ".

The rule of the economist unbridled would mean, in the existing complexity of the trading world, " planning " in both its phases, the short-term plan of the fiscal year and the long-term plan of generational development. Bridled only by the exigencies of the demands of sectional political supporters it already means spasmodic and uncorrelated planning from diverse motives. (I take my liquor at a time and price dictated to me by a haphazard combination of brewing and distilling combinations, temperance reformers, State spenders who must tax and licence to obtain revenue, and sociologists to whom liquor is a dangerous drug and a public house not an inn but an infamy. I take my amusement at the dictates of controllers of film quotas and actors' unions, of local bodies who open or keep shut at their elective will the pleasure grounds for which I and my fellows must pay. I select my viands under the correction of devisers of quota schemes. I school my children under compulsion designed to shape them to a mould of which I may not approve. I launch, or do not launch, my enterprises, however beneficently conceived, in ways laid down for me by bureaucrats lacking all knowledge of my means and purpose. But these various restrictions are not unified, and were not unified at their conception. They have come, so to speak, at haphazard, and sometimes accidentally, as when my convenience as a drinker, or a games player, or a reader, is affected by the incidence of some arbitrary boundary like that between the City Police area and the Metropolitan Police area or one municipality and the next.) The spasmodical planning of the existing haphazard régime must, as Sir Josiah Stamp implies, give place to something different, and, as he warns us, is likely to give way to some new mode of planning in which the vital question of what is to happen to the fundamentals of human liberty, and the still more vital question of whether the benefits of the planning are more desirable than even what little is left of our old individual rights, are to be ignored or regarded as incidentals.

The first of Sir Josiah's questions is the most vital—who is to do the planning ? Planning involves tyranny, no matter how beneficent in purpose. Who are to be our tyrants ? We have already seen displayed what Huxley saw approaching, that a Parliamentary system of delegates gives neither representation to the electors as a community of individual citizens organized as families nor cohesion to a proposed plan in its progress to operation. Are the tyrants, then, to be some caucus-chosen committee of balanced representatives of party delegates, themselves the selection of caucuses ? Or are the tyrants to be some secret college of bureaucrats chosen by academic examination and allotted to their fields of service by a system of grading of marks—the best examinee to the fiscal field and the worst to the inspection of nuisances ? Is the qualification for tyranny to be either the possession of those qualities which make a good party candidate—a glib tongue or a fat purse—or those which enable a man at the later stages of adolescence to pass certain scholastic tests? Neither choice promises well for the contentment of the mature masses who are to be ruled.

In the address to section F of the British Association from which I have quoted, Professor Cannan, without dispute, said, "I think the biggest change in economic theory during the last hundred years is to be found in the treatment of the subject of population." Are the new tyrants to be drawn from the available body of professed economists—a judicious mingling of the school of Gregory with the school of Keynes? And, if so, what guarantee have we that the egregious mistakes about population made in the past century will not be made in the next? Is the control of family life and the direction of knowledge of contraceptives to be entrusted to economic eugenists as capable of misdirection as their forerunners?

Or are the new tyrants to be practical industrialists and business-men? If so, with what satisfaction will the normal citizen look forward to the gradual transformation of his world to a series of adorned and camouflaged serf compounds, of decorated but recognizable industrial block-houses none the less repressive in their purpose for having roses round the door and twined about the barbed-wire fencing? And is there any guarantee that the race of business men who misjudged the permanence of the rail roads, who abandoned under protest the system of free competition for that of cartellization only to find the replacement system no more effective for the prevention of the slump cycle than its predecessors, who veered from an advocacy of protection in fiscal affairs to an advocacy of free imports only to veer back again, allowing a Free Trade Premier to re-introduce the tariffs which a Protectionist Premier had abolished at their request, who with generous enthusiasm supported the modern Universities as breeding grounds of highly educated technicians only to find that the supply of these grew far beyond the demand for their highly trained services, who flocked to the service of the State at the call of Mr. Lloyd George during the world war and helped to produce the worst peace in history —is there, I say, any guarantee that these practical men in their role as tyrants of the new planned State will be any more immune from error than in the past ? The function of the man of business is to conduct his business in such a way that it prospers from year to year : his technique must change with changing circumstances : his methods must vary as new facilities become available to him. That wise political philosopher, the late Professor C. E. Vaughan, wrote[1] :

> Moral duties are comparatively unchanging. Political duties are determined mainly by expediency : in other words, by the circumstances—which, strictly speaking, are always unprecedented—of the given time and the given situation. Even in morals, no one not wholly inexperienced or grossly rash supposes that circumstances count for nothing. But in politics it is evident that the allowance to be made for them is infinitely larger : that, as Burke said, " circumstances, which some men count for nothing, in reality give to every political principle its distinguishing colour and discriminating effect."

In the conduct of business circumstances are even more dominant. A business training is, in many respects, more ill adapted than any other for politics, and is certainly ill adapted for the controlled politics of a planned economy. The very virtues of the business man are the vices of the

[1] See his introduction to *Studies in the History of Political Philosophy*, Vol. I (Manchester University Press).

politician—promptitude and courage in enterprise, flexibility in the making of bargains, inconsistency in action over short periods as day-to-day circumstances dictate.

Are the financiers to be the new tyrants ? They have already shown too obtrusive a faculty for mismanaging even their own business to command enthusiastic obedience. The affair of Clarence Hatry, the affair of Ivar Kreuger, the state of the loans to Lancashire cotton enterprises, the existence of various Standstill Agreements in Europe, the differing voices of the Normanites and the McKennaists on the currency question, the failure of the Joint Stock Banks to fashion a mid-term credit organization to the liking of the Bank of England, the general air of impotence which hangs about the Bankers' Industrial Development Company—these augur ill for contentment under a dictatorship of planning financiers.

Is there any promising combination of these sections ? It is quite obvious that, judging by experience, the aims of the politicians, the bureaucrats, the professing economists, the business men and the financiers are not only irreconcilable but contradictory and mutually exclusive, both one section with another and one division with another within each section. Even where in the past there has been unanimity as to the desirability of centralization, there has been no unanimity as to the kind of centralization desired.

" Do you admit the democratic principle ? " asks Sir Josiah Stamp. Apparently many would not. By an irony which seemed unapparent to those present, the Individualist Luncheon Club recently listened with approval to an address by that great educationalist, Sir Michael Sadler, on the need to organize the leisure of the workers against the great day when leisure would be more liberal. The lust to organize the lives of others has reached, surely, its apotheosis when professed individualists contemplate so little individualism for the common man that even his leisure employments and amusements are to be organized for him.

It needs but little experience of the ways of those who delight to organize the leisure of others to forecast the kind of amusements which would be forced upon the leisured masses—morris dancing for those who prefer whippet racing, educational films for those who take pleasure in the merry gymnastics of Douglas Fairbanks or the buffooneries of Laurel and Hardy, organized British games for those who prefer hiking, and organized hiking for those who prefer solitary rambles with a congenial friend or a sweetheart. There would be, too, the organized educational classes, probably in homecraft, itself veering with the changing whim of the " expert " who once forbade us to use enamel pans for our cooking because enamel is apt to chip and bade us use aluminium, only a little later to disparage aluminium because with certain acid contents it caused a chemical change in the food cooked therein.

But if the democratic principle be not admitted, dictatorship only remains, for government by aristocracy has been destroyed, not by the uprooting of any particular caste of aristocrats, but by a spread of information which no longer permits one caste to assume that superiority which is the first mark of the aristocrat. (" In the one case, that of a Monarchy or a Democracy, a public servant is an inferior set to a task ; in the other, that of an aristocracy, he is a superior who gives rather than receives orders.")[1] Commonalty of garb, education and amusement does not permit, nor does the free gossip of an irreverent Press allow, the illusion necessary to preserve that superiority.

[1] *The House of Commons and Monarchy*, by H. Belloc.

If the principle of democracy is not to be admitted—or the name is to be given to some quite different system, such as a Plutocracy working through caucuses—and the principle of aristocracy can no longer be applied in the absence of aristocrats, dictatorship remains. It involves again Sir Josiah Stamp's first question: Who is to be or choose the dictators?—and a second question: Does dictatorship promise any clearer approach to the good life for the mass of men than the denied principle of democracy?

The political purist may well say that we have not yet on earth seen pure democracy working in anything larger than a city-state. We shall not see it. Democracy can only work by committing its authority to its delegates and watching them closely and critically at their work of administration and government. But the virtue of democracy as a system is that it permits the mass of men to shape the State to their desires by relinquishing authority only for short term periods. It prevents the fallibility of the expert from exerting a mischievous effect for a long time, and prevents the theorist from constricting the ordinary citizen's desire within a code desired only by a minority.

The attitude of democracy has never been better displayed than in a comic-paper anecdote of an old retired Colonel who, having tried for some time to find a pair of shoes, was told by the shop assistant that if he would but visit a chiropodist the shop might be able to find a pair of shoes to fit him. To this the fiery warrior retorted: "God-damn, sir, I came here to get shoes to fit my feet: I'm not going to have my feet spokeshaved to fit your damned shoes!" The charge of democracy to its governors is to fashion a State to fit the community: the charge of Dictatorship to democracy is to fashion the community to fit the dictator's idea of the State. If the sections of the community from whom dictatorial governors must be chosen had in the past shown an aptitude for infallibility, or if existing dictators in other places had demonstrated their power to achieve what the normal man desires in life, all would be well : the faults of any adaptation of the democratic system cannot be denied : the choice would be simple. But the dictators at command must either be elected " experts " or bullies, or a combination of both. The record of the experts, particularly the politico-economic experts, is not such as to invite confidence, and the bully is never a pleasant taskmaster. (If any deny that a dictator who is not an elected expert is a bully, let him carefully study the blood and iron methods of Lenin and Stalin, the bludgeon and castor-oil methods of Mussolini, the pogroms of Hitler. It is possible that the malaise of a nation may be such that these methods are commendable as a remedy against national dissolution, but let none pretend that they are pleasant to endure or even—except to sadists—to administer.)

Is there no half-way house to dictatorship ? Is there no " confederal system " whereby the specialized activities of the community can achieve sectional government under the general direction of a democratically elected House of Representatives, such as the existing House of Commons is supposed to be ? The short answer to these questions is that too many of our present discontents already spring from such a system. It is from the mistakes and misdirections of sectional organizations which an elected House of Representatives has proved powerless either to detect at their inception or to check during their development that many of our troubles arise.

There is, it must be admitted, a tacit responsibility upon any critic of any system to be prepared to suggest a workable alternative. It is a responsibility which this book, for all its designedly ragged form, should not seek to avoid. But he who preaches that imposed collective systems are bad merely because they are imposed collective systems can hardly formulate a new collective system with the bland suggestion that it should be imposed upon the community. It is almost as difficult to suggest merely that Reaction will solve many existing discontents. It has been well said that you cannot " unpull " a man's nose or unscramble an egg. But there is possible what may be called reasoned reaction, a retreat from the morass into which faulty over-organization has led us which will have all the advantages of an advance.

CHAPTER XIV

THE RETURN TO HUMANISM

IN the earlier chapters of this book it has been suggested —within the limits of space imposed by a single volume it could not be proved—that the disappearance of a single ethical authority at the time of the Reformation caused the substitution of a motive of avarice for that of a " right " or " fair " human relationship in the affairs of mankind. From that disappearance grew most of our present discontents. It has been further suggested that when the science of economics came to the aid of the statesman it failed at every test to do more than diagnose a situation which was already passing away at the time of the diagnosis, and that had this not been so the remedy prescribed after diagnosis failed to take into account its own effect upon the psychology of those to whom it was administered.

To sum up: the acquisitiveness of society and the ineptitude of economists to gauge the idiosyncratic reaction of the community to the politico-economic measures which were successively devised combined with a failure by the community to secure a political system which was true to its name. The democracy did not live under Democracy: the House of Commons was not a collection of representatives of the commons.

The reign of the plutocracy from the dawn of the industrial revolution to our own day has favoured the growth of the large unit in affairs. To make easier the collection of capital for large commercial enterprises, hoping to exploit larger and larger markets and to trade in a wider and wider variety of articles from a wider variety of sources, limited liability has become the accepted mode, but has lacked certain checks and restraints, and so has earned the distrust of those whose capital is thereby collected. For the same purpose the legislature has eased the way of both large aggregations of capital and large aggregations of organized labour, with the result that in ordinary working life the individual citizen has been deprived by easy stages of most of the old responsibilities and freedoms which his personal traditions led him to expect and for which heredity and tradition shaped him.

The justification for the large unit is its success in providing a better economic life for those serving it and whom it serves. To a point not easily discernible, the large unit achieved this justification, but within recent years its growth has revealed such weaknesses as to justify the suspicion that it is now defeating its own purpose. The larger the unit, the greater and more numerous the margins of error in management and of possible malfeasance. Since large units imply an absolute dependence by many users upon the services of a single serving entity, the possibility of failure in those services by that unit becomes a matter of the utmost seriousness. A failure, or a strike, in the organization of a large milk collecting and distributing agency, for example, will menace a whole township. A failure in transport owing to some disagreement between large blocks of labour and large unit employers menaces a whole nation. Again, while a large unit may provide a better economic life for its servants, it wields an economic power over them which reduces them to a virtual state of serfdom. Deprived of its employment, they have no alternative employer to whom to turn with an offer of services. Confronted by a reduction of standard or by an order to conduct their private lives by a certain code, they must assent or suffer indignities incompatible with the seriousness of the sin of refusing their assent.

The large unit tends to narrow and stabilize the mental life of the people whom it serves, rather than to widen it. The desideratum of the large producing unit is standardization of demand, whether that demand be for the shape of a collar or for the length of a book or for the nature of an entertainment. In the dissemination of knowledge the large unit makes for stereotyped information. The popular Press and the Broadcaster, for example, tend to shape a common mind rather than to stimulate diversities of thought and knowledge.

This trend towards uniformity is, perhaps, best seen in the shaping of the physical landscapes of towns and cities, each containing the same frontage to its depot of Messrs. Woolworth, Messrs. Montague Burton, Ltd., Messrs. W. H. Smith & Son, Ltd., or one of the well-known multiple stores for the sale of drapery or provisions, and each adorned by cinematograph theatres of depressing external similarity showing, if not the same, certainly the same kind of film.

The duplication of these emporia is not caused by a decision that their methods and goods are those most desired by the locality, or even by the nation at large, but by the need to duplicate to pattern depots for the disposal of goods produced in masses in standardized forms.

It is a possible opinion, and one widely held, that these tendencies, which are at one and the same time responsible for and caused by the large unit, are desirable, and that by their spread mankind is made happier rather than less happy. It is also a possible opinion, still held in some quarters, that these tendencies are undesirable, and make mankind less happy by reducing his personal independence and depriving him of that responsibility for his own life whereby he could cultivate his own temperamental desires and find means to their fulfilment—the contriving of the means being no less a fulfilment than the finding.

It is a possible opinion that there are some things which a man (or woman) must do for himself and which cannot be done for him by any large communal unit if he is to attain to happiness. These include the selection of his mate and the care of her; the choice of his metaphysical faith and his observance of its dictates; the rearing of his children; the allocation of his hours of leisure; the making of his own " background ", by which I mean the atmosphere of his home; and the selection of those who shall govern him in those provinces which are obviously collective. It may be argued that the growth of the large unit hampers none of these things, but the growth of the large unit is towards the single unit, and the single unit is nationalization, whether it be State nationalization in the Russian sense or corporative nationalization in the English sense, as chemicals and certain other common commodities, electricity, broadcasting, totalisator betting and other activities, including passenger transport, have been nationalized. The end of nationalized goods and services is nationalized citizens, and the end of nationalized citizens threatens to be eugenic selection of mates, State rearing of children, sterilization of selected categories —the " unfit " to-day, the merely rebellious to-morrow— and homes to a communal pattern served by communally devised and directed supply and amusement services.

The reward for a tolerance of this trend towards Robotism is a better material standard of life, a larger variety of material satisfactions within the limits of necessary standardization, and the banishment of certain old fears—if the system of large and single units can survive its own weaknesses. Of this capacity to survive there is no guarantee: if, for example, it is the whim of the controllers to-day to produce in the mass for mass distribution "grade A sterilized milk for cherished babies", it may be their whim shortly to produce in the mass for mass distribution grade A mustard gas for the elimination of awkward or unwanted masses.

The alternative to tolerance of this trend is reaction to simpler modes and greater personal freedoms, the price of which may be a lower standard of material comforts. In the days of Voltaire the English had forty-seven religions and only one sauce: to-day they have the one religion (of indifferentism) and Mr. Heinz and his compeers supply them with fifty-seven varieties of sauces. It is not discoverable which proportion makes for the greater happiness of the greater number.

By what means can the alternative be pursued? By two means—of which the first is the inculcation, by those who are aware of the choice, of the lesson that expanding material benefits from large-scale trade are not always coincident with expanding happiness, that a simpler life is often paradoxically a fuller life, and that "want" is a strictly relative term under modern usage. The second is by a revision of our modes of election to Parliament and its restoration to public prestige. By this I do not for one moment imply that we should leave the present method of election for some newer-fangled alternative, but that the exercise of the vote should be regarded as a function and not as a right, that it should be governed by those who supply and not those who use public wealth.

This last is a hard saying. It means, bluntly, that the vote should not be exercised by any who are the servants or the pensioners of the State, lest the taxing body which allocates whatever of wealth is contributed for communal purposes should be tempted to bribe with the public money the potential recipients of public money, and should thus take more and more of the functions of the individual citizens into the domain of the State itself.

If the pensioners of the State are not to vote, the vote must be withdrawn from the dole-drawers. It is impossible! There would be a revolution of all who draw the dole or whose friends and relatives draw the dole or who fear that they may in person need to draw the dole. But this objection only holds good while we tolerate the dole as such.

If a nation can afford to keep in idleness some three million citizens, it can afford to keep them at work. It can afford to keep them at work either by lightening the labour hours of all workers or by finding occupation for them. That this has not already been done is due to one fact, and one fact only—the existence of large units of employers and organized labourers whose interests are menaced by a new distribution of leisure or the influx of workers at lower rates of pay. It is not a fear that the nation as a whole will be impoverished, but that a re-distribution of available wealth will affect certain sections, which prevents the short working week from absorbing the unemployed. The large employing units will not face a re-adjustment of costs; the large units of employed will not face a threat to existing wage rates. Any stimulus which prompts the unemployed to press for employment, such as depriving of the vote those who take State assistance without labour, is so far to the good. There need be no revolution, for the abolition of the dole in favour of shared labour, which means shared leisure, ought to precede the new allocation of the franchise.

The taking of the vote from State servants is no startling innovation. Until 1918 soldiers and sailors in the fighting services had neither vote nor voice. To declare that those who draw public money shall not vote for those who allocate it is an understandable precaution: there need be no fiat forbidding such public servants to take part and have voice in the election of the allocators.

The old property qualifications were unsatisfactory, but they were not irrational. They should be replaced by earning qualifications, since the power to earn in the modern State means the necessity of paying taxes.

That reform achieved, what remains to be done is the exercise through short-term Parliaments of unwinking vigilance in the endeavour to detect and prevent the sacrifice of the freedoms and responsibilities of the general mass of citizens for the benefit of selected groups. It is, for example, illogical that because group finance opens the way to certain undesirable practices, the enterprise of small entrepreneurs should be penalized, and often rendered abortive, by the imposition of checks and restraints, of form-filling duties and obligations, incompatible with the scope of the enterprise embarked upon or projected. It is equally illogical that the whole community should be restrained in its times of merrymaking because some sots must be protected against themselves, and those sots an insignificant minority. This is, indeed, the more illogical when it results in men being able to drink at will when they are rich enough to buy a private store of liquor for use in a private establishment, but not being able to drink at will if they are not rich enough for that, or if they and their friends happen to be at some distance from the store and the establishment. It is absurd that a master craftsman should not be permitted to teach his craft to another except by permission of some large unit of craftsmen, or that a competent craftsman should not be permitted to exercise his craft until and unless he has fulfilled certain requirements of some such unit. It is absurd that a joiner should not be permitted to finish his work by painting it or a plumber to finish a job of work by a little carpentering of which he is capable.

It is absurd that a man should not be able to offer his labour at the dockside until he has paid his entrance fee to a body of organized dockside workers.

But it is not absurd that these things should be in society as we know it, for they are preventives of injustice devised against certain ills. The real absurdity is that for all our hundred years' lust for organization we have not found a less irrational remedy for the original ill. Such a remedy exists, but no single economic or sociological formula contains it. It must lie in a return to the form of government which encourages individual responsibility in the masses of men.

Such a return to responsibility the people themselves alone can achieve. Statesmen, officials, functionaries and pedagogues have a vested interest in directional power. They are unlikely to relinquish any system or any part of a system which takes control from the mass and gives it to selected delegates. The use of power itself encourages a belief, perfectly sincere in the holder, that none but the "expert" is qualified to direct public policy or dictate codes of conduct. It is from this that there arises the most obvious of our modern political paradoxes—that at a time when the education of the mass is most conscientiously devised to perfect the ordinary citizen for a political role, he has the minimum of effective political power: at a time when education forms a type of proletarian who can be trusted to observe standards of decency in conduct, the proletariat is most restricted in its choice of how to behave: at a time when education, both formal and occasional—that is, both through schooling and the acquirement of knowledge through the public prints, the broadcaster and the screen—is most fitted to inculcate standards of taste, the exercise of personal taste is forbidden or made extremely difficult, as any middle-class citizen can testify who has tried to build himself an habitation.

The masses, if they are to be encouraged to demand again the responsibility which was once the prerogative of the individual citizen, must be stirred by agitation, and the kind of agitation which alone can be successful is that of an earlier day—the direct stirring of individual emotions by direct personal appeals. The art of the platform, of the tribune, is almost lost. Few to-day think it worth the expenditure of effort to canvass the public will on isolated items of policy. Men will occasionally address meetings and bombard the Press with expressions of opinion about a party or about large principles of policy; they no longer undertake campaigns against particular measures.

It is said that the broadcaster and the form of popular journalism has destroyed the power of the public meeting. Electors will no longer attend. It is said that electorates are too large to permit the old individual canvass of each particular elector. It is said that the attraction of party politics is no longer sufficient to permit the vigorous life that once pulsated in ward committees and sectional associations. It may be so, but only by a revival of these things can the necessary education of the individual be achieved.

And to what end must that education be directed? The voter must be taught again to watch jealously all proposals that threaten new encroachments upon personal liberty and responsibility; to register disapproval of all measures which permit persons not directly answerable to the public through Parliament to frame instructions or prohibitions affecting conduct and the relation of the citizen to the State; to protest against proposals which make easier the aggregation of economic power and of capital into units so large that genuine supervision by the proprietors of the enterprise is rendered impossible and its bare form a farce. It must be ensured that all legislation is automatically short-term, and that the Expiring

Laws Continuance Act on its renewal is made the occasion for a general revision of Statutes which have become ripe for revision.

In America Grover Cleveland enunciated, though he did not coin its phrasing, the principle that " Public Office is a public trust ". If it is to be observed seriously in any country the populace must be taught to look with care at all shifting of authority from small units controllable by their proprietors to large units whose directors are nominated through or by the political officers of State but yet do not have a direct responsibility to the elected body which selected the nominating Ministers. Such experiments in socialization without nationalization as the Electricity Board, the Totalisator Board, the London Traffic Board, the British Broadcasting Corporation, cannot remain isolated from the general trend. Either they are the pioneers of a new mode or they are abortions within a system of small free enterprises. It may not much matter that the wife of an ex-Cabinet Minister gives place to the wife of a present Cabinet Minister on one of these bodies, but it does matter that such a change can be made without the authority or sanction or approval of those who finance and use the service. It may not much matter that monopolistic and virtually monopolistic enterprises the direction of which is a public service in all but name—the Bank of England and Imperial Chemical Industries, Ltd. spring to the mind as examples of such bodies—are able to change the personnel of the governing body without, unless they wish, immediately notifying the proprietors and the public,[1] but in certain circumstances it might matter exceedingly. If the public is to

[1] Directors are elected and co-opted directors approved at annual meetings, but in law there is no responsibility upon anyone to notify shareholders that one director has resigned and another been substituted until that meeting. For twelve months less a day, therefore, any company may be under entirely new directorial influences without the general body of proprietors being any the wiser. It rarely happens so, of course, in practice.

know who shapes its life, it must be taught to be jealous of this delegation of power from the mass to the few. If the direction of such vast aggregations of capital for the making or distributing of vital commodities (in which credit must be included) is to all intents and purposes a public office—as indeed it is—then it, too, should be a public trust, and not the private hobby or interest of a cabal, however devoted and able. There may be a strong case for refusing the demand of organized Labour for some participation in direction and management ; there can hardly be such a case against the participation of the capital providers.

Finally, the public must be taught again to be dissatisfied with an appeal from those seeking its suffrages based upon little but the promise to restore or maintain prosperity. Such appeals put first things second and second things first. They shape themselves thus : " Let us have tariffs (or no tariffs) and this trade and that will be the gainer." The older methods of appeal shaped themselves rather thus : " My design, if I am elected to a position of power, is to shape the life of the nation in this wise, and to do that I seek a mandate to impose (or abolish) tariffs which is one of the necessary means of reaching my objective."

It may seem contradictory that in succeeding paragraphs it is first suggested that the people must be taught again to concentrate more upon single proposals and next that they should demand a broader appeal from those seeking power to inaugurate proposals. The two are not contradictory, but complementary. It is upon his conception of the future shaping of civilization that a man should be elected, but it is upon the " bricklaying " work of individual measures that he must be constantly and constructively criticized by those electing him, and, if necessary, deprived of his office. The physical inconvenience seems in our time to have ruled out of men's desires the short Parliament of the Chartists, but there is much to be said for the interpolation into our electoral system of some means of ensuring an expression of electoral opinion during the life of a five- or seven-year Parliament, whether such means be the Referendum or the power of recalling a Member to face a bye-election.

It is widely said that the people of the present generation hunger for dictatorship and its imposed discipline and are disillusioned by what experience they have had of democracy. This is to say that democracy has failed. It is a saying true in the same sense that the saying that Christianity has failed is true—it has failed to secure a working trial. It has failed to secure a working trial largely because the exponents of democratic government who achieved the first steps towards it failed to realize that democracy is much more nearly akin to anarchy (not, of course, in the popular usage of that term, but in its exact and philosophical usage) than to oligarchy. What was loosely described as democratic government between, roughly, 1870 and 1914 was in reality oligarchic government, and in a world organized in large units any form of dictatorship must be oligarchic. The oligarchs will be different, perhaps, but the method must be the same. Communities are themselves now too large for a dictator to control them by any other method than that of small oligarchies culminating in a supreme oligarchy of which he is the head.

The tendency of dictatorship is obviously towards ever-growing units until all units become one—the managed State. In the managed State are two dangers to personal happiness. The first is the obvious danger that organization for planned productivity may clash with the traditional appetites and fulfilments of the individual citizens. The second is that in the multiplication of dictatorships may lie the thwarting of that world dictatorship of which imaginative novelists so frequently write and which is the logical progress from national dictatorships. If dictatorships breed rivalry which finds expression in war, the end of civilization is at hand. The return of mankind will not then be to a simple civilization, a civilization of hard-living simplicity, but to barbarism.

A world unity under a single command would obviate war in any sense known to human experience, but it is a concept harder to translate into fact as each national *bloc* solidifies under a dictator who owes his power to a growing sense of nationalism. A unified world in which each national *bloc* achieves government by a succession of governors changed without strife, and in which the foreign policies of the nation are modified both by such changes and the fear of such changes, may manage to obviate war by the perfecting of its common instrument, the League of Nations, for settling disputes as they arise and for avoiding conditions that lead to disputes. The negative permission given by democracies to economic and governmental units to grow larger, to drift, that is to say, further and further away from the older ideal of a maintained human relation in all functional relations and from the effective control of life by the mass as a mass, has not even the excuse that it makes the foundations of peace more sure.

One aspect alone will make this point clear. Time was when treaties between nations were what they purported to be—treaties between nations. To-day treaties are more and more treaties between various industrial or trading *blocs* within nations arranged through the States involved. In the early eighteen-sixties peace between America and England was said by one mordant satirist to

> . . . hang by a rotten
> Fibre of cotton.

That exaggeration may well be aptly true in the nineteen-sixties, for International relations are more and more bound by ties woven for the sake of this or that group of producers or distributors of commodities, and every tie in world politics means a potential cause of rupture. And this tendency owes its being entirely to the large-scale organizations born in an age when the economist dominated and overwhelmed the humanist in politics. It is the economist who hungers for rigidity in trading relations.

Lest the use of the words " economist" and " humanist " be misunderstood in that context, let us define them by analogy. Two traders operate in one town. Of these, one is a disciple of modern efficiency methods. His office is arranged solely with an eye to efficiency or work. The filing cabinet, the position of the table, the very contents of the office are selected and arranged from motives of minute saving. The other, knowing that more than a third of his life, and more than half his waking life, is to be spent in his office, arranges the room with an eye to comfort. The first trader is a little richer than the second, but he has purchased his increased profit margin at the expense of personal comfort. If he grow to like the efficiency expert's arrangement of his room he has purchased the increase at the expense of a certain quality of taste. It would be equally just to say that each has had the same margin of profit, but that one has chosen to expend some of it in the purchase of ease and personal satisfaction. The first is the prototype of the economist, the second that of the humanist. To import another analogy, a household run by that familiar type of domestic economist known as a managing wife may be a most efficient house, but it may give less happiness to its occupants than the home run by some less managing but more human mistress. There may in the second and less technically efficient establishment be fewer 'rows' with the tradesmen and fewer friction surfaces between occupants and staff or between the various members of the family one with the other. The analogy, in this last sentence, with a nation is too close to need apology.

The large unit necessitates many rules, for there must be routine methods if there is to be discipline and economic working. Rules mean standardization, and human beings are not standardized products. Speaking generally, the fewer the rules to be observed, the happier a collection of human beings. It is still possible to regard as strictly necessary only two rules for the government of any community—that law and order shall be preserved and that contracts shall be honoured. These are the minimum functions of any Government, and the nearer the maximum of admitted functions keeps to that minimum, the better for those governed. The army, the convict prison, the school demand many and rigidly enforced rules, because these are organizations which drill their components for a purpose in direct contravention to their personal wills and desires and ideas of happiness. The club and the home need but few and loosely enforced rules, for these are organizations expected to shape themselves to the will and happiness of their members. The nearer a nation approximates to the home or the club, and the further it remains from the barracks or the gaol or the school, the happier will its citizens be.

Governments which appear to their members and to their subjects as bodies to which an appeal can be made for the organization of communal action to meet necessities which are not within the scope and power of sections, make for communal happiness ; those which appear as bodies determined to take into the realm of communal action all that can possibly be done by the State make for communal discontent, even though the result of such abrogation of power results in technically better government as expressed in a higher level of total prosperity.

That paragraph, like so much else in this book, is a dogmatic credo, and is intended to be only that. It is probably a creed to which a majority of persons in the English-speaking countries would subscribe. If it is a creed left unsupported by action in the near future, our present discontents will be perpetuated and increased. That action, this volume submits, must take the form of a determination to diminish and not increase the volume of legislation passed by elected bodies; to diminish and not increase the accepted functions of such bodies and their servants; to limit and not increase the power of elected and selected persons both in politics and in industry; to widen the basis of responsibility by restoring to the individual citizen rights and obligations of which he has been bereft by the evolution of a ragged system wherein the control of property has become more and more divorced from its ownership and the very ownership of property subjected to attack; and to restore again by familiar methods of educational agitation the once general standards of fair work and fair dealings in place of the contending standards of successful avarice and personal aggrandizement which have too long dominated a world now brought to a state of discontent which threatens, on the public confessions of the world's leaders themselves, to precipitate crisis after crisis until ultimate catastrophe and the dissolution of civilization and culture ends all warnings and efforts by an economic and social cataclysm.

INDEX